Ks. 32/50

Bernard Fergusson

RETURN TO BURMA

' It's a poor sort of memory that only works backwards,' the Queen remarked.

Through the Looking-Glass

COLLINS
St James's Place, London
1962

The Author and the Publishers wish to thank
Messrs. Macmillan & Co. Ltd. for permission
to include an extract from *The Soul Of A People*
by Fielding Hall; also The Society of Authors
as the literary representative of the Estate of the
late A. E. Housman and Messrs. Jonathan
Cape Ltd., publishers of A. E. Housman's
Collected Poems for permission to include the
poem *Here Dead Lie We.*

FOREWORD

" Short retirement urges quick return," wrote Milton in *Paradise Lost*. I sent in my papers from the Army and applied for a Burma visa almost simultaneously.

My family's crest is a bee sucking honey from a thistle, and its motto *Dulcius ex Asperis:* " sweeter out of bitter things." Our ordeals in Burma on the two Wingate Expeditions of 1943 and 1944 were severe, and some of the experiences bitter; but they piled up for me many memories, sad as well as happy, which I would not willingly be without. Some of the most precious are of the people who helped us at great personal risk.

The search for a few of them, which this book describes, was successful because of the sympathy and co-operation of many different people. I would thank especially U Aung Soe; Mr. H. V. Hodson; Sir Richard and Lady Allen; Lieut-Colonel Bo Lwin; Major Shan Lone; Colonel U Saw Myint; U Maung Maung and his wife.

Auchairne, 1962   *Bernard Fergusson*

ILLUSTRATIONS

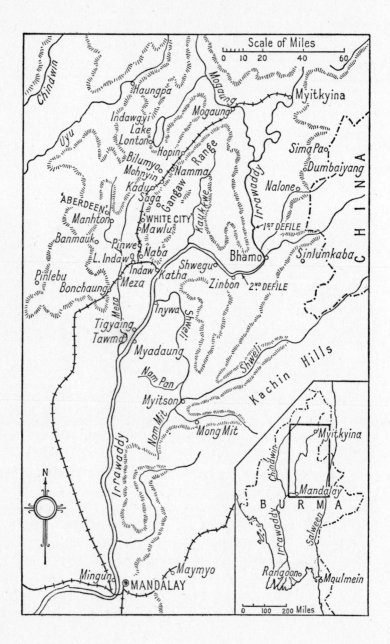

I

IT WAS FIFTEEN YEARS since I had last seen Burma, and fifteen hours since my wife and I had left London Airport. Slowly out of the mist, like a coloured slide coming into focus, there appeared the coast of Arakan, forty thousand feet below us. I could see the whole sweep of it, from Cox's Bazaar to Akyab: the white ribbon of surf along the beach, the three broad rivers with their muddy banks, and the ranges in between, like the backs of prehistoric saurians. My only happy memory of that part of the world was of a glorious swim in the last year of the war: huge translucent rollers curling over twenty naked officers, and drawing off from the sand with so loud a hiss that we had to shout to each other to make ourselves heard.

Our aircraft continued to bore its way through the sky, over the islands of Akyab, Ramree and Kyaukpyu, and the many mucky creeks through mangrove swamps where hearts in dozens were broken during the war. This is nobody's country. Perhaps the Almighty never made up his mind whether his creatures should regard it as land or sea. The result is one's exact idea of a natural home for prehistoric reptiles, dragging their bulk through the mud, with pterodactyls perching on the mangrove branches; the whole place buzzes with mosquitoes, crawls with crocodiles, and stinks.

The country for which Laura and I were bound, on the other hand, I remembered as a sort of earthly paradise. If

9

the swamps of Combermere Bay were prehistoric, then the hills and valleys of Upper Burma belonged to a Golden Age where time had hardly yet begun to tick. It remained to be seen whether the rude irruption we made during the war, two years running, under General Wingate behind the Japanese lines had left its mark; or whether life had resumed the old slow cadence of Arcady. If you cut a track through the jungle, there will be no sign of it after two monsoons. I hoped to find that the psychological scars of our depredations had healed by something akin to the soil's natural process; but equally I hoped that we were not wholly forgotten. Above all, I wanted to seek out the people who had hidden us, led us, fed us and guided us, in those bad times: to supplement the hasty handshake and whispered farewell, often by twilight or starlight, which was all the thanks we'd had time to offer, though I admit that money often passed as well.

I had left the Army a year before; and even before Laura had put away my uniform in moth-balls—Private Graham being no longer available to do it—I was inside the Burmese Embassy in London, asking whether I might travel in Upper Burma. As soon as I saw the Ambassador, U Aung Soe, my nostalgia for his beautiful country was redoubled. His features, his chuckle, his friendliness were the personification of the Burma I was hungry for. He told me with relish how, at the time of our first incursion in 1943, he was a high official at Sagaing, the provincial capital of that " Division " of the country in which we were causing such a commotion. The Japs had suspected him of collaboration, and he was lucky that no worse fate befell him than transfer to another area. Aung Soe was sympathetic but far from encouraging. It was less than three months since U Nu's administration had split in two by dissension, and given place to a military government headed by Ne Win, the

Chief of Staff—and virtually Commander-in-Chief—of the Army. I could hardly have chosen a worse time to propose such a journey. Aung Soe promised to put it to the proper authorities. Within a few weeks he had to pass on to me an official refusal; but he advised me privately to try again in a year or so.

I did, and this time permission was granted. At least, there was no firm promise to begin with that we should be allowed to travel at will; but we were tipped the wink that we might not be wasting our time if we went to Rangoon and tried our luck on the spot. So here we were, Laura and I, whisked in a Comet from the tarmac of London Airport on a crisp January noon, beginning to lose height over the coastal hills and to feel the heat coming up to meet us during our long downward glide over the Irrawaddy delta.

Until the war, 99 per cent of Europeans setting foot in Burma for the first time did so at Rangoon; or, in earlier days, at Syriam, a little way down the Rangoon River. Rangoon was the front door, the respectable mode of entry. Both my entries into Burma hitherto had been by a back door, across the Chindwin at some point or other; and I felt rather smug and out of character as I plunked down our two passports on the Immigration desk, aware that the Burmese peacocks rubber-stamped on their pages as part of our visas were also our certificates of respectability. Granville Brooking, the military attaché, had met us in uniform, and he wafted us quickly through the various hoops and out to his car beyond. Within half an hour we were at the British Embassy, on the threshold of four days in Rangoon as the guests of Sir Richard and Lady Allen.

It was pretty rash of the Allens to put us up, since we had never met; but I think and hope that we didn't disgrace them, and they were extraordinarily kind and long-suffering. They were approaching the end of their third year in Rangoon; and Dick Allen, whose tastes are amphibious, spent all the time he could spare from official and social duties on one sheet of water or another. Their house was lofty, large and cool. The Government House of British days was now the President's palace, and the British Embassy was housed in the former residence of the General Manager of the Irrawaddy Flotilla Company, whose river-steamers, now state-owned, used to ply on all the waterways of Burma. The Chancery, where the Embassy staff worked and the Ambassador had his office, was down on the water-front, ten minutes' drive away.

Although it was still only seventeen hours since we had left London just before lunch-time the day before, it was between tea and dinner, and therefore cocktail-time, thanks to the irresponsible manner in which the earth spins, when Laura and I came downstairs. The Ambassador had a remarkable servant called Lingam, a Burma-born Madrassi, who had served in the Burma Navy during the war, and who now doubled the parts of Embassy butler on the one hand, and skipper and " ship's husband " to Dick Allen's varied fleet of craft on the other. Sometimes he drove the car as well. It wasn't that the Embassy was poorly staffed; it was simply that Lingam was richly versatile. At one moment he would be dispensing drinks in a white coat or livery; soon it would strike you that the chauffeur closely resembled the butler; later it would occur to you that the man with the black face and the broad grin in a yachting cap who was steering the sampan in the Pegu River was somebody you had met before. All three were Lingam.

It was Lingam now who met Laura and me as we came downstairs—beautiful broad stairs of teak—and ushered us through french windows on to the lawn, where the nucleus of a small cocktail party in our honour was beginning to gather. Dick and Juliet Allen met us, and began introducing us to the first comers. Somebody whose face was vaguely familiar brought us drinks on a tray. (Lingam.) And then among the European guests I saw a face which I recognised at once.

Charles Cowie, whom I had met once in Glasgow since the war when he was home on leave, had been with the Chindits as an officer of the Burma Rifles. Almost all the officers of this remarkable unit were drawn from the various Burma firms: either from the big ones, like Steel Brothers, the Bombay-Burmah Trading Corporation, Burmah Oil or the Irrawaddy Flotilla; or from the smaller companies, such as Findlay's or Macgregor's. I had dropped a major brick with Charles Cowie when, the first time I met him, I asked him which of these companies he worked for.

" My own! " he replied, coldly. He was, in fact, the fourth generation of his family in Charles Cowie & Company, a Glasgow house established in Rangoon since the middle of the last century.

The only other guest whom I knew of old was " Rusty " Shan Lone. He too was a former officer of the Burma Rifles, although he never served with the Chindits: having got out to India in 1942, he was reintroduced into the far north of Burma the following year to play a lone hand among his brother Kachins. His war record was legendary. He finished up as a major with the O.B.E. and M.C.; and he was now Secretary to the Kachin State in Rangoon. The modern " Union of Burma " consists of Burma proper, divided into its seven " Divisions," plus several more or less autonomous states represented in Rangoon by a Minister and a Secretary: hence Rusty's presence in the artificial and steamy atmosphere of Rangoon, so far from his blue cloud-capped native hills. He claimed to be moderately homesick, but I had the impression that he was rather enjoying himself.

13

I was so enchanted to see him again, though I didn't know him well, that I behaved rather badly towards the other guests. We sat side by side in cane chairs on the Allens' veranda while I asked after mutual friends and brought him up to date so far as I could about old Burma hands who were now back in Britain. He promised that if I could get permission to travel in the far north—about which he was optimistic—he would alert the Kachins about my impending arrival, and commend us to various officials. From that happy twenty minutes side by side with Shan Lone I date my certainty—I think he must have known more than he told me—that Laura and I were going to achieve our ambition to get up-country. Thereafter it was a question of formal permission, and ways and means. But we went to bed fairly confident that the pilgrimage of our dreams would be realised in fact.

Still, it all hinged on the outcome of an interview which had been arranged for the following morning; and I came down to breakfast with my fingers crossed. Granville Brooking called for me, and we drove together to the office of Colonel Bo Lwin, Director of Military Intelligence, who came out to meet us on the veranda, silent, reserved but friendly. A junior officer brought us maps and an orderly brought us tea; and over both I sketched out to Bo Lwin a square of roughly 200 miles each way in which I was hoping to travel, naming specific villages where I had particular friends or to which I was especially indebted. I had been able to glean little knowledge in London about the state of the country, but I knew there had been a good deal of trouble in this area during the years that had intervened. Obviously I must be completely frank with Bo Lwin, and to leave it to him to decide where I might go.

Burma is slightly bigger than the British Isles and much more elongated. It is shaped like a parrot facing west:

Rangoon is where the parrot's claws would grip the perch, and Tenasserim is the long tail hanging down. Except for a small stretch abutting on China in the north-east, the land frontiers all run through high forested mountains difficult to penetrate, so that the structure of the country resembles an oval dish. The Irrawaddy flows from the mountains in the far north, majestic and mysterious, as the main artery of the country, until it breaks up into the delta some 150 miles short of the sea; and the delta spreads its channels across almost the whole width of the south coast.

Near Pakokku, 100 miles below Mandalay, the Irrawaddy is joined by its junior partner the Chindwin, which also rises in the northern mountains and flows along the foot of the hills lying between Burma and India. For most of the Japanese occupation, the Chindwin was the dividing line between the British and the Japs, and whoever set foot across it was playing Tom Tiddler's Ground. The district I wanted to reach lay mostly between these two rivers, but I also hoped to visit some villages east of the Irrawaddy, where our sufferings on the first expedition in 1943 had been particularly acute. We had got ourselves into a pocket with deep rivers on three sides of us and a main road across the mouth of the bag; the Japs surrounded us with two whole divisions and put garrisons into every village to stop us getting food.

During the ten years of Independence, the internal security of Burma, which was already pretty rocky when the British left, had gone from bad to worse. There were periods when the Government's writ hardly ran outside Rangoon. Different parts of the country were dominated by rival factions. Out of the total population of something like nineteen millions, only about two-thirds are Burmese. There is a mass of other indigenous races, of whom the Kachins, the Chins, the Shans and the Arakanese live in

well-defined territories around the perimeter. It is the
political misfortune of the Karens that although they pre-
dominate in certain areas many of them live intermingled
with Burmese. Under U Nu's Government, some of the
Karens were in the field fighting for complete independence,
while up-country there were sizeable bands of Communists
(who were not always on good terms with each other) and
other private armies whose motives were ill-defined and who
were in fact straight dacoits. There was trouble also in
Arakan, where one faction wanted independence and
another union with East Pakistan. There is nothing new
about trouble in Arakan; it has been with us since the dawn
of history.

When Ne Win was called upon to restore order in the
country, he set about his task with vigour, putting senior
officers in charge of every ministry (*de facto* if not *de jure*) and
prosecuting the war against insurgents of every colour with
thoroughness and energy. The pattern he adopted was not
unlike that which the British under Sir Gerald Templer
pursued during the " emergency " in Malaya. Up-country,
Commissioners and Deputy Commissioners took their
orders from the local brigade commander, usually a colonel.
The year which had elapsed since my first abortive approach
to Aung Soe in London had seen the whole country transformed. There were still patches of resistance, but they were
sporadic; the initiative had passed entirely to the Government.

Colonel Bo Lwin sat at his table, noting down the various
places I wanted to visit and occasionally asking me to point
them out on the map. When I had finished, he pondered
for a moment; and then he gave the trip his blessing.
Provided that we put ourselves entirely in the hands of the
brigade commander at Myitkyina, and accepted any
restrictions that he might impose, my wife and I could

The Irrawaddy from the Guest House garden at Myitkyina.
'Peeping Tom' is beyond Laura's head

Planning our journey with Colonel Saw Myint (*right*) and his staff captain

Myi Tun Hka and Ba Ohn

go anywhere we liked. A civil aircraft flew to Myitkyina every Monday; this was Friday. If we cared to fly north on the coming Monday, he would signal Myitkyina accordingly.

So the last shadow of worry was dissipated, and I left Bo Lwin's office a blissful man. There was a good deal to be done before Monday. The aircraft left at dawn, the shops were shut on Sunday, and there only remained Saturday and what was left of Friday to fit ourselves out and make all necessary preparations. Granville Brooking was dying to come with us, since he had never managed to get to that part of the country; the Ambassador gave him permission to accompany us for the first week, and Bo Lwin raised no objection. The aircraft that flew north on Mondays returned on Tuesdays, which suited Granville nicely; it meant that he could be back at his desk eight days after leaving it, observing the spirit if not precisely the letter of the Ambassador's period of grace.

The luggage we had brought from home was strictly within our baggage allowance; we had calculated that it would be cheaper to buy the necessaries for the expedition in Rangoon than to pay excess. Leaving Granville to book the air passages, we went to the bank and converted a large number of travellers' cheques into Burmese currency of small denominations, which made us feel both bulky and vulnerable. Partly in shops and partly in an open-air market, we bought a supply of blankets and bedding-rolls and pillows, knives, forks, spoons, plates, mugs, medicines, and a host of small presents suitable for headmen and guides —for old friends we hoped to meet, and new ones we hoped to make. By the time we'd finished we could have stocked a modest bazaar. If we'd only known it, we could have got most of the stuff in Myitkyina.

When we next compared notes with Granville, we found

that he had achieved a masterly piece of piracy such as only a cavalryman—he belonged to the 4th/7th Dragoon Guards —would have had the nerve to try. At Mandalay there was a sort of Embassy outpost, the British Information Office, under a young man called John Slimming. He toured widely in the Shan States and elsewhere showing films of Life in Britain, and ran a popular reading room in Mandalay itself. For these purposes he had a motor car and—more important to us—a Land Rover. Whether off Granville's own bat, or with Dick Allen's authority, I was too tactful to ask; but a telegram went from the Embassy in Rangoon instructing poor Slimming to put his Land Rover, complete with driver, on a train forthwith, addressed to Myitkyina, to arrive not later than Monday evening with orders to report to Granville. Granville had also laid in a stock of hard rations to take with us in case we should at any time be stranded away from food supplies. Judging by ear, some of the hard rations were in bottles, and some were harder than others. (It is legitimate to paraphrase George Orwell, since he once served in the Burma Police.)

The Allens' cocktail-party the previous evening had added another string to our bow. Among the guests was Glover, the General Manager in Rangoon of the Burmah Oil Company, which has a network of retailers all over Burma selling petrol in the more sophisticated areas and kerosene everywhere. Glover was leaving at crack of dawn for an inspection tour, but he promised to warn his colleague, Cousins, that I might call on him for help. I duly spent half an hour with Cousins explaining where we were hoping to go, and he furnished me with a sheaf of letters to up-country agents, mostly Indians, telling them to fall in with any requests we might make and to give us credit if necessary. His main agent for the north was at Mandalay, where our aircraft would be calling, and Cousins undertook that this chap would meet us on the airfield as we passed through to discuss ways and means.

But Cousins, who had served during the war with the Chin Levies, did me an even better turn than this. Far and away my closest friend in the country was Saw Chet Khin, a Karen. Our friendship dated from our first meeting in 1942, when we were training in the Central Provinces of India for the first Wingate Expedition. He speedily became one of the best known and best liked officers in the whole of Wingate's Force. He was actually twenty-eight, though he looked ten years younger; he was slight and neat in appearance; and except on the rare occasions when he was cross, which produced a black frown, he had a broad and famous grin. In private life he had graduated from Rangoon University into the Customs, becoming a Reserve officer in his spare time. On the first expedition, after disintegration set in, he took command of over a hundred Gurkhas who had lost their British officers, and brought them out to India, for which he was awarded the M.C. I managed to poach him for my own brigade on the second show, and posted him as Reconnaissance Officer to The Queen's. At one time they were using him as a company commander, and his English troops adored him.

After Independence, Chet became a brigadier in the Burma Army and we continued to correspond. Then I heard the devastating news that he had joined the Karen rebels and captured Maymyo. I was to learn in the course of this present journey the true and very different story of that affair. Later I heard with a stricken heart that he had been captured, tried and condemned to death. Then came news that his sentence had been commuted to imprisonment for life. After seven years he was released and we were free to write to each other again. He was able to find a job wite

Burmah Oil, working in their refinery across the Pegu River in Syriam.

There is no telephone between Rangoon and Syriam, but Cousins had a radio link; and we were able to arrange that Chet and his wife should meet Laura and me for dinner in the Strand Hotel. The Allens sent us down in an Embassy car that evening; and there was Chet, searching for me among the pillars in the hall, as trim as ever. We fairly hugged each other. Never before had we met except under open skies, and he looked oddly unfamiliar in a white dinner jacket and black tie. I knew him better as I had so often seen him: with a pack on his back and a carbine slung over his shoulder; or, as once, lying idly in the sun, stripped to the waist, and eating his way through a huge pile of tomatoes in a village from which he and his companions had evicted the Japs. But it was still the same Chet, heart and soul, in a body which like mine had grown a good deal plumper. Laura and Chet's wife, June, had a poor evening of it while he and I reminisced. We never drew breath until the hour came when he and June had to catch the last launch home, and even then we had barely scratched the surface of all we had to say to each other. But we planned to meet again when we got back from the north; and meanwhile he had told me where to find other friends.

By now everything was in train for Monday, and we could relax. On the Saturday morning Dick Allen took us across the Rangoon River in his speedboat to a sampan which he also owned, moored on the far bank; the skipper, inevitably, was Lingam. Sampan and speedboat proceeded separately to the Pegu River, where two members of the Embassy staff treated us to an exhibition of water-skiing. Laura had tried this performance several times behind our own speedboat at Ballantrae, but had always been defeated by the chill of the waters of the Firth of Clyde. Now triumphantly she did

it, after only two preliminary flounders, skimming past the
sampan with ease while I recorded it, plus an inadvertent
glimpse of Lingam's yachting cap, on coloured film for
posterity. As she preened herself on her achievement aboard
the sampan afterwards, I rather ungallantly pointed out to
her each successive carcass as it floated past on the filthy
waters of the Pegu River in which she had just been wallowing.

We spent Sunday morning in the more conventional
ambiance of the Yacht Club. (Let me disarm Sabbatarian
objections by saying that church services in Rangoon are
held in the cool of the evening.) The club stands on a
grassy peninsula jutting out into a lake studded with wooded
islands. Personally I am a blue-water cruising sailor of the
humbler sort, and not much good in racing dinghies; but
His Excellency was gracious enough to affirm that I made
admirable ballast. Our race was a bit of a drifting match,
but it ended congenially with copious gin-and-limes on the
lawn in front of the club-house.

Rangoon was gay, Rangoon was fun, and the Allens were
wonderful hosts; but I was longing to get up into the real
Burma that I knew.

II

WE LEFT THE EMBASSY at 4.30 a.m., having spurned the Allens' offer of breakfast. I thought in my innocence that gorgeous Burmese air hostesses would be plying us with trays in the aircraft; or, failing them, that sellers of curry and rice would be hawking their wares at our various ports of call. I was to be proved very wrong indeed, and Laura had a good deal to say about it before next we ate. The wily Brooking, having travelled this way before, had demolished a whole plateful of bacon and eggs, a rackful of toast and half a pot of marmalade before leaving his house.

Our aircraft was an appropriately old-fashioned Dakota, such as used to drop supplies on us from tree-top level during the war; and the pilot a fat, jolly Dutch-Malay Indo-European from Sumatra. We lumbered along at six or seven thousand feet, with the hills on our starboard hand and to port the broad Irrawaddy plain, part jungle, part cultivation. Below us ran the road and railway to Mandalay. From the map on my lap I was able to identify various towns whose names were known to me from the days when I was a joint planner in Delhi, and later, but which I had never seen. I peered down with interest at Meiktila, where the thumbscrews really began to turn on the Japs in March, 1945; but I knew too little of the battle to pick out the landmarks.

Our second stop was at Mandalay, and there on the airstrip was a reception committee of two. One was John Slimming, the information officer whose Land Rover had

been reft away from him so abruptly. He was bearing his
loss with fortitude, and actually invited us to stay with him
for two or three days on our return journey. The other was
Keith Gregory, the Burmah Oil agent for the whole of
Upper Burma, who had been alerted by a telegram from
Cousins in Rangoon. He was born in Burma and educated
in Maymyo; he knew the country well, and was more than
willing, on the strength of Cousins's telegram, to drop
everything and join us as courier-cum-interpreter at any
time or place on our journey that might suit us.

We all adjourned to the hut that served for airfield office,
and spread out our large-scale map of Burma on the only
article of furniture in the place, a rickety ping-pong table.
Our plans depended entirely on the whim of the brigade
commander at Myitkyina, but I had a fair idea of where I
wanted to go. There was no question in my mind of trying
to follow our war-time routes at any stage. I had grown
much too fat and idle and sybaritic to want to slash my way
up hill and down dale just for the hell of it, and there was no
longer any need for concealment. I wanted rather to cut
across these routes at various points. With a few exceptions,
the most exciting episodes had always happened at easily
accessible places, where the Japs had made efforts to inter-
cept us: on the Irrawaddy, on the railway and on the motorable tracks. These last were few and far between. It was at
these places also that we had had most help from the local
inhabitants, and at most risk; and although I would dearly
have loved to trek up to some of the more remote and delect-
able bivouacs, where we had lain with our shirts off beside
some pleasant stream, secure in the knowledge that there
were no Japs within miles; or to such fastnesses in the
Kachin hills as Pakaw, where the Kachins themselves
guarded all the tracks, and the Japs were too terrified to
venture, and we ourselves could relax entirely: I still thought

that we could accomplish most of what we had come to do without departing very far from the main lines of communication. I pretended to myself and everybody else that I was thinking chiefly of Laura's comfort. Laura at any rate was not deceived.

The Mu Valley Railway runs north from Mandalay as far as Myitkyina. I had crossed it several times and sabotaged it once, when we blew up a bridge and blocked a cutting. Gregory explained that we could communicate with him by telegraph from any of the railway stations, and we made a vague provisional rendezvous to meet at Katha in a fortnight's time. Katha is a biggish town on the Irrawaddy, and capital of Katha District. It would make a good central base for part of our journey, since it can be reached not only by river, but also by rail; a spur from the main line runs down to serve the steamer station. The Deputy Commissioner there was one Bill Maung Maung, by all accounts a character, to whom Shan Lone in Rangoon had promised to commend us; and it turned out that Gregory and he had been at school together in Maymyo.

Meanwhile an argument developed as to whether it was possible to drive from Myitkyina to Katha. The others said it wasn't; I obstinately maintained that it was, because I remembered the Japs building a road roughly parallel with the railway in order to reduce their dependence on the latter, which was for ever being attacked by the Royal Air Force from the air and by Chindits on the ground. The fact that I hadn't been in Burma for nearly sixteen years wasn't going to deter a chap like me from telling people who lived there all about it. The argument ended with the pilot saying that it was time to get back in the aircraft, and we walked out to it in a flurry of last minute arrangements.

Keith Gregory promised to warn by telegraph some of his B.O.C. sub-agents in the Railway Valley that we might be coming; we promised to telegraph Keith Gregory whether or not the Katha rendezvous was to hold good; John Slimming made us promise to accept his invitation to stay with him on our way south; and I made John Slimming promise to get hold of two Karen friends of mine who were said to be living in Mandalay. I asked him also to try and get a message to Sao Man Hpa, a slim, handsome Shan prince who had come in with us on the first expedition, and who eventually slipped away with Wingate's permission to his mountain kingdom up near the China border. I hoped there might be a chance of inducing him to meet me in Mandalay in three weeks' time.

As we took off from the air-strip, waving to our friends on the ground, I got my first glimpse of Pagoda Hill and of the famous fort. The fort was knocked to smithereens in the fighting of 1945, but its outer walls and the moat were still intact. We climbed over the hills above Mogok, where the rubies come from, and Bernardmyo, called after a namesake of mine in the last century. *Myo* means city, and there are other towns in Burma called after British founders: such as Maymyo, after Colonel May, and Allanmyo after Major Allan. These names are at least more euphonious than their equivalents in India: McCluskieganj, for instance, in Bengal.

The character of our fellow-passengers had changed perceptibly at Mandalay. The prosperous and sophisticated, mostly in European clothes, had alighted there, and their places had been taken by passengers in Burman dress, with bundles rather than suitcases for luggage. Laura had been watching a patient old woman, humbly attired, squatting in the shadow of the aircraft's wing with an enormous, shapeless load beside her. When the passengers were called forward she picked up her bundle and took her place in the plane. Most of the new passengers, including the old lady, got out at our next stop, the modest little strip at Mong Mit, the capital of the Shan State nearest to the Irrawaddy. There are something like twenty Shan States, of which a handful are in Siam and all the rest in Burma, thanks to a famous figure of the eighteen-nineties, Sir George Scott— " Scott of the Shan Hills." Under the British régime they were more or less autonomous under their rulers, or *Sawbwas*, several of whom went to English public schools, and one at least of whom married an English wife. Now they have been integrated into the Union of Burma, though with separate representation, and with most of the *Sawbwas* sitting in the Upper House. Sao Man Hpa, whom I was hoping to see in Mandalay, was either brother or uncle to the *Sawbwa* of one of these states.

The single runway at Mong Mit, where we had another complete change-over of passengers, had been built by the Japanese during the war, and the place was as rustic as a country railway station in England. It was now well on in the morning, and Laura and I were famished with hunger; there wasn't so much as a banana to be got. But I had other distractions. I was beginning to get really excited, for the next few minutes of flying would bring me over country I knew. My own column had got near enough to Mong Mit during the war, in 1943, to see the Japanese aircraft which were scouring the country in search of us, descending towards this very strip on which I was now smoking a cigarette. I buttonholed the pilot and declared my interest; and he agreed to fly a little bit west of his course for the first few minutes of the next stage. There were one or two old haunts I thought I might identify. As soon as we were airborne, I was invited forward to the cockpit for a better view.

And so, five minutes after take-off, I spotted the large village of Myitson, lying at the precise point where the Shweli—" The River of Golden Sands "—turns abruptly to the northwards, after flowing 250 miles south-west out of the mountains of China. Joining it from the west was the Nam Mit, *nam* being the Shan word for stream. In March, 1943, during a very hot spell, I had bivouacked four miles up the Nam Mit from where it flows into the Shweli at Myitson: the southernmost point in Burma that I reached during the war. We arrived on it after three days of marching through country so thirsty that we had been reduced to digging for water at the corners of stream-beds which had dried up weeks before; for some reason water lingers at the corners longer than on the straight reaches. This is a painful process. After hours of excavation with your mouth dry and no moisture in your body to sweat with, you still have to exercise a stern patience until the mud in the holes has settled and the water can be scooped up and drunk: no joke for 300 men and 70 animals with their tongues hanging out, and the mules and ponies fighting and plunging to break away and bounce the queue. But the Nam Mit was two feet deep, with cool clear water running freely over clean sand. Having mounted guards up and downstream on either bank, to make sure that we weren't caught literally naked, we took turns at lying for half an hour in the water, washing away even the memory of scum on our tongues and at the corners of our mouths.

From that idyllic bivouac we sent out two pairs of Karen scouts in native dress. One lot never came back, and we heard later that they were prisoners; I fear they were executed. The other lot came scurrying in to say that they had seen Japs in Myitson, that the locals estimated their strength at 700, and that rumour reported more on their way from Mong Mit. (We now know from the Official History the identity both of the battalion already in Myitson, and of the other, from a different brigade, which was coming up to reinforce it. Both had been dispatched to the neighbourhood for the specific purpose of hemming us in.) I reported this by signal to Wingate, and asked for an air strike on the village. Two hours later we heard the bombers going over, though the jungle was too thick for us to see them, and we hugged ourselves when we felt the ground thud in sympathy as the bombs went off. So far as I know, this was the first time in history that bombs were called down on to a target behind the enemy lines by troops on the spot. We were 140 miles by crow-flight from the nearest British outposts, and 260 from the airfield where the bombers were based. It was a purely fortuitous business; but the following year we developed a highly elaborate and effective technique based on this experience, with a squadron of B 25 Mitchell bombers with American crews always standing by for such calls.

Now, from the air, I could see the motorable track running west towards the Irrawaddy which our scouts had told us about. From Myitson to the Irrawaddy is a mere thirty miles; and this track, easily patrolled, formed the mouth of the Irrawaddy-Shweli bag into which that first expedition of ours contrived to get itself. Neither river is fordable. The Japs confiscated all the boats they could find on our side, and sealed us off with two divisions. The astonishing thing in retrospect is that so many of us were able to slip through; though I myself had to abandon forty men while crossing the Shweli farther north two weeks later, and it was the blackest moment of my life. Some were drowned; most of the rest died in prison. But before our aircraft reached the point on the Shweli where that happened, the pilot indicated that he must get back on course; and I was glad to be spared a sight of the place.

The Irrawaddy runs from north to south for all but a hundred miles of its course; and those hundred miles are the stretch immediately below Bhamo, where it runs roughly west almost to Katha. We saw it coming up now, across our

front instead of parallel with our course. The pilot began to
let down, and soon we were skimming along with our
wheels only a few feet above the sandbanks in the river, as
we approached Bhamo air-strip. Here again all our fellow-
passengers left us, and a new lot, eyeing us curiously, was
waiting to get in. I noticed that this time they were nearly
all Kachins.

Among the trees a mile or so away we could see the tops
of the pagodas and taller buildings of Bhamo town, the
nearest sizeable place to the China frontier. It has an
ancient history as a staging post for traders and travellers.
There is some evidence to suggest that Marco Polo visited it
at the end of the 13th century; certainly the Dutch tried, but
failed, to establish a " factory " there in the 17th. It is
primarily a Burmese city, but the country to the east, south
and north is all Kachin. From the east the town is dominated by the towering heights of the Sinlumkaba Hill Tracts,
a Kachin stronghold which the people of that tough race
look upon with the same sort of fierce affection as Clan
Campbell has for Cruachan. It is the native district of
Rusty Shan Lone, and of many another Kachin fighting man
well known to my own generation. The spelling may be
ugly, but the name itself is euphonious: pronounce it
Sīnn-lōōm-kǎ-bāh, with the accent heavy on the " bah."
The town itself is 6,000 feet up; the cleft in the hill above
it is visible for sixty or seventy miles. I had often seen it
from afar, but never before had I been so nearly under its
shadow.

Soon we were airborne again on the last stage of our
flight to Myitkyina. Our Kachin fellow-passengers were
evidently experienced air travellers, since they were looking
out of the windows with far less eagerness than we were:
in fact, I can claim in all modesty that they found Laura and
Granville and me much more intriguing to look at than the

jagged hills and deep glens and plaited jungle above which we were flying.

I had never been to Myitkyina, any more than I had previously been to Bhamo or Katha. In war-time they were all occupied by hefty Jap garrisons. We knew them by name, only too well, and all about them; it was our business to have an intimate knowledge of what was going on in them, the habits of the garrisons, which buildings were being used as billets, the routes in and out, and everything that was happening in the environs. To the towns themselves we gave a wide berth, although in 1944 I had some columns operating close in to Katha. I had never been within sixty miles of Myitkyina, but its geography and lay-out were well known to me. The town (which, by the way, is pronounced Myi-chi-nāh, and means " riverside ") has no ancient history like Bhamo: it only came into being in 1901, when the railway reached the Irrawaddy and halted there. It at once became the natural centre of that part of the world, the seat of the Commissioner and the headquarters of the Frontier Police. It was ideal for the purpose, since the famous confluence of the two rivers which join to form the Irrawaddy lies only thirty miles to the north. Both their valleys could be easily administered and a watchful eye kept on all that stirred in them. The trade routes from the north to Bhamo and so into China, both legitimate and clandestine, were all within easy reach, though it was impossible to prevent a prosperous contraband traffic in such commodities as opium and gold. Although every sort of race is included in its population, it was the obvious choice to be the capital of the new Kachin State established after Independence.

The mountains were closing in on us from all sides as we approached the air-strip in our Dakota, to make the fifth and final landing of the day. From the air the town looked much

as I expected, but more beautiful. I could see the sprawling
bazaar, the neat lines of the cantonment, and on the northern
edge of the town some biggish houses, in their own gardens
on the river's edge. A train was standing in the station
breathing steam. There were upturned faces in the streets,
and bullock-carts moving on the tracks outside the town.
We circled and came in to land, with the bushes speeding
past just below us. We touched down, taxied to a halt and
stopped. We had arrived.

Thirty or forty men were standing around on the strip, in
front of an iron hangar, a dozen yards from where our pilot
had switched off his engines after a final revving-up. The
first to greet us was a shy young man, perhaps the Airways
agent; but he was superseded so quickly that we never discovered who he really was, and we never saw him again.
He was thrust aside by a stocky, cheery, broad-shouldered
Kachin in European clothes, who rushed up and introduced himself; but I am always deaf when I step out of a
Dakota, and I didn't catch his name or function. He
introduced us to the Deputy Commissioner, a Burmese,
whom we never saw again either, and who was busy anyway
supervising the loading into our late aircraft of a pile of tin
boxes from a corner of the hangar. Apparently they were
ballot-boxes for the impending elections, which our Indo-
European was going to fly on to Fort Hertz, the Ultima
Thule of Burma, 200 miles farther north. I asked whether
we couldn't do one more hop in the aircraft to see from the
air that last cranny of Upper Burma, the happy hunting
ground of such famous travellers and naturalists as Kingdon
Ward and J. K. Stanford; but there wasn't enough room for
both us and the ballot-boxes. We submitted ourselves to
being hustled by the Kachin into a large car; he had
already detailed an underling to bring in our belongings.

We were now being driven at speed into the town, with

no idea of where we were going or into whose hands we had fallen: though it was easy to deduce that this was the doing of Shan Lone. Just as we were reaching the fringes of the bazaar, and craning our necks to see the crowded stalls and the polyglot populace, our Kachin twisted round and said to Laura: " Not very much like Ayrshire, is it? "—a remark which took the breath out of us. After enjoying our surprise he confessed that he had only lately come back from a spell in Britain; five months earlier he had been in camp with some boy scouts from Edinburgh on the estate of one of my neighbours only thirty miles from Auchairne.

The car turned in at a gateway, and drew up before a fine two-storey building, in a garden running down to the river. In style it was a compromise between Burmese and British, standing not on lofty stilts but on modest supports two or three feet above ground, with steps up to the veranda, and built of solid teak. On the lower floor were a hall, a large dining-room and a sitting-room; upstairs were three bedrooms, complete with balconies, a bathroom (though only a tin bath), and a genuine plug-pulling water-closet. A pantry was attached to the main building, and the kitchen and servants' quarters were a few yards away. The walls were adorned with large photographs of Aung San the Liberator, Ne Win the Prime Minister, picturesque views of various places in the Kachin State, and catches of mammoth fish. A *durwan*, or major-domo, in spotless white appeared, and our anonymous host asked if we would like some luncheon. It was now mid-afternoon, and Laura and I, who had eaten nothing all day bar a digestive biscuit with our early morning tea eleven hours earlier, said " Yes " rather faintly. Our host gave some orders—I was beyond caring which language he was using—and said he would come back and see us in the evening.

We still didn't know where we were, or who it was that

Myi Tun Hka and I drink a toast at Saga

The men who hid us at Saga ; N'gum Hdu the headman in the middle

The Indawgyi looking east

The pagoda and the gum tree at the Second Defile, where
Robert's party crossed in 1943

had brought us there. Our meal, a luncheon in the European
style, arrived in about twenty minutes; and after we had
eaten I felt recovered enough to put some questions to the
durwan. Our benefactor was none other than Kumje
Tawng. I had never met him, but like most people who
served in the less conventional forces in Burma during the
war I knew him well by reputation. Like his father before
him, he had served in the Burma Rifles, marching out to
India with them in the withdrawal of 1942; then, after
parachute training, he had been dropped into Upper
Burma, and done great things against the Japanese, as an
independent operator, as second-in-command to Shan
Lone, and as an officer of the Kachin Levies: ending the war
with the Military Cross and the Burma Gallantry Medal.
What I didn't know was that since Independence he had
been Deputy Commissioner Myitkyina, until about a year
earlier; and he was now in the service of the Kachin State.

The building we were in was the State Guest House, as
we had more or less deduced. But when the *durwan* volunteered the additional titbit that it was formerly the bungalow
of Steel Brothers' Forest Manager, the penny suddenly
dropped. It was here, in this very building, that my close
friend and companion John Fraser was held and tortured
by the Japanese officers in May, 1942; they were using the
place as their mess. And it was from this compound that he
had escaped.

John Fraser was my second-in-command on the first
Wingate expedition, and my Senior Reconnaissance Officer
—a position I created for him out of thin air—on the second.
His father was an Assam planter from the Scottish borders;
he himself was an employee of Steel Brothers, and a reserve
officer in the Burma Rifles. In 1942, after every kind of
hairbreadth escape from the first moment of the campaign,
he was sent to Myitkyina as station staff officer, to help

organise the air-lift of women and children and other refugees from Myitkyina air-strip. Except for Fort Hertz, which few of them had any prospect of reaching, Myitkyina was the last place from which air evacuation was possible: the other landing grounds had been swallowed up one by one. John drove up there in his own car, and functioned until the Japs arrived and put a stop to everything, when he fell into their hands like everybody else who still remained.

The story of his escape will justify a digression. On the second night, after the Japs had finished with him, he managed to convince his jailer that owing to his sufferings he was physically unable to bring his wrists together to be bound as tightly as before. When left alone he managed to release himself; he also freed Serjeant Pratt of the 7th Hussars, but he dared not do the same office for a third man, who had gone off his head and was raving. Pratt and he then scampered off into the dark, and got clear away. The only place worth making for was Fort Hertz, which so far as they knew (and they were right) was still in British hands. John had lost his spectacles while the Japanese were bashing him about, and was walking in a mist. At Sumprabum, a hundred and thirty miles north of Myitkyina, John found, by the roadside, his own car, which somebody had pinched in an effort to get away, and abandoned when it ran out of petrol. He remembered that he had left a spare pair of spectacles in the dashboard locker. He fumbled for them. There they were.

Fraser and Pratt never reached Fort Hertz. They joined forces instead with a party they encountered which was trying the desperate measure of getting out over the Chaukan Pass, which leads to the head-waters of the Dihing, and so into Assam. There were several such parties; theirs consisted of about a dozen. Only five Europeans had ever made this journey, all between the years 1892 and 1900; and it had never been attempted in the monsoon, which was now in full swing. For a hundred miles there was no trace of man or beast, and precious few of bird. The pass itself is at 8,000 feet, without a vestige of a track. When they could, they waded along the rivers, and this was for about half the time; when the rivers were unwadable, they cut their way through the hills, where the jungle grew solid. Their daily march averaged five miles. They had to cross or go round twenty-three tributaries in full flood; where they crossed them, it was done by felling trees for bridges; and all they could muster between them for the job was three Burmese *dahs* and two *kukris*. The journey lasted more than seven weeks in constant rain. The hardest physical part of it coincided with their shortest commons. One of them was drowned half-way; John himself was washed away, and got stuck below a log under the surface of the water; he was saved by Ritchie Gardiner plunging into the water and cutting off his equipment. Another of the party died two days after they reached safety. They were saved in the end by the dumps of food brought into the hills under incredible difficulties by the organisation set up by the Indian Tea Association, under Gyles Mackrell, and by the heroic work of the Assam Rifles, the Rangpang Nagas, and many others equally unhymned. And within a few weeks after all this, John Fraser was posted to me, to come back into Burma for another go.

John used to tell a story about his fabulous journey over the Chaukan, in which I still delight. One of the party who, to do him justice, pulled his weight throughout the ordeal, was a senior official, and conscious thereof. As the survivors neared civilisation, he said to Serjeant Pratt:—

" Pratt! We've been through a lot together, and I shall not forget how well you've done. But now that we are practically back in the civilised world again, you must realise that I am, in fact, a senior official. Will you therefore, please stop calling me X, and address me from now on as Mr. X? "

And according to John Fraser—but you can never quite believe all he says—Pratt replied:—

" Very good, Mr. X. And would *you* mind addressing me in future as *Serjeant* Pratt? "

It was difficult to realise that in this comfortable building, where we had just unstrapped our bedding-rolls and eaten a large meal, John Fraser had been mishandled as a prisoner, and had barely escaped with his life. It was the more difficult because, only three weeks ago, we had spent a night with his wife and three children, one of them my godson, in their snug farmhouse in the borders, six miles from Galashiels, with his turkeys and north-country Cheviot sheep all around.

Highly contented with our lot and still slightly incredulous about everything, Laura and I strolled down across the lawn, where a man was watering the herbaceous border, past the white flag-pole to the wooden post-and-rail fence at the bottom of the garden. Immediately beyond, the ground fell away in a twenty-foot drop to a narrow beach and the Irrawaddy. We leaned on the fence and admired the view. We were on the outside of a great sweeping curve. Downstream a ferry was plying ; upstream were the high blue mountains in which John Fraser had found his freedom in war, and Kingdon Ward and Stanford theirs in peace. Away to the north-east stood a mountain like a broken tooth, the twin brother of " Peeping Tom " in the Imatong Mountains of the southern Sudan—so called because wherever you travel in Equatoria it always seems to spring up in the distance to peer at you. The colours were astounding: a mass of flowers in the garden, the river a Mediterranean blue, the sandbanks bright gold, and on the far side of the river luscious green vegetation. It was so hot that I seriously considered a swim, and slithered down the bank to try the water. I put in my hand, and found it as cold as snow.

Even if we'd wanted to—and we were happy enough where we were, for the moment—we couldn't have left Myitkyina that afternoon. The brigade commander, without whose fiat we couldn't go anywhere, was away until late that night, so Kumje Tawng had told us; and our Land Rover hadn't yet reported for duty. But a car, complete with driver, now arrived from Kumje Tawng to put itself at our disposal in case we wanted to go somewhere in the town. Laura, Granville and I climbed into it and set off for the bazaar, to buy oddments for our journey and to add to our stock of presents for giving away. I have always had a soft spot for bazaars and particularly for those, like pre-war Damascus, where sellers and buyers alike come from many different races, and have travelled a long way to do their business. The bazaar at Myitkyina didn't disappoint.

In the wooden shops with their plaited roofs, and on the dusty unmetalled earth roads between them, hundreds of people, whose birthplaces were thousands of miles apart, were engaged in buying and selling, although at this evening hour the tempo had dropped and the jostling had abated. There were Kachins, Burmese, Shans, Indians, Chinese and Gurkhas in profusion, and some wild-looking, long-haired creatures whom I couldn't identify: I thought they might be Mishmis, but they might equally have been Lashis, or Marus, or Yawyins, or Nungs, or any other of those northern races whom even ethnologists hesitate in identifying. Certainly there were numerous Tibetans.

There is in Burma this extraordinary profusion of races, all hugger-mugger, many of them divided into sub-tribes, and many of them on top of each other. The Mons of

Lower Burma, for instance, have been in the country far longer than the Burmese who conquered them; in the 18th century they made a serious attempt at ejecting the Burmese, advancing several hundred miles up the Irrawaddy and keeping them at bay for more than a decade until swept back and finally overrun by King Alaungpaya: since when they have been submerged, though still identifiable. In Upper Burma, from Mandalay northwards, you can deduce from the place names on the map the preponderance of a race in any particular area; but if you travel fifty miles in any one direction you may pass through villages belonging to several different races—and through some inhabited by a mixture. Intermarriage is rare.

In broad outline, the Kachins or Jinghpaws, with smaller offshoot tribes, came into Burma from Tibet some fifty generations ago, evicting Chins, Shans and others from the northern hills. To-day the Kachins stretch from Assam in India right across Upper Burma into China; they number about half a million in Burma, and certainly more in China. To the south of the Kachin belt there is an almost equally wide sweep of Shans, from the Upper Chindwin at Singkaling Hkamti (which I by-passed on tiptoe in 1944 because there were Japs in it) through the Shan States into Siam itself: Shans and Siamese are both Thai. At one time the Shans had a kingdom in Assam; but the Kachin invasion was accompanied by such slaughter that there is little trace of it to-day. The Hukawng Valley, which leads from near Myitkyina towards Assam, derives its name from the Jinghpaw word meaning cremation mounds, and refers to the disposal of Shan corpses after massacre; the word Jinghpaw itself is said to derive from the Tibetan word for cannibal.

All this is so compressed and over-simplified that any right-minded ethnologist will hereafter box my ears if he can get within reach of them; but I will defend it as being roughly right. The Burmese domination of the country, punctuated with ups and downs, has lasted since the middle 1550's. The earliest precarious European foothold was that established by the Dutch in 1647, which lasted a mere ten years. In the 18th and early 19th centuries the French and British were in hot competition; in 1852 Lord Dalhousie, my great-grandfather, annexed everything up to a line fifty miles north of Prome; and in 1885 Lord Dufferin took over Upper Burma. Here endeth the shortest and most inadequate account of the enthralling history of Burma that has ever been written; but this much at least is necessary to understand the complexity of a country which is not much bigger than our own.

Concerning the size of Burma there hangs a tale which is perhaps worth telling. Throughout Burmese history there has run a strong thread of self-confidence, intertwined with a mistrust of foreigners: traits of character which are still present to-day. During the Crimean War, King Mindon once asked to be shown Britain on a map of the world, and when he saw it commented: " Yes, I always knew it was a very small country. Now show me Burma." When he saw that it was much the same size, he flew into a rage, and was only pacified when his courtier, losing his nerve and fearful of losing his head, hastily added most of Asia to his sovereign's putative dominions.

And thirty years later, when King Theebaw, egged on by his Queen Supayalat—"Soup-plate" to the British soldiers— was defying the British, he refused to believe that we had it in our power to overwhelm him. The sagest of his statesmen, the Kinwun Mingyi, had been to London, and had also been Queen Victoria's guest at Windsor; he had seen something of our strength. He tried in vain to persuade the King and Queen to desist from their provocation. The King ignored

III

BACK AT THE GUEST HOUSE we found that our Land Rover had arrived. It was painted a delicate cream, and bore the legend " British Information Services " in English and Burmese: Burmese script is the most elegant and graceful that I know. The driver was a small, friendly, rather anxious Burmese from Mogok called Kan Gyi Maung (" The Man from the Big Pond "): he wore a white shirt, a black jacket, a scarlet *loongyi* and no hat, and his English was good enough to enable him to act as interpreter, provided one kept the matter simple. He might well have been less friendly and even more anxious had he known what was in store for his precious vehicle and its paintwork; more than once he was to beat his breast and moan; but he was a good little chap, and I remember him with affection.

Granville and I abandoned Laura, who by this time was more than ready to " put her toes up," as she calls it, and set off to visit the army headquarters, to make sure of an appointment with the brigade commander when he got back. This was my first view of the modern Burma Army, and I was very well impressed. The sentry on the gate was smart, and the guard commander treated us with exactly the right mixture of deference and suspicion. While he quite properly kept us waiting, having sent a runner to tell somebody of our presence, I looked past the barrier and saw how the lawns were flanked with flowers; the stones along the road inside the perimeter were whitewashed to perfection and so were the ropes that drooped from post to post. The notice-boards indicating the various offices were neatly painted and inscribed in English as well as Burmese. I noticed that the Signals Office used the same shades of blue and white as our own Signals do, to proclaim their whereabouts. My spirits rose as I heard a bugler faultlessly sounding Defaulters—our own British bugle call; although in Highland regiments, where we do these things better, our defaulters on the rare occasions when we have any are summoned by a piper playing " A Man's A Man For A' That."

The orderly returned and spoke to the guard commander; the barrier was raised, to let Granville and me through on foot; Kan Gyi Maung and the Land Rover remained at the guard room. It was only fifty yards to the trim two-storey building, where we were ushered down a passage. Above each door projected a wooden sign inscribed Brigade Major, Staff Captain and so on, still in both languages, but otherwise exactly as in a well-run British brigade headquarters. We were ushered into a small square ante-room and abandoned. In a couple of minutes there appeared a young staff captain. He was shy, and I had to make the running; but he confirmed that there had been a signal about us, and that the brigade commander, Colonel U Saw Myint, and his brigade major were expected back late that night. I told him in outline what I hoped to do; but he was evidently rather embarrassed, and uncertain as to whether he was empowered to discuss things with us: so we contented ourselves with making a provisional appointment to see his boss next morning. Back at the Guest House we heard and saw a helicopter coming in over the town to land, and deduced that this was Saw Myint returning.

Our evening in the Guest House was enlivened by new

arrivals: U Bo, the Inspector-General of the Burma Police, and his wife, and the wife of the German Ambassador in Rangoon as their guest. It struck me that U Bo might have come to keep a professional eye on me, but I was flattering myself unduly. The unexpected appearance of this party threw the staff of the Guest House into something of a tizzy. The *durwan's* reaction was to move Colonel Granville Brooking's bed into the room designed for the use of my wife and myself. This in turn threw Colonel Granville Brooking into something of a tizzy, and he dragged his bed out on to the veranda, where he must have been extremely cold. With nightfall the day-time heat which had almost tempted me to swim in the Irrawaddy had given place to a biting chill, and I lamented having deliberately left my tweed suit behind in the Embassy.

U Bo and his party had come up from Rangoon in a special railway coach. Their food was being cooked on the train and brought to the Guest House in containers. We had already made inroads on the European-style dinner prepared for us, but we looked with envy on the succulent curry, chicken, pork, fish and fruit, Burmese style, being eaten farther down the table. Our envy must have been obvious to the point of ill manners, for we were soon invited to move along and join the others. With the U Bos was U That Tin, the local Deputy Inspector-General of Police who had come along to join them, and whom we were to meet later on in our travels.

After dinner Kumje Tawng dropped in to see us, and we broached some of the softer of Granville's hard rations. We were sitting over a dram when there was a fuss at the sitting-room door, and an Indian pushed his way in past the protesting *durwan*. He was tall, tousled and incoherent, and his English was patchy; he seemed frightened of everybody, and especially of the two high-ranking police officers. He turned out to be the Burmah Oil Company's sub-agent from Hopin, down the Railway Valley, and he was brandishing a telegram from Gregory saying that we would be coming through Hopin, and that he must stand by to give us any help we needed. Thoroughly fussed, he had hopped on to the first train to Myitkyina to find us.

It took us an appreciable time to discover what was worrying him so much. At last we prised out of him the 64-dollar question: could we eat Indian food, or must we have European? The vital importance of knowing the answer had made, to use the war-time phrase, his journey really necessary. We opted for Indian food, stipulating only that the curry shouldn't be too hot. He relaxed at once, just like a man against whom a serious charge has been preferred and then dropped. His visit illustrated, at any rate, that the telegraph service was pretty good: it was less than twelve hours since we had parted from Gregory on the air-strip at Mandalay, which was more than 200 miles from Hopin, and Hopin was ninety miles from Myitkyina.

Having calmed him down, we explained how, subject to the brigade commander's approval, we hoped to spend to-morrow night at Mohnyin, and would lunch with him at Hopin on the way. He reckoned that by road it would take us two and a half hours. From our experience on the morrow it was to become quite obvious that he himself had never done the trip except by rail; but this knowledge was still in the womb of the future.

With the Indian soothed and gone, and another issue of Granville's whisky in our glasses, we got Kumje Tawng to talk of his war-time adventures. After marching out of Burma in 1942, he had trained in India as one of a team of four parachutists under Rusty Shan Lone. The other two were a wireless operator and a demolition man; all were Kachins. They were intended to drop north of Myitkyina and to work their way down through Kachin areas, gathering intelligence and assessing the situation, to a rendezvous near Sima Pa, a well-known Kachin village just over the frontier into China. Here they were to meet a party from our own first Chindit expedition, under " Fish " Herring, formerly of the Bombay-Burmah, and Lezum Tan, a Kachin lieutenant of the Burma Rifles with long service in the ranks, both friends of mine. But this rendezvous was never kept, since shortly before they were due to be dropped Shan Lone broke his ankle playing hockey. The other three, with Kumje Tawng in temporary charge, were dropped according to plan, with orders to operate independently until Shan Lone could join them.

Now Kachin loyalty is proverbial. The only case I ever heard of where a Kachin co-operated with the Japs was rather special, and almost forgivable. This wretched man, of importance in his own neighbourhood, had a complaint against the Government some years before the war, and went down to Rangoon determined to see the Governor and win redress. He got into wrong hands and was induced to part with sums amounting to five thousand rupees, about £350, by way of bribes; he had never moved in such circles before, and was easily persuaded that this was a necessary preliminary to seeing His Excellency. He might not have even grudged the money; but he very much grudged paying it over and still not getting his interview, and he returned to his native village (which one of my columns occupied in 1944) with a natural chip on his shoulder. When the Japs first appeared, he did all that he could to help them until he was chased out by his own people. I tried to discover his subsequent history from Kumje Tawng and others; but either they didn't know, or they knew and wouldn't tell.

The area where Kumje Tawng and his party dropped was solid Kachin, and they received an ecstatic welcome. They moved south to a safe hide-out near Myitkyina, and Kumje Tawng took to haunting the railway between there and Mogaung in the congenial disguise of an opium smuggler, reporting his discoveries back to India through his own radio. His biggest day was when he found four ammunition wagons on a siding near Mogaung, and got the R.A.F. to bomb them. He found time also to travel down to Sinlumkaba, to tell Shan Lone's father and brother that he would soon be calling on them in person. This was especially welcome news, since the last they had heard of him was his capture by the Japs in Mergui eighteen months before; they knew nothing of his subsequent escape, or the fact that he had reached India.

It was now getting late. We had had a long day, and were all of us ready for bed; but when Kumje Tawng took his leave, Laura and I couldn't resist a last walk down the garden to the river before turning in. The moon was only a few days short of the full; the night was wonderfully clear, and there wasn't a cloud in the sky. The outline of the mountains was sharp and chilly, and the fast flowing waters were dappled as they ran past us at the foot of the little cliff. Theirs was the only sound we could hear; the ferry must have tied up for the night. There were some lights in the Guest House behind us, and a few others twinkling downstream. It was only seven days since leaving Scotland; yet already Rangoon seemed more distant still.

When I was in Burma during the war, I used to dream that we were safely out of it all, and my responsibilities over; it was a daily misery to wake up each time, and find that we were still " in." By contrast, for weeks after we got out, I used to dream that we were still " in," and wake up to the joy of finding we were " out." I never seriously thought that one day I would wake up in the erstwhile Japanese officers' mess at Myitkyina, and rejoice at finding myself "in" again.

But that is exactly what I did in the early morning of the 12th January, 1960.

I threw on some clothes and went down to the river again. For two years it had been an enemy and an obstacle; now it was a lodestone and a friend. I made a dawn obeisance to Peeping Tom. Away in the trees on the far side, thin blue smoke was rising from a hidden village, as it was in the town behind me; and downstream the ferry was creaking its way back towards our own bank, its first outward journey of the day already accomplished. I watched the white shirts of the ferrymen swing to and fro through their tiny arcs as they stood and pushed at their huge sweeps. There were clanging noises up in the Guest House kitchen, and I went and asked for some hot water to be sent upstairs.

After breakfast, Granville and I went along in the Land Rover to keep our appointment with Saw Myint, on whom everything depended. Under the military government he was complete dictator in his own territory, and it had been made quite clear to me in Rangoon that his veto, if he applied it, would be final. Large notices carrying photographs of Wanted Men with prices on their heads were stuck up everywhere in the bazaar, side by side with election posters. It was only a matter of months since military operations on a large scale were in full swing. I reminded myself that in my own three incarnations as a brigade commander I wouldn't always have been wildly enthusiastic about giving foreign strangers carte-blanche to wander about my parish while I had an internal security problem on my hands. I was therefore a little nervous when I found myself waiting in the same small square ante-room where we had met the staff captain the evening before.

I knew it was going to be all right the moment Saw Myint bustled in and shook hands. He was soldierly and incisive, but the smile on his face was far too broad to be worn by somebody who was about to refuse a favour. He swung round to the operational map hanging on the wall behind him, and said that he imagined I would want to go here, and here, and here. At first I thought he must be telepathic; next it occurred to me that Bo Lwin's signal to him must have been extremely detailed; and then it turned out, most gratifyingly, that he possessed both the books I had written about our war-time excitements, and was as keen as I was that we should be able to cover the old ground.

My provisional plan resembled the *modus operandi* of a cable ship. I wanted to pick up the cable of our route at two or three places, and then to examine either side of it. The first I had in mind was Kadu Railway Station, something over a hundred miles down the line from Myitkyina, and the two or three Kachin villages lying on either side of it. In 1943, when the strength of my column had fallen from 318 to 70-odd, I had split up the remnant into three small parties in the hopes that this would give us a better chance of slipping across the Irrawaddy, despite the Japanese patrols on both banks. Two parties got across complete; the third was less lucky, and most of those who managed the crossing were rounded up a few days later. The next obstacle confronting us was the Railway Valley—not nearly so tricky as the Irrawaddy, but still not easy, for the Japs had Burmese sympathisers in some of the towns and garrisons in all the railway stations; they themselves patrolled the line constantly both day and night, while their partisans watched it and reported regularly. But the hills on either side of the valley were occupied entirely by Kachins, who provided us with relays of guides; and the point where we eventually crossed was a few hundred yards south of Kadu Railway Station.

Mohnyin looked a good spot for our first base and point of departure. It was only six miles short of Kadu, and according to the map there was a Rest House there. Not that this last was much to go on: my maps were war-time maps, and we had been told in Rangoon that most of the old Rest Houses were either requisitioned, or occupied by squatters, or fallen into ruins.

" Not at all! " said Saw Myint. " I've stayed at the Rest House myself. And one of my battalions has an outpost at Mohnyin. They can give you an escort. The very place."

As far as Mohnyin the road wasn't good, though at least it existed. Beyond was less certain, but we could always reach Kadu by rail or on foot, and if we wanted to get up into the hills we should be able to hire or borrow elephants. Our time wasn't quite unlimited, since Granville had to be back at Myitkyina to catch his aircraft south exactly a week later, although we could always pop him on a train if necessary. There was also the question of letting Gregory know whether or not we wanted to keep him to his provisional rendezvous at Katha; but Saw Myint settled that one with a shrug.

" You're in our hands now! " he said. " We'll look after you at Katha too. Just tell us what you want."

So much for all those Dismal Jimmies who had pro-phesied that we would never get beyond Rangoon. I have done a bit of scrounging in my time, and with shameful success. (Almost the last thing I ever did in the Army was to borrow a cruiser and three destroyers off the Royal Navy.) But there was no question of scrounging with Saw Myint, or even of hinting. He thrust everything at us. Had I transport, drivers, cooks, bearers, bedding, petrol, food, maps, money, cigarettes, cheroots? " Yes, yes, yes, yes," I said to every-thing; but even so, as we left his office, he whispered some-thing to Granville, who told me afterwards what it was: " Don't you worry about food."

We decided to drive down to Mohnyin that day, and Saw Myint would warn his outpost that we were coming. We

would base ourselves there for a few days, making sorties to
various villages where I hoped to find friends, and then
come back to Myitkyina to put Granville into his aircraft.
We would then drive down to Bhamo, where—and this was a
really handsome gesture—an Army launch from Katha
would meet us and carry us down the Irrawaddy. At Katha
we would set up Base No. 2, and make further sorties from
there. It was an admirable plan.

"But there is one condition," said Saw Myint, gravely.
Oh dear, I thought: there's going to be a snag after
all.

"What's that?" I said. "Of course: I'll fall in with
anything you say."

"You are not to go around blowing up my bridges," he
said. "Your days for blowing up bridges are over!"

I solemnly promised to leave all bridges as I would wish
to find them, and on this happy note of banter we parted.

Back at the Guest House we found Kumje Tawng, and
with him two middle-aged men in European jackets and
trousers and open-necked shirts. They were squatting on
the lawn, but as we drove in they rose from their haunches
and stood to attention, smiling shyly while they waited to
see if I recognised them. They were two Kachin ex-Jemadars,
of whom I dimly remembered one, Jhan Aw: he had served
in a Burma Rifles reconnaissance platoon with George
Carne, a planter from the Shan States, and Charlie Bruce,
of the Irrawaddy Flotilla, which had done a good performance in 1943. He asked for news of both. I was able to tell
him that George Carne's brother had won the V.C. in
Korea, but I knew nothing of George himself; Charlie was
growing fruit near Tewkesbury, which Jhan Aw rightly
thought was tame stuff for Charlie. Was there jungle
around Tewkesbury? I said I had never been there, but I
believed not.

The other chap had been with Fish Herring and Lezum Tan on their long march to Sima Pa, and had been captured by the Japanese while receiving a supply drop. Fortunately for him he was in plain clothes, and was able to persuade them that he was an innocent civilian working under duress for this one occasion; and the locals, being Kachins, had confirmed his tale. Instead of being shot he was taken away into China to do forced labour; after three months he escaped and made his way through the Kachin Hills back to India. It always amazed me how these soldier Kachins, when they found themselves separated from their units and on their own in their native mountains, and when they could easily go underground among their own people, would make their way back to their parent unit in India. I remember several instances of this.

There was another Kachin whom I knew was in Myitkyina and whom I was especially anxious to find. He served with me as a very senior subedar in good days and bad, and had become a major in the post-war Burma Army. But he always had a taste for the bottle; and somebody had told me in Rangoon that there was a scandal two or three years before, when my old friend was going on leave in an Irrawaddy steamer. He got gloriously drunk, tried to steer the ship and succeeded in knocking out the *serang* or skipper. The result was a court-martial and his disappearance from the Service. I was hoping to see him, and put out several feelers for him during my two visits to Myitkyina; but in the end I was told that he was " away," and I suspect that his absence was diplomatic. I would have loved to see him again, with his heavily wrinkled face and Irish eye and repertoire of stories. I have often wanted to steer ships and knock out skippers myself.

By eleven o'clock we were clear of Myitkyina. For the first

couple of miles, until just beyond the airfield, we bowled along on tarmac, with Kan Gyi Maung's accelerator hard down; and then with a bump we left the tarmac for ordinary metalling. We were still on an all-weather road, solid and hard, but it was deeply ribbed and full of pot-holes, and ten to twelve miles an hour was as much as we could do. It wasn't exciting country yet: just dry, low scrub no higher than one's head; numerous villages where the houses were mere huts, of no indigenous pattern but thrown together from oddments of material. This stretch was part of the road built by General Stilwell's engineers from Ledo in Assam over the Patkai Hills, through the Hukawng Valley to Myitkyina and Bhamo. The Ledo-Hukawng stretch was said to be entirely overgrown, although Group-Captain Peter Townsend had managed to struggle over it two or three years before with a Land Rover; but here it was still recognisable as a road, and the bridges were of metal and intact.

There was a fair amount of traffic: we passed something every four or five miles, a rusty bus or lorry, or a jeep. The chassis and engines all dated from the war, but the upper works, as sailors would say, were all home-made and variously quaint. Only natural mechanics of genius could have kept such contraptions in working order; and they were by no means being nursed along, but driven flat out.

We soon realised that our estimated time of arrival at Hopin had been wildly optimistic. It was two hours before we got abreast of Mogaung, which was only two-fifths of the way and lies some miles east of the road. As we reached the cross-roads and saw a sign-post in Burmese pointing to Mogaung, Kan Gyi Maung announced that we were about to run out of petrol, confessing coyly that it had not occurred to him to fill up before leaving, and that he had brought no spare cans. There was nothing for it but to turn off to Mogaung.

I should have been more reconciled to this waste of time had I known more detail about the Mogaung fighting. Mike Calvert's Chindit brigade had captured it in the closing stages of the 1944 monsoon, after two months of bitter fighting with heavy losses under appalling conditions of bad weather and ill-health. They won three V.C.s there. When they finally took the place, the B.B.C. ascribed the success to General Stilwell's Chinese, which inspired in Mike a signal which became a Chindit classic: " Understand from B.B.C. that Chinese have taken Mogaung. My brigade now taking umbrage." Stilwell's staff is supposed in Chindit mythology to have spent hours looking for Umbrage on the map.

As we drove up and down the town looking for the B.O.C. depot I noticed that every building was new, evidence of the destruction of the war. We found an enormous reclining Buddha, lying on its elbow and dreamily contemplating us as we went about our mundane business. I don't know whether it had been restored, or whether it had escaped damage by some miraculous chance. Squatting Buddhas of all sizes are ubiquitous; reclining ones are rare. Pagodas you see everywhere: in every town and village, by the roadside, in unexpected places like a jungle clearing, high up and miles from anywhere on mountain features or spurs; they may be 320 feet high like the Shwe Dagon or not much taller than a man. I used to think before I first knew Burma that you could go inside a pagoda, as you can a mosque; but in fact they are solid, built usually of brick, which is then covered with mud and finally whitewashed. The more fancy ones, with *poongyikyaungs* or monasteries attached, are often plastered with gold leaf by the faithful.

Medium or big pagodas are guarded by two or four

Chinthe, big *couchant* beasts, half lion and half dragon. It was this word that Wingate had in mind, but misremembered, when he wanted a name for his men. He hoped it would help persuade the Burmese that we were coming back into their country as protectors of their rights, both civil and religious. By the time he realised he had got it wrong it was too late: " Chindits " we had become, and Chindits we remained, though we all disliked the word, and referred to ourselves as " Special Force."

Old Burma hands got a lot of fun out of this solecism. One Steel Brothers man, H. E. W. Braund, who got an M.C. while serving with the Chin Levies, wrote an excellent lampoon in the News-Letter which Steels circulated throughout the war to keep their scattered people in touch with each other. I must explain that *S.E.A.C.* was the daily newspaper edited for the forces by Frank Owen, and distributed by parachute to the more inaccessible units; and that a D.C.3 is the same as a Dakota—or, if you are an American, as a C.47.

A *S.E.A.C.* set free from a D.C.3
   In the maw of the mad monsoon
Had a hectic day while the blast held sway,
   Then sank like a pricked balloon.

As it spiralled down on a Burmese town
   The breeze, with a last caress,
Chose a Chinthe's face as the resting place
   For this page of the Allied press.

When Maung Maung Galay pulled the bandage away
   The Chinthe's face was glum,
And turning its head to its mate it said:—
   " They're calling us CHINDITS, chum! "

Our diversion to Mogaung in search of petrol cost us all

of fifty minutes, from cross-roads back to cross-roads. Those cross-roads, by the way, are a fateful and historic spot. It was here in 1942 that the refugees, pouring northwards in their terror before the onrush of the Japs, had to make up their minds which way to take. The choice before them was Myitkyina or the Hukawng Valley. Myitkyina offered a chance of air evacuation, or failing that, the long walk north up the Fort Hertz cul-de-sac. No doubt the refugees could see aircraft in the distance, flying to and from the west; but they must have known that their chances of getting a passage out of Myitkyina were slender, with so many competing; and they knew also that it was only a matter of time before the Japs would appear in Myitkyina from Bhamo. The route to the Hukawng Valley, on the other hand, looks deceptively gentle and easy from the cross-roads, with no hint of how difficult it becomes later on; the tracks and defiles over the Patkai Range are lower than the Chaukan, but still almost impassable in the monsoon. Nobody will ever know the exact figures of how many men, women and children took the decision to turn west, hoping to reach India by the Hukawng. Something over 22,000 got through, but many thousands died.

We now turned south from the cross-roads, taking leave of Stilwell's metalled road, which turned west to follow the path which the refugees had taken. Our progress became dismally slow. The road was never less than six inches deep in dust, and deeply scored lengthways with bullock-cart ruts. A bullock-cart's wheel-base is much wider than a Land Rover's, but not wide enough with all the hazards of the track for a Land Rover to be navigated safely between the ruts. So the knack of driving was to straddle a rut, which meant brushing the bushes at the side of the track and inflicting the first of many indignities on Kan Gyi Maung's paintwork. Another point in favour of the bullock-cart as against the Land Rover is its high clearance: it will rumble cheerfully over mid-track obstacles against which the Land Rover will belly.

My spirits rose as Kan Gyi Maung's sank. The suburban environs of Myitkyina were far behind us, and we were getting into decent country. There were no longer any signs of motor vehicles. Single bullock-carts or convoys of three or four drew off the track into the bushes as we approached or overtook them, the bullocks snorting, tossing their heads and rolling their eyes in nervousness as we went past. A line of three elephants with their *oozies* (which is Burmese for *mahout*, which is Urdu for elephant-man) plodded off the road to let us by. Unlike the bullocks, they showed no fright but merely looked at us over their weather-beaten cheeks like cynical admirals.

Laura was sitting in the front beside Kan Gyi Maung, Granville and I in the back, hanging on like grim death to the rail in front of us. Half the time we were airborne as we went over bumps. Behind us rose a cloud of dust which in the old days would have attracted every Japanese aircraft in South-East Asia; now it merely enveloped each party of pedestrians that we met, and settled in their open mouths as they gazed at us. I remember one party of gaily-dressed Shan women in their enormous hats the size of a cart-wheel; several groups of men bent double under panniers of rice; and various hunting parties carrying their trophies. We met and photographed two young men bearing on their shoulders a pole from which was slung a dead porcupine.

We were now well into the jaws of the Railway Valley, though at this point it was still about eight miles wide; the trees were taller here, but we could get occasional glimpses of the hill-tops, three or four thousand feet above us. The streams which the track crossed were getting more frequent. Now that we were no longer on Stilwell's road there were no more metal bridges, and the numerous wooden ones were liable to be damaged or washed away every monsoon. We didn't dare cross any of them before first testing them for weight. In Granville Brooking and myself, both of us men of presence, we had two people admirably qualified for these experiments.

Some of the bridges simply didn't exist; an odd abandoned pile survived to show where they had been. Four streams out of five had to be splashed through. There was always a well-defined ford, just upstream or downstream, but the approaches were muddy and soft. It was a matter of pride with Kan Gyi Maung never to engage the four-wheel drive of his Land Rover until after his first failure to negotiate a ford without it, by which time he was usually stuck.

By now we were hours overdue at Hopin. It was no good worrying about it. I kept remembering Mike Calvert's abominable war-time pun, when he stood up in front of a map in Wingate's Operations Room with a pointer in his hand to outline his proposed campaign, and had the nerve to say: " Here's Hopin '! " But where the hell *was* Hopin? We began to ask passers-by how far it was, and received that familiar answer which used to infuriate us so much in the old days, and which now served to confirm beyond challenge that I was now back " in ": *ma we bu*, " it's not far." Pressed, one informant said five miles; the next said seven and it looked as though Hopin were gaining on us.

It struck me that there was something familiar about this conversation; and then I remembered: the opening chapter of *Guy Mannering*. I have just looked it up:—

Our traveller questioned more closely each chance passenger on his distance from the village of Kippletringan, where he proposed to quarter for the night. . . .

The answers, when obtained, were neither very re-
concilable to each other, nor accurate in the information which they afforded. Kippletringan was distant at
first " a gey bit ": then the " gey bit " was more
accurately described as " ablins three mile "; then the
" three mile " diminished into " like a mile and a
bittock "; and extended themselves into " four mile or
thereawa "; and lastly a female voice assured Guy
Mannering " It was a weary lang gate yet to Kippletringan, and unco heavy for foot passengers."

I finally deduced from the behaviour of my compass and
a sudden glimpse, across a stretch of paddy, of the hills, now
crowding in more closely, that we had overshot Hopin. We
found it eventually down a turning we had missed, and a
couple of miles east of the track, which bore no relation to
the map. There were no more sign-posts; the one which
had helped us find our way to Mogaung was the last for
200 miles.

It was well after three o'clock when we got to Hopin,
almost as hungry as the day before at Myitkyina. As we
drove up the main street, " Lo, the poor Indian," wringing
his hands, the same as had come to see us the previous
evening to ascertain our taste in food. He was returning
from his second visit to the railway station, where he had
been telegraphing anxious inquiries up the line for news of
three lost Europeans in a Land Rover. Most, though not all,
of the worry departed from his face as he greeted us and led
us to his father's shop, a brand-new building built of teak.
We were taken to an upstairs room where the dutiful
photographs of Aung San, U Nu and Ne Win were flanked
by others of Gandhi and Nehru. Here for half an hour we
sat and drank warm beer, not liking to hint that what we
wanted was grub and plenty of it.

In due course we got it: a lavish curry. I thanked my stars that I had stipulated the evening before that it wasn't to be too hot: it was hot enough in all conscience as it was. Laura's first mouthful must have contained a chilli. She sat bolt upright as though she had been stuck with a hat-pin, went the colour of sunset, began to play like a Versailles fountain, and coughed fire like a salamander.

Our Indian hosts, who consisted at the time of the father, three sons and the wife of the eldest, had fled to Hopin in the evacuation of 1942, along with their cousins, the B.O.C. agents at Mohnyin, whom we were shortly to meet. They had offered enormous sums, which had been refused, for air passages, but in the end had been flown out from Myitkyina for nothing, which seemed to them anomalous. They had spent the next few years in their native Lahore, returning to Burma after the war to recoup their scattered fortunes; then Burma had become independent, Lahore had fallen to Pakistan, and they were thoroughly bewildered about which country offered them the best and securest terms for citizenship. Nor do I blame them. They were faced with a problem which has never confronted subjects of the United Kingdom, and they had no precedents to guide them. They could choose to become citizens of the Union of Burma, with full voting rights; but they would never be wholly assimilated, they might never be entirely accepted, they might even be always resented: the more so because their acumen in business made it probable that they would usually be creditors in their community, which is never a popular role. For the moment they had adopted a compromise, whereby one son was a citizen of Burma and the rest Pakistanis.

They had shared at least one calamity in common with the rest of Hopin: their houses and all their possessions had been demolished in a heavy bombing raid in the spring of 1944. With a pang, I remembered how, and when, and why,

I myself had asked for it. At least it had been effective, in that the Japs had suffered casualties. It sometimes happened that a town got bombed for no useful purpose, on the strength of reports that the Japs were in it, when in fact they were in cosy bivouacs a couple of miles outside.

We drank coffee and smoked cigarettes on the veranda, looking down on the street below. From a shop opposite there emerged a Chinese woman on her tiny four-inch feet. She was surprisingly young to have followed so obsolete a custom; it has lingered far longer among expatriate Chinese than in China itself. We watched her precarious progress along the street to buy something and back again, marvelling that she could keep her balance at all.

Filling up with petrol was a long business: there were petrol pumps, but they weren't connected with any tanks, and we had to pour laboriously out of drums. We still had twenty miles to go before Mohnyin, and couldn't hope to get in before dark, so we borrowed some hurricane lamps and bought some torches off the Indians. Back on the main track we noticed the tyre marks of a lorry, which hadn't been there before; we had no means of knowing which way it was travelling, but at least it was confirmation that the track was motorable. And this was comforting, for it got worse and worse and the fords more frequent. At last, just at dusk, Kan Gyi Maung, changing gear too late in the worst possible patch in a muddy ford, got us stuck again, and this time well and truly. We climbed out into mud half-way up our shins, and pushed and heaved forwards and backwards, but in vain. Kan Gyi Maung walked up and down keening and beating his breast, but that didn't do any good either.

Certain that we were there for the night, I chose a bivouac site before it got too dark: twilight is brief in those latitudes. At that moment there came the first boom of a monastery gong, in deep melodious waves through the swiftly falling darkness. There was perhaps half a minute between each stroke, yet the vibrations of the last had never died away before the next. It wasn't eerie, but deeply moving, and of the purest essence of worship.

Then ghostly in the gloom four white figures came along the track from the Mohnyin direction, villagers returning home from their cultivation. With their help we got out of the mud and were on the move again. Soon we were approaching the lights of a large village which we took to be Mohnyin; but no, it was Namma, barely half-way and two miles off course. A few miles farther on we skirted another big village, Bilumyo, where I was surprised and rather shocked to see a large pagoda picked out in green neon lighting: an attractive anachronism, we decided in the end. I hadn't expected to find electricity at the back of beyond. And at last, an hour before midnight, stiff and sore from all our bumps, we drove into Mohnyin.

IV

THE TOWN was dark and deserted, but we met a group of youths who showed us the way to the Rest House. There was no sign of life, but at least the door wasn't locked. We unloaded the bedding-rolls and other impedimenta; and while Granville and Kan Gyi Maung shipped one of the youths as a guide and set off in the Land Rover to find the Burma Army's outpost, Laura and I lit two hurricane lamps and started to shift the gear into the house. The Indians in Hopin had told us that there were some English missionaries at Mohnyin, and we knew that we could cast ourselves on their mercy if all else failed.

For one thing, we had no means of cooking. This isn't as improvident or incompetent as it sounds. In Burma there is never a moment when somebody isn't cooking something somewhere; one can always stock up with cooked rice, wrapped in leaves or packed in bamboo; and it had seemed pointless to burden ourselves with a clutteration of pots and pans. I hadn't taken into account a belated arrival at an unmanned Rest House. In any event we could always fall back on Granville's emergency rations, which were not entirely liquid.

As Laura and I sat, a little despondently, on our bedding-rolls, we heard the unmistakable clatter of army boots; and in came four soldiers, in full marching order, rifles, packs and all. They saw us, stopped dead in their tracks and looked at us curiously. Then they all put their heads together, still looking at us, and whispered. At last one of them took a pace forward, and standing strictly to attention addressed me in what I have no doubt was excellent Burmese; but it included none of my limited vocabulary until I caught the words " B.O.C."—Burmah Oil Company.

" B.O.C.! Yes! Where is it? " I said, talking Burmese like a native. Unfortunately I couldn't understand a single word of the answer.

There was more whispering, and one of the soldiers dumped his pack—but not his rifle—and ran off out of the house and into the night, while I continued my idiotic attempts to converse with his comrades. The only sentences in Burmese of which I can claim to be a master are:—

" What is the name of this village? "

" Where does this track go to? "

" Is it far? "

" Is it so or is it not so? Do not prevaricate."

" Are there any Japanese about? Are there, or aren't there? "

None of these seemed applicable to the present situation; and even in the days when they had come in handy, the answer had always defeated me. I just used to nod sagely. Incidentally, I can order two eggs in Swahili; but not one; and not bacon.

The soldier soon came back, thank goodness, with an Indian and a Singhalese. The former was the B.O.C. agent, and cousin to our hosts at Hopin. The latter, who spoke good English and was therefore useful as well as being a crashing bore, was the manager of a local Government rice mill. Hard on their heels came Granville, with another soldier: the N.C.O. in charge of the four whose acquaintance we had made already.

Out of all this initial muddle, it turned out that Colonel

Saw Myint, as we might have guessed, had turned up trumps. Without a word to us, he had despatched to Mohnyin a 15-cwt. truck, bursting to the seams with food, and carrying in addition to the driver two cooks, two mess-waiters and the N.C.O. in charge. It was obviously this vehicle whose tracks we had seen; it must have caught us up and passed us during our prolonged meal at Hopin. Maung Tu, the N.C.O., had been in the British service as a mess-waiter; he spoke English of a sort, and knew our quaint European ways. He was a splendid little chap, and during the five days he was with us he looked after us like an indulgent nanny.

Late as it was, there were no fewer than three runners in the Hospitality Stakes. We were hours overdue; but the B.O.C. agent claimed that he had a meal half-prepared for us, Maung Tu was itching to start on his new duties, and Granville during his sortie had found and visited the English missionaries, who had also offered us a meal. They too had heard of our impending arrival from some tendril of the ubiquitous and omniscient Burma grape-vine, and had prepared dinner for us. They had then heard a false report that we were arriving, not by Land Rover but by the 4 a.m. mail train. They had therefore scrapped, or perhaps eaten, the first feast, and were now planning in most Christian fashion to meet us at the station at that intolerably pagan hour with the offer of another. Granville had been in time to save them from that barren act of kindness, and had promised that we would be round to call on them the first thing in the morning.

We resisted the blandishments of the B.O.C. agent. After our long day in the Land Rover our hinder parts were suffering from an advanced state of taxi-driver's cramp, and we were in the Jorrocks mood of, "Where we eats, we sleeps." We therefore succumbed to the offer of Maung Tu's ministrations; and it proved to be a sensible choice. In the twinkling of an eye the gloomy and deserted Rest House became a cosy home from home. Hot water appeared in the bathroom annexe, along with a tin tub, bucket, basin and dipper; and we were able to wash off the dust of a hundred miles of Burma. By the time we were clean, food was ready: not a blistering curry, but a gentle savoury rice and vegetables, the real, good, genuine Burmese food I had been boring Laura about ever since we married. Soon the rest of the B.O.C. clan joined us for a gossip over a bottle of Mandalay rum, until we pleaded our far-from-bogus weariness, wished them good night, and went to bed.

It was far, far colder than at Myitkyina, and the blankets we had brought were too few and too thin. My war-time journeys in Burma had both begun a month later in the year, when two light blankets stitched together to make a rough flea-bag were perfectly adequate to keep one warm even in the open air. I am now prepared to testify that the difference between January and February is considerable. By 3 a.m. Laura and I had donned every stitch we had brought with us; we were still shivering but managed from sheer exhaustion to get to sleep.

But not for long. At 4 a.m. a stationary train a hundred yards away gathered up all its steam and proceeded to whistle. I deduced that this was the mail train which might have brought us from Myitkyina: the one which the missionaries had planned to meet. I deduced further that it was due to change crews at Mohnyin, and that this banshee screech was designed to act as Reveille for the reliefs. It went on for three-quarters of an hour through the whole gamut of scales and arpeggios. As a murderer of sleep Macbeth had nothing on the Burma Railways.

With dawn there came down on the valley a heavy blanket of mist. Of course! Sixteen years had wiped this phenomenon from my memory, but it came back to me now like an old friend. Every day at this season the mist would shroud the valley from dawn until ten or eleven o'clock; it had been a major factor in all our tactical calculations, and presumably in those of the Japs. In most respects the night was our ally, and this morning mist in the Railway Valley extended it by several hours. It prevented the Japs from sending up reconnaissance aircraft, and enabled us to march boldly by compass across broad stretches of paddy which might otherwise be whipped by machine-gun fire. The very name Mohnyin means Valley of Mist, and I had forgotten all about it.

Maung Tu's team brewed up hot water for washing and shaving, and rolled up its sleeves to set about giving us a European breakfast. But they were forestalled by the B.O.C. Indians, who arrived and carried us off to eat at their house. It was a replica of that of their cousins at Hopin, and so was the meal: curry, and trimmings, and an endless succession of hot, fresh chupatties, and ultra-sweet tea with condensed milk. As we champed our way through it, making polite conversation the while, we heard feet on the stairs; and two Englishmen appeared. They were from the Mission. One was Stephens, newly ordained and only six weeks out from home; two years before he had been doing his National Service as a subaltern in the 7th Hussars; he was broad, powerful and full of high spirits. The other was a doctor, a layman called Hobson, tallish, spare and quiet, who had been in Mohnyin for several years. He and Granville eyed each other in a puzzled sort of way as we finished our breakfast; and soon they realised that, although they had only overlapped for a few weeks, Hobson had been medical officer to Granville's regiment during the war. A certain cavalry atmosphere now sprang up, and I found myself relegated, though in the nicest possible way, to a sort of psychological infantry zareba. I was never much good with horses; or tanks, either.

I began to try out my half-formed plans on Hobson and Stephens, but they declined to be drawn. Their job in life was to stay in Mohnyin and run the Mission; or, to be more precise, Hobson ran the hospital, to which the sick came or were brought, while Stephens was still learning the language and helping to teach. The two members of the Mission who really knew the district and could advise me were Dansey and Darlington; Darlington was away, but Dansey was there, and his were the brains to pick. I pricked up my ears at the name Darlington: two brothers Darlington had been much talked about in General Stilwell's area in 1944 when my brigade was getting ready to march in over the Patkais; they were missionaries with the Kachins in the north, and highly esteemed for their guts and their knowledge of the countryside and people. This was indeed one of them, who had married a Kachin wife; and when Hobson and Stephens took us along after breakfast, we met two dusky little Darlington children playing in the garden.

The Mohnyin Mission is run by the Bible Churchmen's Missionary Society, or B.C.M.S.—from the Evangelical flank of the Church of England. It was staffed by these four men, of whom only Darlington was married (or if any of the others were married, their wives were not present), and two very nice women. Stephens and Miss Paine, the Matron, showed my wife around while Dansey and I talked journey over a map. The other woman was a Miss Mitchell, who had been in Upper Burma for thirty years, apart from the war. For several she had lived in Pinlebu, all by herself, travelling everywhere on foot and talking about the Gospel. She made me feel fairly small, for she had been almost everywhere I had been on this side of the Irrawaddy; she had read both my books, and we talked familiarly of this or that village or

track; and of course she knew infinitely more about them
than I did. All the others except Darlington were post-war
recruits. During the war the women had been flown out
from Shwebo and the men had walked; in the subsequent
fighting the Mission had been flattened, except for the main
ward of the hospital; on what remained of the church when
they first came back to it there lay the carcass of a crashed
aircraft.

They were extraordinarily nice people, devoted and
cheerful. Their life was certainly rewarding, but I respected
rather than envied its austerity. I imagine it derived partly
from sheer want of money, but much more from a genuine
desire to live no better or less simply than their neighbours,
and to channel what money was available into the Mission's
work. I noticed that none of them smoked or drank alcohol,
and I talked with Dansey about their policy on this. He said
that since the war they had made a good deal of progress in
converting to Christianity the Kachins living in the hills on
either side of the railway. These Kachins, whose lands
were not fertile compared with the plains and whose rice
cultivation was all *taungya* patches scratched out of mountain
jungle, had always had to buy much of their food. Their
chief means of raising the wherewithal to do so were trading
in opium and brewing rice spirit. The first of these activities
was anti-social by any standard: it weakened health, shor-
tened life and stunted the will to work. The second might
be less evil intrinsically, but according to Dansey the art of
drinking in moderation was rare: drinking was apt to take
the form of recurrent orgies. The Missions had therefore set
their face against both these industries; and as a group of
individuals or a complete village became converted, these
methods of making money were debarred. The result was
that many Christian Kachins had come down from the hills
to settle in the predominantly Burmese valley, where

fortunately there was land enough for all; they were clearing jungle and making paddy-lands in its place. And because there was plenty of room, there had been surprisingly little trouble between Kachins and Burmese. The country here was still part of the Kachin State; the boundary with Burma proper was near Mawlu, another thirty miles down the railway.

Some of the foregoing would certainly be disputed by many people who have lived among the Kachins; but I hope and believe that it is a fair digest of what Dansey said to me that morning, as we compared our maps, and that I haven't misrepresented him. His map was covered with all sorts of notes and symbols in red ink; new villages had been written in, and old ones scored out. There is nothing unusual in Burma in hill villages changing their site every few years; the country is so rich and under-populated that instead of going in for scientific rotation of crops, the tradition has been to work the lands round a village to the point of exhaustion, and then to move a few miles, after fifteen or twenty years: which is why you can never expect with confidence to find a village where it is marked on the map. It wasn't surprising, therefore, to hear Dansey saying that such and such a village had shifted. What came as a shock was the number of instances in which it had disappeared altogether. Sentiment-ally this depopulation of the Kachin Hills is much to be regretted, and there may be a danger that in the easier life of the plains the people will lose that hardy highland vigour which has given the race so many of its qualities. This is not to denigrate in any way the work of the Mission; if their wisdom is equal to their sincerity and devotion, they are very wise indeed; and opium is certainly a curse.

I confess that I had been looking forward, all the same, to my little drop of rice wine; it had been highly acceptable as a stimulant in the old days. I have an old photograph of myself which I rather fancy, sitting in a chair in the open, in the middle of a village, with a splendid view of my Adam's apple under an upturned bamboo mug. I couldn't remember the village's name, but I knew exactly where it was, and described it to Dansey, who shook his head and said: "There's no village there now." I asked if he would like us to regard ourselves as having signed the pledge while in his neighbourhood. He laughed and said:

"Far be it from me to put a ban on you. I will only say that if you accept *zu* in a Christian village, they might think it rather odd, and it wouldn't help us." It reminded me of Sir Walter Scott's story of the beggar on the Scottish side of the border who, having begged in vain, asked: "Are there nae Christians in this village?" and got the answer: "Na, we're a' Johnstones and Jardines." I promised to respect Dansey's wishes in any Christian community we might find; but I didn't give up hope of finding some Kachin Johnstones or Jardines while in the neighbourhood.

I told Dansey why I hoped to pick up the threads of my journey at Kadu. We had come over the hills from the eastwards through a Kachin village called Shiamdebang (it existed no longer, said Dansey) and down to another called Saga (which Dansey hadn't been to, but thought might still be going). I think there were twenty-three of us at that stage, including John Fraser and me. We were just buying rice and asking advice about how to get across the Railway Valley, when a tall Kachin in a Gurkha hat came running up the hill saying that fifty Japs were marching in. I was anxious to avoid trouble, partly in the interest of the Kachins, partly because other parties might be coming that way. We were hustled off into a bamboo clump five hundred yards outside the village, while the Kachins obliterated our tracks with their bare feet. The Japs spent most of the day there, and then went on up the trail down which we had come.

Meanwhile, the Kachins not only fed us and regaled us on the lies they were telling the Japs; they also brought in to me an officer and four men of my own column whom they had intercepted on the fringe of the village as they were about to walk into the arms of the enemy.

When night came, they took us down the hill and handed us over to another set of guides. We marched all night, mostly along a series of very narrow tracks, but some of it along a road; and then once again on a track. Suddenly we heard a baby cry; the guides checked nervously, said it was Kadu Station, withdrew a little way, and then through thick jungle brought us to the railway where it ran along an embankment. At that very moment a train came down the line from the north, and we lay at the foot of the embankment watching it pass. Then we crossed. Soon after dawn the guides left us, but a mile farther on we encountered another man who happened to come along on a bicycle. He led us up into the hills on the west side of the railway, and in the course of the morning revealed himself as a Lance-Naik of the Burma Rifles, who had been wounded in the leg in 1942 and had made his way home. He agreed to come back to India with us; we slipped him a couple of hundred rupees to give to his family, and he promised to catch us up. We never saw him again—for a year.

In 1944, on the next expedition, he reported for duty when we were based on my " stronghold " at Aberdeen, of which more later. Less than five minutes after leaving us, he had bumped into twenty Japs who were tailing us. They had taken his money off him; but he had had the sense to exaggerate our numbers, and they had gone back for reinforcements. In 1944 he served us extremely well, and came back to India at the end of the campaign. Although I couldn't recall his name, I remembered him clearly, partly because of his good looks and soldierly bearing, and partly

because of the relish with which he told his story when we
met again the second year.

Obviously Kadu was the place to go for if I wanted to
renew my friendship with Saga and with the man we always
referred to as " The Missing Lance-Naik." And Dansey
knew the headman at Kadu, a Kachin called Myi Tun
Hka, though he was not of Dansey's flock. He gave me a
letter to him in Jinghpaw, which for some reason I still
have: it is in English, not Burmese, script, and begins:—

Ndai BRIGADIER FERGUSSON *ngu ai Inglik Upyen du
Kaba gaw. . . .*

The second and third words are the only ones I understand,
but I suspect that the sixth deprives me of my Scottish
nationality.

We had taken advice from the B.O.C. agent as to the
possibility of hiring elephants to take us up to Saga, and
learned that there was a timber contractor at Kadu who
was working some. We had received a message, I forget from
what source, that we were to pick up an escort before leaving the town. It proved to consist of two armed Kachins,
very smart in jungle green, each with a rifle and happy at
the prospect of a day in the country. The Land Rover
having been emptied of bedding—for the trip to Kadu was
only a reconnaissance, and we intended to sleep at Mohnyin
—there was room for them in the back behind Granville and
me.

The last wisp of mist had disappeared by the time we
crossed the wooden bridge over the Nam Yin, the stream
which runs through Mohnyin, on the way to Kadu. Its
modest beaches were dotted with women doing their washing, and bathers their ablutions, as we turned south. We
got to know the track by heart before we left the district,
but on this first trip we had some difficulty in finding our
way. The first village we came to was Nyaunggaing, big

and prosperous, whose stockade we had to skirt to find the proper track after two false starts; and just beyond Nyaunggaing it led to the bank of a river perhaps thirty yards broad, where bullock-carts were obviously in the habit of crossing. I rolled up my trousers above the knee, and splashed about to confirm that the sand was hard, and to find the shallowest line; and Kan Gyi Maung drove in a gingerly fashion down and across. The current was swift, and the Land Rover left a broad white wake on its beam rather than astern. We crossed that river five more times in the next two days; and Laura was unkind enough to record in her diary that only once—and that was the last time, when she anticipated me—did I fail to say: " The Shweli was flowing as fast as this when we crossed it, but *that* was up to our necks! "

The six miles to Kadu took two hours that first day; we made better time thereafter. It felt odd travelling so overtly by daylight through country which had always been rather sinister to us. The track ran through a mixture of scrub and paddy-fields. Paddy, by the way, is only another word for rice—strictly for rice before it has been husked; and paddy-fields are divided up into small sections by turf walls or *kezins* about eighteen inches high. When the rains come, these sections fill up with water; and there grows the rice, a startling green in colour. The rains in Burma are from May till October; in January the fields are dry and dusty. Most paddy-fields boast a watchman's hut—a few poles with a roof of leaves to keep off the sun.

A mile short of Kadu the track improved and we bowled along at twenty miles an hour. The scrub had given way to teak: tall and noble trees casting a generous shade, as cool and quiet as the aisles of a cathedral. A deer plunged suddenly on to the track; half-way across it saw us coming, jinked wildly, and sped off into the shadows.

The jungle thinned, sure sign that we were getting near the village. In another minute we saw blue sky ahead of us and we were emerging into the open. It was a poor-looking village with shoddy houses, but we pulled up in front of the village tea-shop on the left. It had no outer walls and was open to the world; some tables and chairs were inside, in the shade, and others on the road. You can always get a dish of curry and rice in such places, and probably chicken and hard-boiled eggs and *ngapi*—stinking fish paste; and you have a choice between warm sweet tea with condensed milk, such as soldiers love and first-aid people force on you when you have had a shock, and thin transparent Burmese tea drunk neat.

We ordered Burmese tea for the whole party; I offered the escort curry and rice as well, which they accepted. A large crowd appeared from nowhere and eyed us with astonishment. They were chiefly women and children, for most of the husbands and sons were away in the fields; but there were a few youths, and I wondered which if any of them might have been the baby whose midnight squall had alerted us seventeen years before. The people were a mixture of Burmese and Kachins. The women, some of them with babies keeking out of the shawls on their backs, puffed at their cheroots, fat cylinders of local tobacco eight inches long and an inch and a half thick, bound in a single leaf: to smoke them is an art in itself, since in my experience the end always falls off and burns a hole in your lap.

Soon there was a stir in the crowd as a man pushed his way through. He was wearing a brown Balaclava helmet; he introduced himself as the station-master, and he spoke English. He sent a boy running off to look for the headman, warning us that it would be some time before he could arrive; and then he accepted our invitation to join us at our tea.

Before we said good-bye to him the following evening we had come to have a very soft spot for this gentle, pleasant man. Ba Ohn was a native of Mergui in Tenasserim, and looked like a coffee-coloured edition of Alastair Sim. He was the first person we had met on our journey who had been literally " on the other side of the hill " during our campaigns. Throughout the war years he was station-master at Naba, the junction where the spur line leaves the main one to run down to Katha. It must have been almost as unpleasant as being at Ham, that marshalling-yard in Germany which was forever being bombed during the war, and about which somebody wrote in *Punch:*

> What a disaster!
> I've been made station-master
> At Ham.
> Damn.

He was at Naba in 1943, when we blew up the Bonchaung Bridge. My feelings were rather hurt by his insistence that this dastardly deed was carried out by parachutists. As we had walked over 300 miles to do it, carrying 65 lb. packs, I was damned if I was going to let him get away with that; but he took a lot of persuading, and I don't think I convinced him. He was still at Naba when my brigade was operating all round it in 1944: I made a major attack on Indaw, only three miles down the line, at the end of March, when the fighting lasted three days; and later one of my columns occupied Pinwe, the next station up the line and about eight miles from Naba. All his station staff had decamped, and I don't blame them.

" I'd have got away myself, if I could have," said Ba Ohn with a grin, " but the Japanese put a guard on me. I was porter and everything, just me."

" How long were you on your own? " I asked.

" The Japanese brought forty persons in lorries to work
for me," he said in his precise English, " but they all run
away, sometimes two, sometimes three, till none left. The
bombs came down boom-boom-boom. We thought there
would be no human being left, ha, ha, ha! "

Out of the blue he suddenly asked:—

" From whom you get cash to come to Burma? "

I parried this question on a delicate subject; and the next
thing he asked was:—

" You know Mr. Castens? "

Indeed I knew Bertie Castens, a burly man with a black
beard and twinkling eyes who used to appear mysteriously
at G.H.Q. New Delhi when I was a planner there before
joining Wingate. One used to see him going up and down
stairs from time to time to some cloak-and-dagger establishment on the top floor. We didn't know who he was in those
days, though we all used to speculate. He was in fact the
Forest Officer of Katha District, who spent most of the
Japanese occupation wandering about his old stamping-
ground with a wireless set reporting on enemy movements.
It was he who told Wingate of a little-known track along a
forest boundary which led from the basin of the Uyu River
across the Zibyutaungdan Range to within three days'
march of the railway. The use of this track by the bulk of
the Force in 1943 enabled us to slip unobserved through the
screen of outposts of the Japanese 55th Division, whose dis-
positions had been designed to prevent just such a movement. The name " Castens's Track " is branded on the
memory of everybody who trod it or waded it, or crawled it:
parts of it followed streams, and other parts were almost
vertical. It was frightful going, but it did the trick.

The following year, when we were at Aberdeen, Bertie
used to drop in for a drink and a gossip and a bit of company.
The life he led was really astonishing. He had induced the

powers in Delhi to commission his former assistant, a
humorous and cynical Kachin whose name I cannot for the
life of me remember, as a captain; and the two of them
roamed about casually as if they still owned the place, keeping an eye on the forests as well as on the Japs. Ba Ohn's
inquiry after Bertie Castens was only the first of many.

"You *do* know Mr. Castens? Is true he now running
biggest dacoit gang in England?"

I said that I hadn't heard it, but knowing Bertie Castens I
thought if it were true he would certainly be doing it very
well—like everything else he tackled! Ba Ohn agreed fer-
vently. He said that the big bungalow Castens had built in
Katha while District Forest Officer was still in use; and then
went on to tell me rather sadder things. One of Castens's old
forest employees near Kadu, who had given shelter to him
and his wireless set, had been betrayed to the Japs and shot;
and several others of his men, who had worked for him in the
old days, had been rounded up and executed on the mere
suspicion that they might have aided and abetted him. The
worst feature of all resistance movements is this constant risk
of reprisals. It was the thing I had most dreaded hearing,
and the only consideration which had given pause to my
determination to come back to Burma. Fortunately we were
to come across much less trace of it than I had feared.

At this moment a messenger arrived for Ba Ohn from the
railway station, which we could see fifty yards farther on
down the street, and gabbled something in Burmese. Ba
Ohn swallowed what remained of his tea, rose to his feet, and
made an announcement in a voice as solemn as a toast-
master's.

"It is The Sugar Cane Special," he said. "I return
when it is gone through."

We all felt we must see The Sugar Cane Special. It
sounded like a train out of a fairy story. With any luck Noddy

might be driving it; or failing him, Andy Pandy. We accompanied Ba Ohn to the station. So did most of the crowd. Perhaps they were accompanying us. We may not be V.I.P.s in Ayrshire, but we certainly were in Kadu.

The railway ran straight as a die north and south through the station, along a track edged with teak as far as the eye could see. It was single line, except for its passage through the station, where it became double and threw off a few sidings, on which some trucks loaded with cane awaited collection. There was a fairy-tale appearance about the whole place: the square station office, the precision of the tracks, the squatness of the trucks on the sidings, the symmetry of the teak trees; the feathery palms and the paw-paws, even the people, looked nursery-floor and Noah's-Arkish. The very smoke out of the funnel of The Sugar Cane Special's engine, when at last it arrived, had something of the quality of cotton-wool.

But it didn't arrive just yet, and it wasn't in sight up the line as we stepped across the tracks to await it in the assistant station-master's garden. I paused for a moment to gaze south, wondering exactly how many hundred yards away we had lain hidden while the train puffed past us before we tiptoed over in the dark. By the time I had caught up the others Laura was sitting in a chair, and a boy had been sent shinning up a tree towards the blue and cloudless sky to pick a paw-paw for her: he set it on a long pronged stick which was thrust up to him from the ground and then lowered with care with the prize stuck on the end. Everybody else was given a stick of sugar cane, which is the stock sweetmeat of Burma, equivalent to chewing-gum, lollipops or peanuts. Children peel off its outer skin and throw it away without fear of prosecution for being litter-louts, and spit out the stringy residue when they have chewed and sucked the sugar.

A prolonged whistle from up the line announced the advent of the train. It arrived, shunted, added trucks to its tail and departed southwards, whistling with every movement. As its final farewell screech came back to us from down the line we all returned to the tea-shop, to be ringed in afresh by the crowd. We had hardly resumed our drinking of tea when there was a bustle. Myi Tun Hka the headman had arrived.

He was short, thick-set, well-built and at first his face was quite expressionless. He spoke no English. Ba Ohn told him the gist of our story; and when he said that I wanted to find whoever had led us across the railway, Myi Tun Hka at once said: " It was me." I thought this a trifle too slick to be true. Whoever had taken us across had bobbed up in the middle of the night, when our guides from Saga had handed us over, and had vamoosed soon after dawn, when we were all tired and sleepy. I looked closely at Myi Tun, and I honestly couldn't remember him. Perhaps he had led a different party; others had crossed the Railway Valley not far from here. Myi Tun went on to describe the composition of my lot; he said, in Ba Ohn's translation, " There were mostly British, with Karen people and Gurkhas." I said we were twenty-five British, one Karen and two Gurkhas. That was right, said Myi Tun: too slick again, I thought, and still wasn't convinced. Then he suddenly launched into the story of the missing Lance-Naik, and got it completely right in every detail, except that according to him we had given the Lance-Naik sixty rupees and my recollection was of two hundred. The Lance-Naik was his brother-in-law.

At this stage I bethought me of twenty copies I had brought of a photograph taken at Imphal the day after we got out. It showed me in a bush hat and a heavy untrimmed black beard, almost as good as Bertie Castens's. My wife produced one of these, and handed it to Myi Tun.

79

At once his face lit up with a broad smile; this was how he remembered me; his suspicions were so completely allayed that I was now equally sure of him. He began to talk rapidly and produced a lot of confirmatory detail which nobody could have put into his head: the baby crying, the train going past. " All your shoes were broken." This was the chap all right; we shook hands afresh with great warmth, and settled down to more tea-drinking. I asked him if he had got into any trouble over helping us; the Japs had come and asked him questions, but never connected him with our escape across the line. As for his brother-in-law, the amount of Indian money found on him had made the Japs suspicious, but he had managed to convince them that he had been helping us only under duress, and that he was on his way to tell the Japs.

When I said how anxious I was to see the former Lance-Naik, a chill came over the conversation, and there was a bit of chat between him and Ba Ohn before the latter said apologetically: " He is a silly man, he is with Naw Seng." This was the first time I had heard of Naw Seng, and Ba Ohn was not too keen to talk about him, beyond venturing the opinion that he and the missing Lance-Naik were probably both in China. I was to learn a lot more about Naw Seng before I was much older: he was a Kachin captain in the Burma Rifles who had led a revolt, part mutiny, and part rebellion, shortly after Burma became independent, and carried most of his company with him. Whether his motive was originally to establish some sort of Kachin-Karen-Shan state independent of Burma I am still not quite clear; certainly at one stage he had both Kachin and Karen backing; certainly, too, he drifted into the Communist orbit, either from conviction or because he was unable to get support from any other quarter. The accounts conflict; but I was sad to hear that my Lance-Naik, one of the people whom I had been especially anxious to find, was now an outlaw and beyond my reach.

I asked Myi Tun how we had got into his hands in the first place. He said that he and the Kachin element of Kadu had left their village because of the Jap garrison there, and were living in the jungle. This was common practice during the occupation, and indeed during other troubled periods of Burmese history. " Sir, in those times life is nothing! " put in Ba Ohn. The Saga people had known the whereabouts of their improvised temporary village, and had sent him a message to arrange a rendezvous where they could hand us over. I remembered very well that whispering encounter in the dark.

By this time our meeting had become almost a *ceilidh*, with Myi Tun, Ba Ohn and me all retailing memories of the old days, in full hearing of the crowd. Myi Tun had much natural dignity, and was held in great respect by the listeners. Later in the war, when the main British forces were working down the railway, he had helped them. Pulling up his *loongyi*, he showed us a bullet wound in his thigh, got near Mawhun early in 1945. When I asked if he could give us a guide to Saga, he said that it was too late to go to-day but that he would willingly take us there himself to-morrow. Remembering the shaggy and precipitous path down which we had come that night so long ago, I asked if it would be possible to hire elephants. He said he didn't think we'd need them: since my last visit Saga had moved; it was now farther down the hill-side than it used to be, and he thought we could get there in the Land Rover. So we made a date to pick him up at 9 a.m. the following morning, and left for Mohnyin in a glow of satisfaction that all was turning out so well. We supped with our friends at the Mission, who were as rejoiced as we were at our success; Dansey's bow at a venture had scored a gold at the first draw.

V

THE NEXT DAY began much earlier than we had intended.
Before going to bed, Maung Tu had come and asked:
" What time Bed Tea? " We were a trifle slow-witted, for
it took us a moment or two to realise that he was referring to
early morning tea; and we talked over timing for the
morrow. Now that we knew the way to Kadu we reckoned
we could do it in a little over the hour: we decided to forgo
breakfast to save time, to have Bed Tea at 7 a.m. and to get
going at 7.30. Actually Europeans in Burma, outside
Rangoon, usually telescope breakfast and luncheon into a
single meal which they call Breakfast and eat at about
11 a.m.: we thought we'd emulate them, and take food with
us.

Owing to a faulty alarm clock, Maung Tu arrived with
our Bed Tea at 4 a.m. on the dot. He was stricken with
remorse when he found out what he had done. We didn't
want to hurt his feelings, so we drank it, intending to sleep
again; but our first sip coincided with the first screech of the
down train howling for its relief crew, exactly as on the day
before. The Mission was even closer than the Rest House to
Mohnyin Station. Presumably volunteers for the mission-
field are prepared to risk finishing their careers in a cooking
pot; but I doubt whether the B.C.M.S. warn their recruits
about steam-whistles every morning at 4 a.m.

We got away at 7.30, having decided to dispense with our
escort; there seemed no need for one, and we feared it

might put some constraint on the people we were going to visit. We paused in the bazaar to try and buy some sandals big enough for my feet; and while we were so engaged our B.O.C. friends waylaid us with a number of trays, laden with coffee, bread, biscuits and hard-boiled eggs, which they insisted on us eating in the main street, in full view of the population. Breakfast was a success, the purchase of sandals a flop. Feet as big as mine had not previously been seen in Upper Burma, and were not catered for.

At Kadu, Myi Tun Hka was all ready and waiting for us. He was dressed up to the nines in his best Kachin attire, complete with headgear of black silk and a huge sword with a silver hilt, in addition to his working *dah*. Everybody in Burma outside the cities carries a *dah*, a slashing knife about two feet long and always beautifully balanced; it is so much a part of him that it is virtually an extension of his right arm, and is used for every conceivable purpose: clearing a path, chopping wood, personal defence, digging a latrine, slaughtering an animal, or spitting a carcass to roast over a fire. With Myi Tun were two strapping Kachins, one of whom had been with him as fellow-guide on that famous night.

A sizeable crowd, including Ba Ohn, saw us off from Kadu in the Land Rover. Close to where we had seen the deer the day before, Myi Tun pointed out a track emerging on to the main road along which we were driving. It was by this less-frequented route that he had led us, in order to avoid the Jap patrols. Later on he showed us another point where the Land Rover was crossing our former line of approach. As we passed through the village of Ywathit, he told us that there had been 400 Japanese in it the night we passed by. This may have been putting it high. One thing I learned during the war was that static garrisons tended to have their numbers exaggerated by the local inhabitants, whereas the numbers of a column on the move were usually accurate. This is natural enough. Imagine yourself as a foreign spy, sent into Aldershot for a week to find out how many troops were quartered there: it would be difficult to assess. But if the authorities were to oblige you by causing the whole garrison to march past a given point, your job would be much easier and your report pretty close to the mark. Myi Tun assured us that in April, 1943, at the moment we went through, there were garrisons not only in Ywathit and Kadu, but also in Mohnyin and Mawhun, sending out constant patrols; and this is probable: the Japs knew we were trying to get back, they had already picked up a number of our men on the Irrawaddy and Shweli, and they must have deduced that most of us were nearing the railway.

At Ywathit we left the floor of the valley and began to climb into the foothills. It took us three hours to do five miles. The track was fine for bullock-carts; but it ran through bamboo, and this had two drawbacks. Old bamboo roots with their multiple stumps stuck up in mid-track; bullock-carts with their high clearance would miss them with their axles, but our sump and underbelly were vulnerable. Secondly, on a bamboo track the branches interlock over your head, and the arches were so low that our windscreen and hood kept fouling them. Myi Tun cut away valiantly with his sword, proving that it was no mere costume article, while his henchmen dug out the stumps with the long mattocks they carried as well as their *dahs*. We had to make many diversions round fallen trees and boggy patches, in one of which Kan Gyi Maung, impatient as ever, got the vehicle stuck; but with six of us to push we cleared it. We were never wheel-borne for more than a couple of hundred yards at a time.

It wasn't long before we realised that the Land Rover was

a complete encumbrance, and a stupid thing to be lugging
into the Kachin Hills when we could go twice as fast without
it; I was wearing an equally stupid hat, a floppy white
thing I had bought in Rangoon. It was a replica of something Dick Allen had worn out sailing, when it was entirely
appropriate; but not even a billycock hat and a rolled-up
umbrella could have looked more out of place here. Yet
getting the Land Rover up to Saga had become a challenge.

About noon, sweating like pigs, we came to a fork. One
branch of the track, said Myi Tun, through Kan Gyi Maung,
led up the hill to the old abandoned Saga where we had lain
hidden; the other, which we could see dipping into a gully,
led to the new Saga where our benefactors now lived. It was
the people rather than the place that I was looking for: so
we took the lower track. After ten minutes we came out into
a clearing, and there we were.

It was a typical Kachin village, such as I had remembered
all these long years, though smaller than most and smaller
than the old Saga of blessed memory. Tall posts, surmounted
by baskets containing little offerings to the wood-spirits,
stood sentry where the track ran into the clearing. There
was no stockade such as the Burmese and Shans build;
long-snouted, perky little black pigs were running about
everywhere: the Kachin loves his pork. There was one
main long-house and two outlying ones. A Kachin house
stands six feet off the ground—long, narrow and thatched,
with a roof-tree along the middle. The door is at one end,
giving on to an open platform, to which you climb up a
ladder of the kind we use for hen-houses. Under the stilts
are all the paraphernalia of the village.

Pigs and piglets ran squealing for cover at the sight of their
first Land Rover (or perhaps at the sight of us?), and the
chickens fluttered clumsily off the ground. A nervous,
wrinkled woman in strict Kachin black appeared at the door

of the long-house, to be appeased by Myi Tun Hka whom she appeared to know. She called back over her shoulder, and was joined on the platform by two or three more women and a couple of men. One was a stranger from Sumprabum, whose business in this corner of the Kachin Hills was almost certainly private; the other was a local. Among the women was one very odd one, who didn't look to me like a Kachin at all. We were to be in her company for several hours, and photographed her half a dozen times; nobody with ethnological knowledge has identified her race, and I suspect that she was simply and literally an idiot. Poor soul, she was certainly a nuisance, and her moping and mowing was a tedious and recurring interruption to an otherwise idyllic three hours in Saga.

Three hours, I calculated, was the longest we could wait if we were to drop Myi Tun Hka at Kadu and get back to Mohnyin before dark. The men were away at the rice planting, and it would take some time to summon them back. The local man loped off up the hill by the track which had brought us into the village, and the rest of us settled down for a long wait. Stools were brought out of the house for us to sit on, and we ate away progressively at our haversack ration of cooked rice. We had bought it in Mohnyin bazaar, ready cooked in lengths of bamboo, one of the two standard methods of carrying it. First catch your bamboo; cut it in two-foot lengths; fill one third of it with rice and the rest with water; add some salt; put it in the embers of a hot fire and leave it for twenty minutes. You then have it perfectly cooked and packed; and when you want a nibble, you tear off a few inches of bamboo, like peeling a banana or a sugar-cane. The rice, when it emerges, is covered with a thin membrane; and it retains some of its heat for at least a couple of hours. Delicious.

Myi Tun Hka was beginning to look restive. The sun was

high in the heavens, and the day was hot; we had expended much energy in the ludicrous task of heaving the Land Rover up the hill. The chickens and the pigs had got used to us, and had long since resumed their habitual pecking and rootling about the houses and the long grass of the clearing. At last Myi Tun murmured something to the woman who had first received us. She disappeared into the house (which Laura had already explored to its darkest recesses) and returned with some bamboo mugs and a large wooden jug of *zu*, locally known as *zakho*. Evidently this wasn't a Christian village, and we were among hospitable Johnstones and Jardines. Myi Tun looked at me with a raised interrogatory eyebrow, and his face lit up in response to the sudden illumination in my own. The stuff is white in colour and tastes like a mixture of very strong cider and aniseed. I like it. So does Myi Tun Hka.

The time now passed more swiftly. From time to time the jug was handed up into the house for replenishment, and passed back down to replenish in its turn Myi Tun, Granville, Myi Tun's henchmen and me.

An alert reader might think that we should have deduced Saga to be a non-Christian village from our having seen offerings to wood-spirits on its threshold. In point of fact one still sees such offerings in avowedly Buddhist Burmese villages in the remoter parts of Burma, just as old superstitions took an unconscionable time in dying out in Britain. People of recent conversion see no great harm in hedging, or in reinsurance, even in more sophisticated countries. It implies an instinct for seamanlike precautions rather than a flagrant disloyalty to the new faith. After all, it is not unknown for church-going people in this country to hang up a horse-shoe for luck.

Just after two o'clock our emissary returned with three men, the headman and two others. I scanned their faces and found I knew them all; and they knew mine. There was much hand shaking. Our mutual reminiscences had to be conducted through Kan Gyi Maung, but there was much mime, much pointing, much digging in the ribs. It was an extraordinarily happy occasion. When later on I asked N'gum Hdu the headman how he recognised me without my beard, he pointed without hesitation to a minor gap in my front teeth, caused by a blow from Malcolm Wolfe Murray in my regiment twenty-eight years before, when we were subalterns: I was trying to pull his nose at the time. Most people are too tactful to notice it; with N'gum Hdu it was my passport and my badge of recognition.

I remembered N'gum Hdu clearly; but I had an even clearer recollection of the tall man in the Gurkha hat who had run uphill into the village as we were lying there eating our rice, warning us of the advent of the Japanese. He had a straggly black beard and thin cheeks. I asked for him, but alas! he was dead two years; and so, apparently, was the headman of Hpatwat over the hill: the first Kachin village we had come to, and the first link in the long chain of helpers which had passed us on so faithfully from village to village for eighty or ninety miles.

There was much talk and more *zakho*, and every so often a new flood of reminiscence from N'gum Hdu, appealing to Myi Tun for confirmation about events of those far-off years. Their talk was all in Jinghpaw; and when they wanted to compare their recollections with mine, they had to pause, and allow Myi Tun to turn it into Burmese (which N'gum Hdu didn't speak) so that Kan Gyi Maung could pass it on to me, Kan Gyi Maung having no Jinghpaw. It was evident that N'gum deferred to Myi Tun in social status, allowing himself no familiarities; and I realised for the first time that N'gum had not only risked his own life and those of his villagers in passing us on in 1943, but had also taken it on himself to assume the willing support of his superiors and to embroil them in the ploy.

N'gum looked over his shoulder, and gave an order to one of his men, who went into the long-house and returned with a roll of pieces of paper. They turned out to be a series of chits. I smoothed out the first, which was written in indelible pencil, on a page of graph paper torn from an army note-book, and read with some difficulty:—

A most helpful and excellent man who fed us well when our tummies were flapping against our back-bones.
May, 1943   W. P. Scott, *Major*

This was a real thrill, for I knew exactly the circumstances in which this note was written. Scotty (who began the war as a private soldier and finished it in command of a brigade) was in command of No. 8 Column, which for various reasons was about a fortnight behind me on the way out. When I reached Imphal, where the British Corps Headquarters were, on the 26th April, I found they were in touch with Scotty and about to drop supplies on him; so I wrote out a full account of the route I had followed, the villages I had found helpful, and the location and patrolling habits of the Jap garrisons so far as we had established them. This was duly dropped to Scotty in his then position twenty miles east of the Kachin Hills, and he had profited by following in my footsteps all the way through them.

I sought in vain for a similar chit from myself; there wasn't one. But there were two, both dated 1944, signed by officers I knew. One was from Peter Taylor of the West Yorkshire Regiment, who had been my pupil at Sandhurst, who was in my brigade in 1944, and who was to serve under me again in another brigade in 1958, just before I left the Army. The other was from Jon Musgrave-Wood, better known as Emmwood the cartoonist, who took part in both expeditions: serving with No. 7 Column on the first, and with the Burma Rifles on the second. There was also a carbon copy of an undertaking which N'gum Hdu had given to Musgrave-Wood, promising " to assist the British Government in defeating the Japanese, and to be honest and truthful in all I do. I shall receive Rs. 50 per month for my work, and one rifle, No. 1234567," or whatever it was. This was signed 26th April, 1944, which was during the period of two months during which Mike Calvert was holding the White City at Henu against all comers.

There was one odd point in N'gum Hdu's recollections which I can't account for, and I think he must have been confusing us with some subsequent party: he said they had got into trouble with the Japs because they smelt English tobacco smoke. We had run out of English tobacco weeks before we got to Saga; I distinctly remember where and when I smoked my last cigarette, a De Reszke, in a dry *chaung* on the far side of the Irrawaddy. Scotty's men having had a supply drop at the same time as my letter would have been well stocked with English tobacco, and I think this incident must have happened during their transit rather than ours.

It was time to go. I gave N'gum Hdu a copy of the bearded photograph, and slipped him an envelope containing twenty *kyats* (about thirty shillings) for old times' sake. We drove away out of the clearing, scattering pigs in all directions, while N'gum and his diminished clan looked after us, still rather bewildered at this apparition from the past. They were obviously very poor: all the more wonder that they should have risked so much for us. The Kachins always liked the British, partly because we left them very largely to run their own show, and partly because the quality of man that we sent among them was high, whether soldier, administrator or teak-wallah.

On the return journey we no longer regretted having brought the Land Rover. Thanks to the sterling mattock-work of the forenoon we were able to drive at a good pace, and our Kachins relaxed and enjoyed the ride. Getting down to Kadu took a tenth of the time it had taken to come up. Myi Tun took us to his house for tea. I was by now deeply ashamed of having doubted him the day before, and more conscious than ever of the risks he had run on behalf of us, whom he didn't even know. And now, out of the goodness of his heart, he had given up a full day's work at the busiest time of the season. He was still rather silent, but all smiles.

I put fifty *kyats* surreptitiously into an envelope, and tried to put it in his hand as we said good-bye. I suppose he had seen me tipping N'gum Hdu, and guessed there was money inside it. He waved it away, saying, " You paid me too much seventeen years ago."

We felt we couldn't depart from Kadu without taking leave of Ba Ohn. We found him in the open space on the hither side of the railway station, with a large number of children playing all about him. We had already begun to make a practice of carrying a supply of boiled sweets to ingratiate ourselves with children, most of whom had never seen a European, and to whom such sweets were a rare luxury. We gave Ba Ohn a bagful. The last we saw of that kindly man as we drove away—I can see him now—he was throwing handfuls of sweets in the air, and laughing as the children scrambled for them in the soft, fading evening light.

Back at Mohnyin, supper wasn't quite ready, and Laura and I went for a walk. It had been a surprise to find electric light in so remote a place; I hadn't expected it even at Myitkyina. We were to find that every town of any size— Mohnyin, Bhamo, Katha—had its own engine, producing

light for streets and shops and houses until ten or eleven
o'clock, when it closed down. Our stroll from the Rest
House brought us to a large dark house on the bank of the
Nam Yin which was shaking and shuddering and emitting
a shattering noise. I pushed cautiously at the door, which
opened, and poked my nose inside, to find a mass of rather
Heath Robinson machinery and two or three Burmese
minding it. By this time we were well-known figures in
Mohnyin, and we were made welcome. We were shown
round, by means of mime and gesture, the municipal
electricity plant of Mohnyin; and our guides were kind
enough to demonstrate how to switch it on and off, as well as
various stoppages and how to cure them. It must have been
a *mauvais quart d'heure* for the subscribers, but it was all very
interesting for us.

Next morning we went along to the Mission, to say good-
bye, to thank them for their kindness, and to report the immense success of the previous day's sortie, which owed so
much to Dansey. We were easily persuaded to accept a
farewell cup of coffee with them in their communal sitting-
room while we told them about our visit to Saga. Darlington
was back, and I enjoyed making the acquaintance of a man
whose name I had known and honoured for so long. He was
quiet and unassuming. His colleagues hadn't hinted at any
feeling of exile; but with Darlington alone one felt that his
roots had sunk so deeply into the Kachin Hills that they
were his real home, now and for ever.

The missionaries told us of two Englishwomen who were
running an outpost of the Mission at Indaw; and we
promised to look them up when we passed that way. Before
we left, Dansey asked me to come and talk to his bible class
of fifteen or twenty young men, all Kachins: one of them, to
be precise, was not so young, but rather what the English
Prayer Book calls " of riper years." It wasn't difficult to

know what to say to them. I told them simply what their kith and kin had done for us at the peril of their lives, at a time when we were underdogs, friendless and hunted; and that this was Christianity at its best and highest.

We had already decided where to go next. There were other Kachin villages which I would have dearly loved to see again: notably Pakaw, which had shared in our fortunes with the utmost loyalty two years running; but Pakaw was two or three days' hard marching from every direction, the Land Rover could never have made it, and we had neither the time nor the energy to tackle the journey on foot. I contented myself with sending affectionate messages to its headman and people.

We were bound instead for Lonton on the In-Daw-Gyi, the Great Royal Lake. I had never been to Indawgyi, though two of my columns had passed that way in 1944; and my own regiment, in another brigade, had established a base there during the monsoon in the same year. The onset of the rains had made it impossible to fly out the sick and wounded from air-strips, and somebody had the bright idea of running a shuttle service of flying-boats between the Indawgyi and the Brahmaputra River. To that anonymous brainwave something like fifteen hundred officers and men owed their lives, including Lord Wavell's son, who was flown out after losing his right hand. Other and more romantic nations would have christened the two flying-boats which ran that service by such names as *Espérance* and *Bon Secours*, or *Nurse Cavell* and *Florence Nightingale*. In fact they were known as " Gert " and " Daisy," after two gallant and popular Cockney music-hall artistes who had endured much discomfort in coming out to India and cheering up the troops with their ribald and nostalgic back-chat, reminiscent of fish-and-chips, Saturday night, and everything else that we were fighting for.

The beauty of Indawgyi was famous; Granville wanted
to see it; the road to it was known to be good; and there was
a Rest House. We felt slightly guilty about not having
warned Colonel Saw Myint of our intention to go there but
it had only grown up on us since we had seen him. We
assumed—and it turned out rightly—that he wouldn't mind;
we dispatched Maung Tu and his party ahead of us; and
we announced our intention of joining them there in the
course of the afternoon.

Kan Gyi Maung and the Land Rover, with all our gear
aboard, rolled up at the Mission to collect us; we made our
farewells, clambered on board and sailed away. We were
now doing by daylight and in the reverse direction the
journey we had done in the dark three nights before. We
paused at Bilumyo, where we had seen the green neon
lighting on the pagoda. It was large, prosperous, Burmese;
a town rather than a village; built round a dusty isosceles
triangle. At the apex stood the truly fine pagoda. Swarming
in the dust at the base end, where we entered, was a mass of
children of every age from two to ten.

I had never seen Bilumyo before, but I remembered
that my regiment had sent a patrol there during the monsoon of 1944—a strong patrol of ninety men, travelling
across country, often up to their waists in mud. It took them
four days to get there, and when they arrived they found
the Japs had abandoned it four days before, just about the
moment they had set out. They returned to base by the
main road, the very route we were now about to follow, and
did it in a single day. We stayed in Bilumyo for twenty
minutes, distributing boiled sweets by the Ba Ohn method:
chucking them in the air, and letting the children scramble
for them. I took pity in the end on one minute infant, in a
battered European hat and little else, who was consistently
unlucky; I shoved three or four sweets into his shyly cupped

hands; he tottered away overcome by his luck, looking nervously over his tiny shoulder to make sure that nobody was following him for plunder. By the time we climbed back into the Land Rover and went on our way we hadn't a sweet left; but we had a splendid coloured film in our movie-camera, which we still enjoy, of those vivid happy children in their bright clothing, the white pagoda above them, and the blue hills beyond.

The state of the track no longer worried us: we had beaten it once, and the wheel-marks of Maung Tu's truck ahead of us were there to encourage us. A few miles short of Hopin we turned west into the hills, and found ourselves to our surprise on a really good metalled road, well graded and carefully maintained, with steel girder bridges over the glens and gullies that scored the hill-side. My eye was out of practice, but the jungle looked to me like primary stuff, where the axe had never been. At each gully we got a view out over the Railway Valley: mostly wooded, but here and there a broad patch of cultivation and the occasional white finger of a pagoda pointing to heaven. The gradient was steep, but the road was so good that we climbed quickly; and less than half an hour after leaving the floor of the valley we halted in a cutting and clearing where the road ran over the crest. We had reached the summit of the Kyusunlai Pass.

The Kyusunlai is the front door to the Indawgyi. The Indawgyi Lake itself is thirteen miles long and five wide, and lies in a broad wooded basin. The villages on its shores are inhabited by Shans, the hills around by Kachins. When Brodie's brigade established its base at the southern end of the lake in 1944, it was essential to hold Kyusunlai in order to keep out the Japs. In monsoon conditions the going was so bad that it was almost impossible to move, even on foot, except along either the road or the crest. Brodie's battalions, including my own regiment (though it was two long years since I had served with it), took turns at holding the pass in May and June; The Black Watch were up there for three miserable weeks; the Japs attacked every day, and often at night, and had to be evicted twice from the main water-point. The unhealthiness of the climate at that time of the year may be gauged from the fact that in The Black Watch alone over seventy men died from typhus in a single month. It was a particularly virulent form of scrub fever which Stilwell's Chinese had encountered previously in the Hukawng Valley, and for which at that time there was no known inoculation or antidote.

Among the minor casualties suffered at the top of the pass was the index finger of the left hand of Hewie Dalrymple of my regiment, my exact contemporary at school and now my next-door neighbour in Scotland. When we got down to Nammun at the southern end of the lake, where the main base had been, and began to cross-examine the villagers about their war-time recollections, I made a feeble little joke to raise a cheap laugh and get them into a good humour: I said I had come all the way from over the seas to look for my neighbour's missing finger, and had anybody seen it? I fear this wretched joke was made to work overtime for the next twenty-four hours, though Kan Gyi Maung went through the motions of laughing loyally every time he put the question for me.

Actually the villagers could tell us little about the occupation. They were friendly but timorous people, and as soon as the trouble began they had all lit off for the bush, and remained in the jungle until peace returned to the Indawgyi. But they remembered and described with many gestures the frequent visits of Gert and Daisy, pointing out where they used to land on the lake, and how they taxied along its surface.

We found the Rest House, with Maung Tu's crew already installed and established, half-way up the western side of the lake. It was beautifully sited on a promontory, thirty feet above the shore. A mile to the north, in mid-lake, was a pagoda on an island, casting a shimmering white reflection on the dazzling blue water. Looking across the lake we saw villages by the water's edge, and behind them the high wooded range, with a little dip to indicate the Kyusunlai. There were hills all round us. The highest were to the south, and a two-day march that way would have brought us to Pakaw; but there was little *va-et-vient* in that direction, for the Shans are still nervous of the Kachins.

We had passed, coming in, a track running westwards through another dip in the hills; it looked passable for the Land Rover, and I toyed with the idea of following it. A mere fifty miles would take us to the Uyu River, which I knew and loved, and I had long nursed an ambition to float peacefully down it on a raft to the Chindwin. But it wasn't practicable: it wouldn't be playing fair with Saw Myint, it would mean Granville going absent without leave, and it would upset all our tentative arrangements for Katha. Another time, perhaps; yet I knew in my heart of hearts that there would never be another time. We were lucky enough in all conscience to be having this one.

An hour before dusk we went out for a stroll. The first person we met was a domestic elephant with a wooden bell round its neck, and a chain hobble attached to its forelegs. It was placidly champing its way through tall grass near the water's edge, and continued to champ despite our presence, though eyeing us humorously. At Lonton, half a mile away, some villagers were baling out a long narrow canoe, and we induced them to paddle us back along the shore in the dusk to the Rest House promontory. There was no breath of wind nor ripple on the water, and the evening smoke from the village was rising straight up in the air.

We had our supper in an inner room of the Rest House, and thereby unhappily missed the rising of the moon over the eastern hills. When we went out on the veranda afterwards, it was some fifteen degrees up and illuminating all the lake.

" You should have seen it when it was more downstairs," said Maung Tu; but even so it was a sight never to be forgotten: with the lake all silver, the hills and the island deep black, and the pagoda an almost luminous white. We sipped our evening dram with great content.

VI

WE REACHED MYITKYINA without incident about three o'clock on the following afternoon, having stopped at Hopin to return to our Indian friends various articles we had borrowed. We were terribly stiff after our four days in the Land Rover; and finding that we had the Guest House to ourselves and nobody to be polite to, we all turned in for a siesta.

At six o'clock I roused myself and dressed. I was half-way downstairs when I heard Granville's voice outside the front door, saying:—

" Are you looking for somebody? "

A voice from the past, which I could recognise but not identify, replied:—

" I am told Brigadier Fuggusson is here."

" Here I am! " I called, and nipped down the stair and on to the veranda. A globular, cheerful figure was looking up from the gravel sweep with a grin the size of a shark's but infinitely more amiable; and as he saw me his arms spread out widely. I hesitated a couple of seconds: there was something not quite right; but I heard my voice saying:—

" Samson? "

And at once I knew that it was, and each of us shouted so loud that Laura, still on her bed upstairs, got up and put on her shoes and came down to investigate.

Subedar-Major (Honorary Lieutenant) Saw Samson of the Burma Rifles had thirty years' service when he marched out to India with the 2nd Battalion in 1942. He was a Karen of Karens, with a pair of moustaches which were the pride of the regiment. These had disappeared: hence my failure to be sure of him at first sight. We were fast friends ever since our first meeting in the Central Provinces of India while training for the first expedition. He taught me many a trick of the trade of living in jungle: how to cook rice in bamboo, how to build rafts, how to make lashings from twisted bark, and many other esoteric practices.

I had last seen him at the time of the Victory March in London in 1946. I was serving in Combined Operations Headquarters which, with the onset of peace, had been expelled from its war-time home in the smartest reach of Whitehall to a requisitioned block of flats in Princes Gate, overlooking Kensington Gardens. From my office window I could see the vast mass of tentage being erected to house the several thousand soldiers of all races, many of them from overseas, who were being brought to London for the March; and I left a message for the Burma contingent, when it should arrive, asking the officer commanding to get in touch with me.

I arrived one morning in my office to find him awaiting me. He really belonged to the Highland Light Infantry, but for the last three years had been serving with the Chin Levies. He was in a rage.

" Do you realise, sir," he said, " that you're the only single bloody person who has taken the slightest bloody interest in us at all? Nobody met us at the station; nobody told us where to go. When we found our lines, they were all muddled up with the Indian Army—apparently they think we're part of it; and the only question we've been asked so far is whether we want Hindu or Moslem rations! "

I soothed him and put him into a chair. It would be libellous to give the name of the very senior official of great distinction, and still in the public eye, whom I then rang up. He had snubbed me once in Simla, and now I had him on toast. He apologised profusely, but I heard later that it took him only thirty seconds to find a scapegoat for his own shortcomings.

Going over to the camp with the Chin Levies colonel, I was greeted with a roar of " Brigadier Fuggusson! ", and there was Samson, still with his great moustaches in those days; and for the next couple of weeks, with relays of friends, I showed the Burmese contingent some of the sights of London and its environs. Few of the men had ever previously been so far from their homes as Rangoon. We started with a visit to the Zoo, and the first hazard was the moving staircase. To begin with, we couldn't induce our forty charges to get on to it; and then, after one brave spirit had ventured, we couldn't get them off it. Up and down they went for a quarter of an hour, the station echoing to merry shouts in Burmese, Jinghpaw, Karen and Chin as they passed each other in their broad-brimmed khaki hats. When at last we got them to Regent's Park, they were puzzled by the interest which other people were taking in such an everyday sight as an elephant; and the excursion looked like being a flop.

The star exhibit in those days was the Giant Panda, which had lately arrived with much publicity; so I took them to its cage.

" This," I said proudly, " is the Giant Panda. It has been brought here all the way from China, regardless of expense."

They looked at it, and then at me, and asked:—

" Why? "

Our next sortie was more successful: a church parade one Sunday at Sandhurst, and on to Windsor and Eton; the Tower, and other obvious places of pilgrimage in London. One warm evening I was strolling through their camp when

I met two young Kachins coming in, rather hot, with compasses in their hands. They had been out for a walk, and through a Jemadar who spoke English I asked them where they had gone. The brighter of the two explained in great detail, exactly as if he had just returned from a reconnaissance patrol.

" We first went south-east," he said, " for a mile and a half until we came to a big *myit*, or river." (I recognised the Thames.) " We turned downstream for 1,500 yards, and came to the big *poongyikyaung* (monastery) the *Thakin Gyi* (me) showed us yesterday." In other words, they had got as far as Westminster Abbey.

A few days later we had the first Chindit Officers' Reunion Dinner at Claridge's, an annual event which petered out after a few years. That was the first and best, and memorable largely for Samson's speech. It was punctuated with guffaws of laughter, led by himself. His tipple was always rum, an unusual demand in those august halls; but we got it. Except for a tendency on the part of the diners to go through the motions of cooking rice on the floor, our behaviour was impeccable.

Some time that same year, 1946, a letter appeared in *The Times*, signed by one Aubrey Buxton, asking that all those who had the interests of the Karens at heart should get in touch with him. I knew nothing of Buxton, but I certainly had the interests of the Karens at heart; I owed them so much, as I did also to the Kachins and the Burmese. I wrote to Buxton, and in due course met him. He belonged, as I had guessed, to that great East Anglian clan of Quaker descent which is inextricably intermingled with Gurneys, Hoares, Barclays and the like, with a bottomless tradition of public service behind them; he had served during the war with Force 136, which had sprinkled parachutists as though from a pepper-pot all over South-East Asia to raise and arm the locals against the Japanese. Independence for Burma was very much in the air, as I well knew; but Buxton told me that a delegation of Karens was on its way home to plead with the Government that they should be allowed to opt out of this plan, and to stay within the Commonwealth.

It was obvious that the Karens would find themselves in an awkward position when Burma became independent. The tradition of hostility between them and the Burmese went back for several centuries. Many of them were Christians. They had supported us in the various wars which we had fought against the Burmese in the 19th century, and again in the Burma Rebellion of 1931. What they were asking for was a Karen State, with its capital at Moulmein, which would be a part of the Commonwealth. They reckoned that it would be self-supporting from the sale of timber and rice, and from the products of various mineral resources which lay in areas predominantly inhabited by Karens. They were opening their mouths far too wide when they laid claim to huge chunks of the Irrawaddy Delta, where there was admittedly a large Karen population, but with Burmese majorities superimposed. Nevertheless, they had some sort of a case, and they certainly had a claim on our gratitude.

One plan was the establishment of a federation of states, shaped like a question-mark or a sickle, stretching from the Chin Hills on what is now the Pakistan frontier, through the Naga Hills, the Kachin areas, the Shan States, Karenni and down through Tenasserim to the borders of Siam, still with Moulmein as the capital and the principal outlet. The idea had its attractions. It might have worked; but it would certainly have been deeply resented by the Burmese, and would therefore not have contributed to stability—and instability has been the curse of South-East Asia ever since the war.

The Karen delegation, when it arrived, consisted of six or seven very likeable men, none of whom I knew. Its leader was Sydney Lu Ni, and one of its most forceful members Saw Ba U Gyi. I attended several parties given for them, including one at the Overseas League with Lord Mountbatten presiding. But the highlight was a luncheon somewhere when the principal host was the Prime Minister, the then Mr. Attlee. The time came when Mr. Attlee made a speech. It was a good speech. None of us, he said, would ever forget the friendship which had existed so long between the Karens and the British, nor what they had done for us during the war. Lu Ni rose to his feet to reply; what he said was this:—

" Mr. Attlee has said some very nice things about the Karens. Everybody has been very kind to us since we came to London. There have been cocktail parties, dinner parties, receptions, and much generous hospitality. But we cannot get the answer to the question that we came to London to ask. We have only one question. Some peoples want to leave the British Empire. We Karens don't. So here is our question, and it's all we want to know. May we please stay in the British Empire? "

Mr. Attlee looked at his watch, and said that he had an urgent meeting for which he was already late. He left the luncheon table. A few days later the delegation returned unsatisfied to Burma. Burma was granted unrestricted independence. Shortly afterwards Saw Ba U Gyi took the field as a rebel.

I wish I could remember him better, but I can't. He was a patriot and a brave man, but he was not a realist. A few months later, on leave from the Palestine Police, in which I was then serving, I tackled Lord Listowel, Secretary of State for Commonwealth Relations, with a plea for the Karens. He had been a big boy in my house at Eton when I was a small one, and he was kind enough to give me an hour's hearing while I pleaded the case of the Karens for staying within the Commonwealth. He had just been out to Burma, and had his own case at his fingertips. Gently and courteously, he knocked me for six. He distressed me most when he said that the British public were not informed about the Karens. When I suggested that steps should be taken to inform them, his own suggestion was that I too must learn to be more realistic.

So Burma was given its independence, and Ba U Gyi took the field. And I, in Jerusalem, in police uniform, complete with whistle and note-book, received the first of two letters which caused me great distress as to what I should in conscience do. Both were unsigned. Both bore the postmark of Penang, in Malaya. Both, presumably, had been smuggled out of Burma to a neutral post-box. Both urged me to plead the cause of the Karens before the world. I knew that the best service I could do them was to do nothing at all.

The advice I wanted to tender was that the Karens should make their peace with the Burmese. The question-mark plan was no longer feasible. The Union of Burma was an established fact. The best thing the Karens could do was to throw in their lot with the Union, and make a go of it: they had, with their skills, their honesty, their integrity, so much to contribute. But there was nobody I could write to, and no way in which I could communicate. It was then that the news reached me of Chet's alleged defection and subsequent arrest.

Meanwhile, here were Samson and I together again; and when we heard that his wife, whom I had never met, was near at hand, we dispatched him in the Land Rover to bring her back to sup with us. She turned out to be a charming little old lady who, like so many Karen girls, had been in British service as a nanny, and had actually spent two years in that capacity in England, in the New Forest.

After supper we sat around and talked, over a bottle of rum. Mrs. Samson sipped hers daintily like a nanny who has been pressed to drink champagne on the occasion of a family wedding. Apart from being clean-shaven, Samson hadn't changed at all. Even the lamentable story of his troubles was punctuated with gales of laughter, as if it had all been a comedy of errors rather than a tragedy. He had been caught up with Chet Khin in the tangle of misunderstandings which had almost led both of them in front of a firing-squad, and which had in fact interned them along with twenty-odd other officers and seven hundred men. After forty years' exemplary service he had been stripped of his pension, and of the annuity due to him as a member of the Order of Burma, and was now penniless. Hitherto he and his wife had been living on the charity of the American Baptist Mission at Mandalay, for he was well over sixty and without qualifications for a job; they were proud people, and didn't like it. Now their daughter Anne had qualified as a Government midwife, and gone to an appointment at Meza not far from Indaw; she had acquired a little house, and they were going to live with her, supported by her pay of something like seven pounds a month. Their elder boy had been among the first batch of cadets to go to Sandhurst from the post-war Burma Army, and had been sitting pretty for a career; but after the disgrace of the senior Karen officers his services had been dispensed with; he now worked for the Baptist Mission. Their younger boy, aged eighteen, had run away when his father was arrested, and had never been heard of since.

They were a tragic couple; but like so many Karens they were Christians of a totality which puts the rest of us to shame, and their resignation and lack of bitterness was extraordinary. Only Mrs. Samson said gently once or twice:

" They have all lost their pensions. For the young ones it

is not so bad; they can earn their living; but my man is an old man."

I asked Samson what rank he had reached before his abrupt retirement, and how I should address him.

"Never you mind," he said. "You just call me *Bo Gyi*, as you always used to."

Bo Gyi literally means "big leader"; it was the proper form of address to a subedar-major by his subordinates, and British officers would use it as a matter of mixed courtesy and affection.

Next morning was a Sunday. Kumje Tawng had warned us that he wouldn't be available to say good-bye: he had made arrangements to spend this particular week-end at a prayer meeting—he was a Baptist—somewhere well away from Myitkyina; but he had promised to warn Lezum Tan, who lived on the road between Myitkyina and Bhamo, that we would be coming his way, and hoped to see him. Sunday is still a holiday in Burma; I knew there would be no Kumje Tawng, and I imagined there would be no Saw Myint either; he would be enjoying his day off. We had been told that the army launch he had promised us would reach Bhamo that Sunday evening, all ready to take us down-river the following day. I wrote him a long letter, thanking him for all he had done for us, and reporting in detail the success which had attended our sortie to Mohnyin and Kadu; and I added that I didn't propose to disturb his Sunday with an unwanted visit. I was just licking the envelope when he drove up, dressed exactly as his counterpart in our own Army might be dressed on a leisure day: in flannel trousers and a pepper-and-salt hacking-coat.

We all had a cup of coffee to celebrate this latest kindness, and indulged in an orgy of mutual photography in the garden. Saw Myint had brought with him the tall young staff captain whom Granville and I had seen the first day;

and he had to work overtime operating the three cameras belonging to Saw Myint, Granville and Laura. This is the sort of thing that always happens to staff captains.

We said good-bye to Saw Myint in an agony of inadequacy. He had done us superbly well, and all that we were hoping to achieve in Katha District would also be under his auspices. He brought with him a pencilled note from Bill Maung Maung, the D.C. Katha, whom he had seen while we were away: it promised us a warm welcome to his parish, and included a suggested outline programme.

Maung Tu and his team had left us; I think they had enjoyed the jaunt as much as we had, and Maung Tu gave us a terrific salute on parting. They were a cheerful lot, and it was a pity that a military frost came over all their faces when we posed them for their photograph: the result wasn't at all how we remembered those beaming looks.

We were now bound for Bhamo, leaving Myitkyina by a road we hadn't travelled before, but which was the continuation of Stilwell's: grown a bit rough, but still goodish going. For the first seventeen miles it ran a little to the west of the Irrawaddy, and it can't have been interesting since it has left no impression on my memory. But after fifty minutes we drew up at right angles to the river, where we had to wait half an hour for the ferry. The wooden jetty was built on piles, and a good cross-section of society was hanging around, waiting like us for the ferry's return from the far side.

There were characters of all sorts. Some were hawkers selling tea, some cooked rice, some fudge and sugar-cane and sticky sweetmeats. Some were soldiers travelling as individuals, or pedlars: these offered a nice contrast in packs, since those of the pedlars were bulging and shapeless, while those of the soldiers might almost have passed muster at the Guards' Depot at Caterham. There were lorries laden with sacks or with long, whippy lengths of bamboo sticking out at the back; bullock-carts with sacks and baskets, and porters with panniers; and there was a man fishing by means of heavy stones. He would peer down into the water from the wharf, and every now and then would dash his stone into the depths; but his optimism wasn't rewarded during the twenty minutes that we watched him.

The ferry came back, and various vehicles lurched on board: our own, an army lorry, a big rusty bus with no vestige of paint and no glass in the windows, a number of bullock-carts. It was the third time in my life that I had crossed the Irrawaddy, and by far the most dignified: the first time was by failing daylight and under fire at Tigyaing, the second by night and surreptitiously, dodging enemy patrols a few miles below Shwegu. We were first on the ferry and first off, driving up a ramp to the top of the bank where there were a few small shacks; and then we were on the road again, and making good time.

Stilwell's road followed an ancient trade route, trodden for centuries by travellers, smugglers, traders and invaders. It ran southward, twenty miles east of the Irrawaddy, through the foothills of a range whose peaks rose to 8,000 feet and in which lay the frontier with China. Frontiers are artificial things in this part of the world, where races straddle them without concern; but hereabouts, except for a few miles in the neighbourhood of Sima Pa (where Shan Lone and Kumje Tawng had had their base in the last war) successive boundary commissions in the twenties and thirties had more or less finalised a line. Farther south a few villages were still in dispute; and while we were passing through Rangoon General Ne Win was on the point of flying to Peking to discuss this very subject with the Chinese.

At the forty-eighth milestone from Myitkyina, or thirty-one miles south of the ferry, we came to a village, where a

broad river, the Nam Sang, tumbles over rocks in its hurry
to reach the Irrawaddy. It is spanned by a fine steel
girder bridge, another relic of Stilwell. There were several
houses on either bank. We rolled through the first lot without slowing down, but on the far side we spotted several
women and children dressed in gaudy reds and yellows
on a black silk base; and we called on Kan Gyi Maung to
stop: he stood on his brakes, and we slithered to a standstill.
They spoke no Burmese, and Kan Gyi Maung couldn't
make himself understood; they showed signs of extreme
nervousness and of wanting to move off. Fortunately a
young man, who might have been the schoolmaster, and
twenty or thirty children, came running across the bridge
from the north bank to look at the strangers, and he
proved to speak Burmese. Thus reinforced, the women
stood their ground, though obviously ready to take off at a
second's notice.

This, I decided, was the time to air one of my Burmese
sentences.

" What," I asked, " is the name of this village? "

I knew it already from the map: for once in a way, it was
exactly where it ought to be. Thereafter I had to resort to
Kan Gyi Maung to interpret.

It was Dumbaiyang, and the inhabitants were Lisu: one
of the many minor races of the north, which some say and
some deny are a sub-tribe of the Kachins. The dresses and
gewgaws of the women and children were highly coloured,
and the background of the bridge and river were picturesque.
Through the young man, we bribed the children with a
promise of sweets to go back over the bridge, and then to
romp across it towards us, so that we could film them. They
were a canny lot, and reluctant to leave us in case we were
giving them the slip, but we persuaded them to comply.
Even the women consented at last to be filmed; but they

didn't like facing the cameras, and kept pirouetting so that their faces shouldn't be seen. Fortunately both Laura and Granville were equipped with cameras, and the one was able to follow the women clockwise while the other went widder-shins.

An old cow water-buffalo was lying in the shallows of the river, wallowing in the noon heat. These are surely the ugliest beasts in the world, with their muddy colour, clumsy rumps and misshapen horns; they are entirely " functional," as a source both of milk and traction. We threw stones into the river to get this one on the move and be filmed; she took a lot of stirring, but at last she got disdainfully to her feet and waddled up the far bank with her tail switching.

Ten miles farther on we stopped to lunch at Nalone, where there was a tea-shop. It was merely a roof supported on four poles, but it produced a good curry and rice, which we shared with the passengers of a north-bound bus, and a heavily-laden south-bound jeep-and-trailer, painted bright yellow—the first motor-vehicles we had seen since the ferry. Our map, which was dated 1916, marked a frontier post here; but we saw no trace of one, nor of any police or soldiers, although this is the nearest to the frontier that the road normally goes. At present, however, the bridge over the river was down, and after luncheon we had to make a detour. Turning upstream, we followed a well-defined track to within a mile of the frontier, where there was an " elephant bridge "—a causeway of tree-trunks rolled into the water lengthways, so as to lie parallel with the bank. The blue mountains towering over us were in China, but they looked just as benevolent as those through which we were travelling.

It was a source of surprise that we had not seen a single soldier all morning, nor did we until we reached Bhamo.

This tract of country has such a rich agricultural potential, and is so sparsely inhabited that if I were the Burmese Government I would be extremely nervous: the more so because land-hungry China has laid claim to it for centuries. Neither here nor in Rangoon did we find the slightest misgivings; indeed, General Ne Win got back to his capital shortly after we did, completely satisfied with a pact of eternal friendship sworn between the two countries. There is of course a thick cushion of Kachins on the China side who regard the frontier as a bureaucratic fiction. Some of them probably don't even know it exists.

As we splashed across the elephant bridge we were within artillery distance of Sima Pa, and it was tempting to play Tom Tiddler's Ground; but we had no wish to risk internment, and carried on south. We were emerging from the hills and therefore better able to see them: the huge mass of Sinlumkaba loomed ahead on our port bow. Villages were becoming more frequent, and we began asking for Lezum Tan. Everybody knew his name, and at last we came to his village. We were directed to leave the main road; a young man sat himself on the Land Rover's bonnet and steered us down a side street on to some paddy, where he pointed out a little group of buildings half a mile away close under the hill. We crossed a ford where some naked children were splashing in the shallows, and drove up a slight incline to an imposing mill. Over the door was the inscription: " Brigadier Lezum Tan, M.B.E.": and various people looked down at us out of windows as we pulled up in the yard with a screech of brakes.

A pretty young woman emerged with a baby in her arms. I deduced that she was Lezum's second wife; I knew that his first had died during the war. When in 1943 he and Fish Herring reached the neighbourhood of Sinlumkaba, Lezum had heard of his wife's death, and his two motherless

sons had joined him and marched with the party for two or
three stages. The last time I had actually seen Lezum was
when he and Fish bumped into my column in the Upper
Mu Valley in February, 1943, early in their journey; as near
as a toucher we had opened fire on each other.

Lezum was not at home, and for the best of reasons: he
had received Kumje Tawng's message, and gone down to
Bhamo to meet us. We made our usual distribution of
sweets to the flock of children who had issued from the recesses of the mill, and climbed back into the Land Rover,
glad of having stretched our legs. The road became steadily
better and more frequented, and within the hour we were
in the outskirts of the fabled town of Bhamo. We found the
Rest House close to the vast pagoda, with its unusual
rounded dome, whose massive covering of gold leaf flashed
and sparkled in the sun. Five officers, all in uniform, were
awaiting us: two soldiers, two policemen and an officer of
the Immigration Department, who wore a blue reefer jacket
and a yachting cap. Two of them went away disappointed:
they were hoping to see some other Fergusson or Ferguson
who had served with them in Force 136, and wasn't me. I
had never heard of this particular namesake. If he should
happen to read these words, it may please him to know that
he is still held in high esteem by these former comrades.

There was a message from Lezum. He was staying with
a sister in Bhamo, but would be joining us for dinner. We
had the Rest House to ourselves, and the *durwan* was efficient;
there was hot water in plenty, and tin baths to put it in. We
bathed gratefully, and celebrated our arrival by putting on a
clean change, wondering whether Marco Polo had been
able to do the same; and when we got downstairs, there
was Lezum waiting for us.

Lezum was always small, wiry and tough. The passage
of years had shrivelled him still further. The Brigadier's

uniform, with three rows of medal ribbons, which he was wearing had grown rather big for him, but his bearing was still soldierly. He had much to ask about former British officers of the Burma Rifles, and a good deal to say which seemed to me unsympathetic about the plight in which Chet Khin and other Karens had found themselves. He had actually commanded the force to which Chet and the others had made their submission. We spoke much about the war years, but he was especially interesting as an informed source about the history of Bhamo and the Sinlumkaba Hill Tract. He himself was a Catholic, and a leading one in the district. His grandmother, who had died aged 115 only a few years ago, could clearly remember the first French missionaries coming up to Sinlumkaba, which must have been in the reign of King Theebaw.

I knew from my rather superficial reading of Burmese history that the British had a toe-hold in Bhamo before Theebaw's time, when the gentle Mindon Min still sat on the Lion Throne. Three Burmese kings in succession had gone off their heads. It was during the disastrous reign of the third of these, Pagan Min—who is said to have executed 6,000 people in the course of two years—that the British were goaded into annexing the Province of Pegu: in other words, the whole of Burma below a line running east and west 350 miles north of Rangoon. Mindon deposed his brother Pagan, and in marked contrast to royal Burmese custom suffered him to survive. He then negotiated the best peace he could get from the Viceroy, Lord Dalhousie my great-grandfather.

It is sad that Mindon and Dalhousie never met, for they developed a high regard for each other; Dalhousie described Mindon as " a prince of rare sagacity, humanity and forbearance." In December, 1853, Dalhousie travelled up the Irrawaddy as far as the new frontier, but not beyond; and

he refused to allow Mindon to visit the lost province, even
for the inauguration of the splendid new *hti*, or top, which
he presented to the Shwe Dagon Pagoda: the same that
crowns it to-day. Among the concessions which Mindon was
obliged to grant was the right of passage up-river as far as
Bhamo of Irrawaddy Flotilla Company steamers, although
he made them pay through the nose for the privilege. But
by and large he was a good neighbour, and among other
things he rejected the advice of his counsellors to declare
fresh war on the British at the moment when we had the
Indian Mutiny on our hands. His final claim to fame rests
on his founding of Mandalay, which he made his capital in
1859. It is odd that such a famous city should be so young.

As he grew older his saintliness increased. The moment
came when advancing age and sheer prudence demanded
that he should designate his heir from among his forty-eight
sons; but he shrank from doing so for fear of the carnage
which he was certain would result. If he had made his choice
when he was younger and stronger, he might have carried it
through; but in 1879 he died of dysentery; one of his wives,
ambitious and able, contrived a successful palace plot; and
in the upshot he was succeeded by a drunken weakling of
twenty, with an evil and masterful Jezebel of a wife. These
were Theebaw and Supayalat. They established their place
on the Lion Throne with a hideous massacre of eighty
princes and princesses of the blood royal. Bands played and
the King and Queen feasted while elephants trampled the
victims into a ditch and covered them with earth.

Theebaw's downfall came six years later, and with it the
eclipse for sixty years of an independent Burma. By a sad
miscalculation, he reckoned he could play off the French
against the British; and it was during this period that
French influence reached its zenith, and French missionaries
came to Sinlumkaba. Under Jules Ferry, the French were

time, even in the wild forest villages, begun to understand that we wanted to stay, that we did not intend going away unless forced to. . . . They began to organise resistance. They looked to their local leaders for help, and, as too often these local governors were not very capable men, they sought, as all people have done, the assistance of such men of war as they could find—brigands, and free-lances and the like—and put themselves under their orders. The whole country rose, from Bhamo to Minhla, from the Shan Plateau to the Chin Mountains. All Upper Burma was in a passion of insurrection, a very fury of rebellion against the usurping foreigners. Our authority was confined to the range of our guns. Our forts were attacked, our convoys ambushed, our steamers fired into on the rivers. There was no safety for an Englishman or a native of India, save within the lines of our own troops, and it was soon felt that these troops were far too few to cope with the danger. To overthrow King Thibaw was easy, to subdue the people was a very different thing.

This book, by Fielding Hall, published by Macmillan in 1898, is superb stuff by any criterion, and one of the two or three classic books to come out of Burma; it went through many editions, but is now unfortunately out of print. The author served many years in Burma as a civil servant, and had a deep understanding of Buddhism. His son, who followed in his footsteps, died by his own hand in Rangoon in March, 1942, when orders were given to evacuate the city; he could not bear the tragedy befalling the country to which his father and he had given their lives.

Another authority on Buddhism and on Burma during those troubled years was Bishop Bigandet, the leader of those French missionaries whom Lezum's grandmother remembered. He began his career as ardent an expansionist of French empire as his compatriot Père Charles de Foucauld in North Africa thirty years later; but his patriotic zeal was to yield and his missionary zeal to mellow as he grew to understand the finer points of Buddhism.

The Kachins had little to lose and a good deal to gain from the disappearance of Theebaw and the Alaungpaya dynasty, and from the earliest days of the British occupation they contributed some of the flower of their man-power to the Army and the Frontier Police. Bhamo's population to-day is a mixture of Burmese and Kachins. Trade routes radiate from it. Although a long way from the railway, it doesn't suffer thereby, for the Irrawaddy is its natural artery for the flow of trade; it is the highest point on the river for steamers, since the First Defile a little way upstream is usually only navigable for country boats. A good road runs south-eastwards to cross the Shweli at Nam Kham by a suspension bridge which I once had hopes of destroying, and then turns north-east to join the main China-Burma Road on the frontier, eighty miles north of Lashio. It was the existence of this road which saved the Japanese bacon in Myitkyina and Mogaung in 1944, after the Chindits established their block on the railway at the White City; attempts to cut it by a group of columns operating independently were ineffective.

Lezum, Laura, Granville and I sat late discussing all manner of things, from the history of Burma over the last hundred years to the problems of the present day: the proximity of the China frontier (which didn't worry Lezum) and the alleged trek of Kachins out of China across it into Burma (which he denied). He told Laura among other things how my nickname among the Kachin soldiers used to be " Three-eyes "—a reference to my eyeglass. By the time the party broke up our heads were beginning to nod, and there was no more rum in the bottle.

VII

I HAVE ALWAYS LOVED boats and craft and ships, of any sort, size or shape. The oddest I ever sailed in was a boat built for me by my sappers in India between the two Burma expeditions. It was made of a few planks nailed together, over which was stretched the tarpaulin off a three ton lorry; the keel, which served also for ballast, was an old railway line bent double; the mainsail was made from bush-shirt material and the jib from a couple of sheets, both bought in the Officer's Shop at Bangalore and stitched into shape by a bewildered Indian tailor. She sailed surprisingly well, though she wouldn't go very close to the wind.

But the point is, I love boats; and I woke up that morning in Bhamo supremely happy at the prospect of the day that lay ahead: a whole day going down the Irrawaddy in a launch. Saw Myint had been as good as his word, and an army launch had come up from Katha to fetch us, taking two days against the current, whereas it would take only one to drop down again. Poor Granville was as sick as mud, for his week's grace was up and he couldn't come with us; he was to travel back to Myitkyina over the road by which we had come, so as to catch the Rangoon aircraft the following morning.

I tried to pay our bill at the Rest House, but the *durwan* stoutly refused to accept a cent. An officer had told him that we were guests of the Army, and that was that. Kan Gyi Maung performed his last service by driving us down to the

jetty with our luggage; and there we bade farewell to him
and Granville and the Land Rover, which carried with it
the marks and scars of the track to Saga. We stood on the
Customs jetty as our luggage went on board, with a little
group of officers who had come down to see us off, surveying
our vessel.

She was about thirty-five feet long, with an open deck
just abaft the wheelhouse and up three steps; an awning
was spread above the deck, and two high chairs facing
forward were awaiting us invitingly. The upper deck
ended a few feet short of the stern, where a lower one projected; and here a cook was peeling potatoes and casting the
debris into the water, where they were swept off downstream at a prodigious speed, for the current is considerable.
Right forward was a roomy saloon, complete with heads,
and you reached the saloon down a companion through the
wheelhouse. Both jack-staff and ensign-staff flew the flag of
the Union of Burma.

For crew we had a serang and his mate and an engineer,
and for escort four soldiers. The whole was under command
of a delightful Burmese lieutenant, Sein Win, who spoke a
little English. He was transport officer of the 1st Kachin
Rifles at Katha, and the launch formed part of his charge.
His other and principal claim to fame was that his eldest
daughter had been Miss Katha, 1959.

It was about a hundred miles to Katha, and Sein Win
reckoned that we would get in a little before dark, provided
we didn't get stuck. The river was prematurely and un-
usually low for the season, and one or two of the river-
steamers had already had misadventures with sandbanks.
The channels change from year to year, which doesn't make
for easy pilotage. We were going to stop at Shwegu, to
pick up the headman of a nearby village whom I was
particularly anxious to see; Saw Myint had promised to

arrange it somehow, and Sein Win had been duly briefed: the man was to come on board at Shwegu, travel down-river with us for an hour, and be put ashore again near his home. He, and more especially his wife, had been of great help to us in 1943.

We said good-bye to the officers and stepped on board. The launch was lying with her head upstream, and the serang squatted on a high stool behind his wheel, with his knees almost on a level with his cheeks. (When we tried to photograph him in this picturesque attitude, he spoiled the whole thing by swinging his legs down, sitting up straight, and posing.) As soon as the bow rope was cast off, the current, swirling between the launch and the jetty, swung her head round into the stream, and for a moment we were shooting down-river broadside on, until the engine and the wheel, hard over to starboard, took effect. By the time we were facing in the right direction, the little knot of waving officers was far astern, and we could hardly see them against the sun as it climbed above Sinlumkaba.

The day promised to be hot, but as yet it was pretty chilly; and the awning over the deck not only obscured our view but made things chillier yet, since it scooped in the wind as we chugged along and created a draught. I induced the crew to furl it, so that we no longer had to crook our necks to peer out from under. Looking ahead over the wheelhouse roof, it was difficult to see where we were heading. There were so many sandbanks and islands, and no sort of hint so far as I could detect of where the channel lay. But after a bit I spotted how it was indicated. If the mark was on the bank, it took the form of a white wand; if on a sandbank or in the water, it was a long stick—a " mete," as they call them in Essex—with bits of tin tied on with string, which swung and twinkled in the sun, however light the breeze. Sein Win told us that on every reach of the river they were checked and if necessary altered every couple of weeks.

A quarter of an hour after leaving Bhamo breakfast was announced. Sein Win excused himself on the grounds that he had eaten already. We hadn't the heart to say that we too had done ourselves proud before leaving the Rest House; so we expressed delight, rubbed our hands, smacked our lips and squeezed through the wheelhouse and down the companion into the saloon. We sat down to a light snack, each portion consisting of two fried eggs, three sausages, half a chicken, beans, cauliflower, lettuce and trifle. The cook, a Madrassi, came forward to apologise humbly because there were no peas. We accepted his apologies, and forbore to say that one single pea in addition to everything else would probably have been fatal. We regained the upper deck with difficulty.

The scene had changed. When we went below, the river was broad and shallow, and the land on either hand was flat, and mostly paddy. Now the river was narrowing, and the hills closing in. Between Myitkyina and Mandalay, a stretch of 400 miles, there are three places where the Irrawaddy has had to force its way through a barrier of hills, and they are known as the First, Second and Third Defiles. The First is twelve miles above Bhamo; we were rapidly approaching the Second.

We could see the hills ahead of us, rising to 3,000 feet, but there was no sign of any way through. The placid paddylands on either bank had given way to jungle, and except for a single village on the left at the mouth of a broad *chaung* there were no longer any signs of habitation. Beneath our keel the river seemed to be flowing with more purpose than before, like a horse collecting itself to jump. There were no more wands or metes, since there were no more sandbanks; the river deepened as it narrowed, and there was ample water from bank to bank for the deepest draught of steamer. We were close under the hills, when a small cleft, which looked no more than an inlet, opened up; and in a few more minutes we were entering the gorge.

As we swept in, the river was barely 200 yards wide, and its banks steep-to and rocky. They were bare for fifteen feet above the present water-level—an indication of the difference between January and the height of the rainy season. The cliffs flared up beside us, but above their lip was tangled jungle of deep green relieved by flowering clematis. The passage is three miles long, with several bends in it. There is one magnificent cliff of red rock on the starboard hand which I estimated with the help of a map to be well over 1,500 feet sheer; and shortly afterwards, on the port hand, the single tiny village of Zinbon.

The final reach of the Defile gave promise of the broad flat lands beyond. On the starboard hand, just before emerging, is a lonely graceful pagoda of dazzling white with a solitary gum-tree and a hermit's hut beside it. All three stand together on a promontory and cast a shimmering reflection on the water. I was seeing them for the first time in my life; but they are mentioned in a long letter of thirty pages which has been in my possession since 1946.

It was in sight of this pagoda that one of my parties crossed the Irrawaddy on the homeward journey in 1943. The reader may remember that, by the second week in April, my column had been reduced to less than a quarter of its original strength, and amounted to about seventy officers and men. I made several attempts to cross the Irrawaddy as a single body, but they all failed: the enemy patrolling was too intense, and they had confiscated all the boats they could find. It looked as though we should all have a better chance if we split up into smaller lots. I divided the rump of the column into three parties. Two of them, my own and another, eventually reached India; the third, under Captain Tommy Roberts, did not.

Tommy Roberts had been a serjeant in The King's Liverpool Regiment, of which his father had been Regimental-Serjeant-Major. He was in command of my machine-guns and mortars, though I was never able to contrive for him a worthy target. His letter is dated April, 1946, eight months after he was found a prisoner in Singapore: the Japanese sent him there for interrogation shortly after his capture, but the records show that they got precious little out of him, and that what they got was the most magnificent rubbish.

His letter contains a full account of all his adventures day by day since we parted a mile on the wrong side of the Irrawaddy after two abortive attempts at crossing: I can see the spot in my mind's eye at this moment, and hear him saying: " Good-bye, sir, and good luck. This way, lads." He began by making several efforts to cross more or less where I did, and actually managed to put one party over: it was the survivors of this lot that were brought to me as I lay in Saga. But their boatman never came back to Roberts's hiding-place. There arrived instead another Burmese bearing a letter in English from the Japanese garrison commander at Little Shwegu, five miles away, offering them food, clean clothes and a shave if they surrendered, and ending up:

" The Imperial Nippon Army is everywhere: you cannot escape."

Tommy Roberts, being short of writing paper, replied on the reverse side of the letter, declining the invitation on the grounds of " a more pressing engagement elsewhere," adding that if the Nippon Army were indeed everywhere it would have been more courteous for its representative at

Little Shwegu to deliver the letter in person; and he signed his answer: " T. C. Roberts, Captain."

He despatched the message by the hand of the same courier, and as soon as he was out of sight slipped away from the neighbourhood of the river, to make a wide detour to the south before approaching it at a different point. After much thought he decided to make his next attempt at a crossing near or in the Second Defile, where the approaches were less likely to be watched, and where there were no roads to facilitate Japanese concentrations. But the march was hellish and hungry, and it lasted six days. In the course of it one lance-corporal collapsed and had to be left; with Roberts's permission his especial friend stayed behind with him; and neither has been heard of since.

Three days later Roberts's party had the good fortune to stumble on a village unmarked on the maps, and ungarrisoned by the Japs, where they got a warm welcome, a square meal, and rations for several days. They celebrated this stroke of luck with a sing-song—" not quiet stuff, but full-throated." On the ninth day after parting company with me, they hit the Irrawaddy at Zinbon in the Defile (half-way between the cliff and the pagoda which I have already mentioned) to find it garrisoned by thirty to forty Japs, who were visited twice daily by a motor-boat patrol from Bhamo. There was one bad moment near Zinbon when they were all sitting naked in a *chaung* de-lousing themselves, and a Japanese foot patrol passed within ten yards of them without looking over their shoulders.

There were no boats to be found, and they set to work to build a raft, with the only tools that remained to them: two *dahs* and a single broken British bayonet. Twice a day they watched the Japanese patrol-boat chugging up and down the river, where it was at its narrowest. Two corporals, Eland and Jones, both of whom I remember clearly, took the lead, skeletons as they were, in the raft-building. The result was heavy and cumbersome, and when at last it was launched it proved inadequate for the weight of the whole party. Four good men, all swimmers, volunteered to stay behind and take their chance: Corporal Eland, and Privates Cross, Porter and Blanchard. I remember Eland as tallish with a long chin, Cross as fair-haired, Porter as tall and also fair, Blanchard as studious and academic in appearance, and wearing army issue spectacles. The raft, water-logged and awkward, carried the rest of the party over the river during the night. On the far bank they took stock of their position. They had seven rounds of ammunition per man, and no food. At 2 a.m. they heard shooting from the other side of the river. Nothing more is known of Eland, Cross, Porter or Blanchard.

Roberts's party, originally over twenty, had now shrunk to eight all told. They waited for twenty-four hours, but nobody came over from the other bank. They then began to scramble out of the gorge, not far from the pagoda and the gum-tree. It was—I quote from the letter:—

hard and slow. The slope of 1 in 1 was a killer, and required both hands and feet; however, at mid-day we reached its crest, and once there the going was easy. We bivouacked for the night with the Irrawaddy only $\frac{1}{2}$ a mile to our right hand—but 2,000 feet below, and a hard day's march away.

They pushed on, and next day managed to shoot a wild pig, halting and bivouacking on the strength of it.

The view from there was magnificent—can see it now. Bhamo over to our right, Katha and the southward sweep of the Irrawaddy to our left rear. Away over to the North-West the blue-grey hills which, once " in," would mean the near-end of our hike. Men in fine fettle, self ditto, and going like a horse.

Two days after crossing they descended into the Kaukkwe Basin, and managed to buy ten days' worth of food in a friendly village. But the following day—which was four days after I myself had reached sanctuary on the safe side of the Chindwin—they got caught. I quote this part of Roberts's letter in full.

Day 20. 29/4/43. 10.30 hrs. One mile south of Nanthalung (openish country). Ambushed. Enemy strength unknown. With our trousers down good and proper we got our packs off and began to fight back.

15.00 hrs. With Ptes. Eardley and Rigby killed, Cpl. Jones, Ptes. Chambers, Preston, Porter wounded, myself and Pte. Holiday unwounded (all minus ammunition for over an hour) the Nips came in at us from 30 yards.

There was nothing exciting about the rest. I told my men to sit tight. I stood up and surrendered. There's little more to be said. Subsequent events were, to say the least, unpleasant, but before we moved off as prisoners (blast it!) we had the pleasure of watching a Nip funeral for seven little Nips we'd stopped for good.

On the way back to Mosit (along the weary trail that we'd already marched in such high spirits) I counted the enemy: 2 officers and 34 other ranks. Their numbers left me and my poor men still proud and unashamed.

" Proud and unashamed! " I should think so. Roberts is now a schoolmaster in Lancashire; and if he is half as good a schoolmaster as he was an officer, his pupils are fortunate.

Clear of the Defile, the river celebrated its freedom by
sprawling once again all over the countryside: within a
mile, it was more than that distance wide, with a bewildering
number of sandbanks and an island with a village on it. But
the faithful little bits of tin kept heliographing at us to show
us the way, and soon on the left bank we saw Shwegu. It
was just after noon. The launch swept round in a broad
arc and fought her way against the stream before nestling
her nose against the twenty-foot bank, with a narrow beach
at the water's edge. The mate scrambled ashore and secured
our bow rope with a wooden stake, and we walked off the
launch along a plank.

As always in Burma, whether by a tiny *chaung* or by one of
the great rivers, the bank was fringed with people washing
themselves and their clothing. The Burmese are not only
scrupulously, but passionately, clean by habit, and they
revel in water. They don't bathe naked but in their *loon-
gyis*, putting on a dry one as they step ashore.

The *loongyi* is a garment as graceful as Burmese script.
The word rhymes with a Yorkshireman's pronunciation of
" spongy "; the garment itself is usually cotton, or silk for
state occasions, and cylindrical in design. You step into it
and draw it up to your waist if you are a man, and rather
higher if a woman. The man knots it about his middle, in
front; the national gesture of Burma is a swift adjustment
and reknotting of one's *loongyi*, rather like our own frequent
habit of straightening the knot of one's tie. The kilt is a
handsome garment when properly worn, but uncharitable
towards a paunch; the *loongyi* always flatters, whatever
your shape or sex. There is nothing more ungainly than the
spectacle on British beaches of people changing into or out of
bathing suits; they squirm and wriggle and look apprehensive of disaster; but the corresponding process with a

loongyi is as graceful as a ballet. I suppose one oughtn't to watch, but there is no lovelier spectacle in the world than a Burmese girl emerging from a river, deftly slipping her dry *loongyi* over her wet one, and letting the wet one fall to the ground without touching the dry. As the finishing touch to her toilet she slips a red flower into her black hair; the effect is almost casual, but, my goodness, it is attractive and neat.

Cruising along in the launch, we had created our own little breeze to keep us cool. Climbing up the steps cut in the sandy bank, we realised how hot the day had grown. We found ourselves in a street thirty yards across, running at right angles to the river and ending abruptly at its bank. On either side was a long line of market stalls, some selling food, some clothes, and some the pottery for which Shwegu is noted. It is basically of red clay, as you can see if you look into the inside of a jug; but the outside is painted in bright, even lurid colours. There were jugs and plates and pots and ashets galore, and rows and rows of ornamental owls, peacocks, dragons and *Chinthes*, big and small. Sein Win had invested in a couple of outsize *Chinthes* on his way upstream, and Laura had been in raptures when he displayed them in the launch. We had a minor domestic argument. By instinct and family repute I am the more extravagant member of the partnership, and Laura the restraining influence, but I was beginning to worry about our budget. We compromised in the end by purchasing a few small owls, the cheapest and tiniest *Chinthe* we could find (to give Hewie Dalrymple as compensation for the loss of his finger on the Kyusunlai) and a flower-bowl supported by three defiant *Chinthes* with silver bodies and red tongues. In the end we gave Hewie's *Chinthe* to somebody else, and the bowl was broken on the way home; but the three supporting *Chinthes* still stand in the porch at Auchairne, where they alarm departing guests by affording a glimpse of their red tongues.

It was a long time since a European—let alone two—had been seen in Shwegu market, but there was no jostling for our patronage, and no haggling, just natural good manners. While we were engaged in shopping, the Sub-District Officer presented himself, a Karen called Cushing Po: the only man of his race we met throughout the journey who held any sort of official position higher than that of station-master, although no doubt there are others. He was friendly and obviously well-acquainted with his Sub-District, since he answered many searching questions about tracks, villages and people embedded in my memories of 1943. But he had had no instructions about summoning the headman of Seiktha, who was to have joined us in the launch, and evidently this plan had miscarried.

I was disappointed in this, because the headman, although he proved a broken reed in the end, had symbolised for us the turning-point in our fortunes. The day before we met him we were at our lowest ebb. A long period on ultra-short commons had culminated in several days with nothing to eat at all; then one single disastrous meal, the winning of which cost the life of my adjutant and a good lance-corporal; and then three further days on absolutely nothing. I was losing men at an increasing rate, and another two days of starvation would, I think, have accounted for the rest of us. Then we found, shot and devoured three water-buffaloes, which saved our lives. Next day we met some boys out fishing, who led us to their village, where the headman's wife took pity on us. She gave us a tremendous meal of rice and sugar-fudge, and filled our packs with provisions for several days, which gave us our chance to try and dodge the patrols and cross the Irrawaddy. It was only when we went back to them in an effort to borrow some boats we had seen lying

under the stilts of the headman's house that they went sour
on us; they had suddenly realised that a huge concentration
of Japs had arrived in the area, they had been visited by a
strong posse already, and they were in mortal terror in case
the help they had already given us should come to light.

It is possible that the headman did receive the summons
to meet me at Shwegu, and funked it through doubt about
what sort of reception awaited him; but since Cushing Po
knew nothing about it, it is more likely that the plan mis-
fired somehow during its passage through staff channels.
But I was sorry. I had never borne the chap a grudge, and
indeed looked back on him as a bringer of luck: although,
as often happens in Burma, the wife was the better man of
the two.

We resumed our voyage down the river. A little below
Shwegu it is split by an island more than two miles across,
itself intersected by several creeks. For the next fifty miles
there is a marked contrast between the two sides of the
river: the left bank is mostly cultivated, with a large
number of villages; the right bank has few villages, and the
jungle grows down to the bank or the water's edge.

Between " bank " and " water's edge " there is a distinction. On the Irrawaddy, as on other broad and shallow
rivers, the channel weaves from side to side; on the inside
of a curve the bank is apt to be flush with the water's edge,
whereas on the outside the current scours away at the land
to form a little cliff. This phenomenon applies also to the
sandbanks in mid-river, which change their shape every
season. The optimists who mapped the river were so rash as
to mark some of the larger banks as they were at the time the
survey was made, which I found highly confusing as I sat in
my high chair with my map on my knee; and I often had to
fall back on my small prismatic compass—the same one as I
had in Burma during the war: don't embarrass me by asking

why I never handed it in—to identify landmarks. The process of erosion is continuous, and several times that day we saw a sizeable chunk of sand, perhaps twenty or thirty tons of it, fall away into the river, sometimes encouraged to do so by our own wash. Once we got stuck, and it took us ten minutes to pole ourselves off against the current, with the help of a kedge.

The general trend of the Irrawaddy from Bhamo to Katha is westerly, but curving through a wide northern arc—the only divergence during all its course from strict conformity to north and south. From the Second Defile to a little way above Katha, the country on the right bank comprises what we used to call the Kaukkwe Basin. The Kaukkwe is a deep and wiggly river some thirty yards across, running black and sullen for fifty miles through the thickest jungle (with one exception) I ever encountered. I also once saw in it a flock or gaggle of three or four hundred flamingos. To the west is the range of Kachin Hills in which lies Saga, and to the east is the Kaukkwe Range, also inhabited by Kachins; but the Basin itself, which is twenty to thirty miles wide, is practically uninhabited, and I have never understood why, since it is well-watered by tributaries. In some ways this was an advantage to us on both expeditions. Although it meant that you couldn't cross the Basin, where tracks were few, without carrying a fair stock of food, it also meant that you had a good chance of hiding from view if you wanted to; yet even so it was within the Basin that Tommy Roberts got caught, and Scotty, too, had a fight there in the actual process of crossing the *chaung* itself, and had some casualties. But Scotty also discovered a natural air-strip in a clearing, from which some of his sick and wounded were evacuated by Dakota. Here is the tale.

The survivors of his column, having got across the Irrawaddy, were making their way across the Kaukkwe Basin towards the sanctuary of the Kachin Hills and my own benefactors at Saga and elsewhere. But the moment came when it was evident that some of them couldn't struggle on any farther. One was a lieutenant-colonel, senior to Scotty, whose separate headquarters were accompanying his column. This officer's stout heart and hale body had been overwhelmed by jungle sores, and almost every inch of him was in a state of suppuration.

The decision was taken to abandon these sick and sorry. Wingate had impressed on us all that it was our duty to get as many people out to India as possible, to fight another day, and that we must harden our hearts towards those who couldn't manage it. I never heard of a single case where a man protested at being left; I know of several where the man himself urged it, mindful of Wingate's orders. With a heavy heart, Scotty made these men as comfortable as it was in his power to do, said good-bye, and marched on.

Then came the miracle: the discovery of the natural air-strip, and, by radio, of a pilot with enough guts to make the hazardous landing and take-off. He was Michael Vlasto, a Calcutta business-man in peace-time and a Dakota pilot in war. Scotty sent back men to haul the abandoned to their feet for another half-mile of effort. Vlasto landed, loaded up with seventeen men, and actually brushed the trees as he urged his overloaded aircraft into the air. Although he volunteered to make another attempt for other men in the column, he was overruled, and rightly, by his superiors: it was one of the most hazardous take-offs of all time; and all the others had a reasonable chance of getting out on their feet. Except for a few battle-casualties, all did.

Now I myself had crossed the Chindwin into safety three days earlier, on the 24th of April. On the 25th my party reached road-head; on the 26th John Fraser and I were motored against the one-way traffic, by special privilege, to

Imphal; on the 27th I was sitting at luncheon in General Scoones's mess at Corps Headquarters. My nightmares were to continue for many weeks into the future; but at that moment I was most gloriously aware that I, personally, myself, was "out" and safe, though grievously conscious that most of my men would never be seen again.

We were all sitting at the end of luncheon, with clean white napery on the table, and smoking cigars, with the dregs of good coffee at the bottom of our cups. The door swung open abruptly. A tall, tattered, stinking figure came half-way through it, and then leaned up against the door-post for support. General Scoones, the corps commander, rose to his feet, and gaily called, "Come in!" Scoones knew us all; he had been very good to us on our way through Imphal into Burma four months earlier; and as we were all expecting the colonel, because of a telephone call from the airfield, Scoones recognised this semi-skeleton at his mess door.

"We've kept some luncheon for you!" he said; but this was too much for the colonel. He staggered forward to the vacant place at the foot of the table, collapsed into a chair, and dropped his head on his hands. Scoones could be tough, and often was, but he could be sensitive too. He collected all his officers with his eyes and led them out; at the same time he jabbed with his finger at me and at the colonel, signifying that I should go to him; and I did. I had emerged from our ordeal in the natural way, marching to the Chindwin and crossing it, growing gradually used to the sensation of being home and dry. But the colonel had come direct to the safety and napery and cigar-smoke of Corps Headquarters, having been snatched from a yard or two of space in thick jungle. There, three hours before, in company with sixteen other men, he had been composing himself for the only conceivable prospect in view: death.

This natural air-strip was put to good use in 1944, when Mike Calvert's brigade was landed there by air. It became his stronghold, under the name of " Broadway." Broadway was only two days' march from both the railway and the Irrawaddy, and an admirable place from which to raid the enemy's lines of communication. During the troubled years after the war, the Communist insurgents put it to the same use; and from something Saw Myint said to me at Myitkyina, I suspect that it was still in insurgent hands, though I didn't press him. But I never liked the Kaukkwe Basin; there was no benevolence about it, somehow, either of the times I marched through it: though the first time it spelt safety for me, and the second we were on our way to Broadway to be flown out to India for a rest.

The right bank had now, since Independence, become part of the Kachin State; and as we reached the dark mouth of the Kaukkwe Chaung, where it debouches into the Irrawaddy, I was intrigued to see that a considerable village had sprung up where there was none before.

" Isn't that new? " I asked Sein Win.

" I don't know," he said; " I've only been stationed in Katha for two years. I'll ask the serang."

Apparently I was right. The Kaukkwe was now the boundary between Burma proper and the Kachin State, and the village had grown around a small police post and check point, and become a handy centre for traders. I could see half a dozen country boats on the beach, and signs of timber extraction.

I was now looking with some eagerness for the point at which my own party had managed to cross, after all our abortive attempts. It was from a high unwooded bank, with a clump of trees five hundred yards inland where we had lain hidden all day waiting for nightfall, not daring to light a fire, and wondering why on earth the Japs didn't turn aside to search it. Two boys, each of whom had a boat hidden, were going to meet us after dark and ferry us over in relays, as they duly did. We landed on a sandbank so broad that it took us half an hour to march across it in the dark, and then scrambled up a high bank where jungle grew to the very edge.

The scene was so clearly etched on my memory that I would never have thought it possible to miss; I knew that it was within two miles, at the most, of the mouth of the Kaukkwe; but miss it I did. What diddled me was the absence of any sandbank the size and shape of what I was looking for; in the course of seventeen years the pattern had changed beyond recognition. By the time I realised this we were certainly past the place, and steaming between Kontha and Moda, where the Japs used to operate a ferry.

The sun was getting low. I could still see through my binoculars, a long way astern of us, the familiar nick in the Sinlumkaba Hills; and ahead of us now was the Naba Gap —the break in the Gangaw Range through which runs the little spur line from the Railway Valley to meet the Irrawaddy at Katha. We were overhauling a river steamer, which had left Bhamo some hours before us; her white snub nose was rosy in the setting sun, and her bow wave pink. One of Sein Win's brother-officers was on board with his family: they lined the rail and waved to us.

By the time we got abeam of Katha we were in shadow, for the sun had dropped behind the Gangaw Hills. This year's pattern of sandbanks had blocked the usual access to the Katha foreshore, and we had to go well downstream and back up again. (One of the disputes submitted and settled during our stay in Katha was the ownership of an island which had appeared in the river since the last monsoon: who was to have the privilege of winning a crop off it? Old

men gave evidence about who had been the successful claim-
ants during its last incarnation.)

As always in a Burmese evening, a light veil of blue
smoke hung over the town, testifying to the preparation of a
meal. Not a breath of wind disturbed it. Along the foreshore lay the carcasses of four river steamers, destroyed either
by the British during the evacuation, or by subsequent
bombing; these were not an agreeable feature of the view;
nor was the prison, where some of my men were lodged after
capture. But the general impression was of a romantic little
town, sleepy after a long, hot day, and owing allegiance to
the vast pagoda by the river's edge.

Sein Win thought we were to be the guests of his battalion,
and had positive orders to take us there. This was embarrassing, as we knew that Bill Maung Maung was expecting
us, and that Saw Myint was *au fait* with his intention of
taking us under his wing. Fortunately, in the absence of
Maung Maung, we were met on the beach by three of his
officials: the Sub-District Officer, the Headquarters Assistant and the Chief Clerk. Sein Win was out-voted, and we
were impounded by the civil as opposed to the military
authority.

The Chief Clerk was a big, burly man who quickly won
my heart.

" Was it you," he asked, " who passed through Tigyaing in
March, 1943? "

I admitted it.

" I was sent there the following week," he said. " The
Japanese had many men there. They were very angry."

" Did they punish the people? "

" No, because the people said you had threatened them if
they didn't help you. But the people were laughing at them
behind their backs; and they told me that your men were
very cheerful, and paid for everything they took—paid much

money, much, much money. They said you made a speech in your eyeglass."

I did actually make a speech at Tigyaing, I remembered, because a Jap aircraft had flown over just before we entered the town dropping pamphlets telling us in several languages that it was all up with us, and that we'd better surrender. As the locals had all read it, it seemed to me that a speech was called for. I smirked a bit to hear that it was still remembered.

We thanked Sein Win, his crew and his escort for our memorable day on the river, and promised to meet him again before we left. He told me that one or two of his Kachin brother officers had served with me in war-time days, and were hoping to see me, so I promised to come up to their mess before I left the neighbourhood.

The Maung Maungs' house was a fine, two-storey building in a large garden, standing back a little way from the river. What surprised us—and this is no reflection on their hospitality, which was epic—was how sparsely it was furnished. There was only the minimum of everything, and even the water-closet off our room didn't flush, nor was intended to flush, until one clambered up and sluiced the contents of a bucket of water, which was always filled and ready, through the cistern. The fact is, I think, that the Burmese have a totally different attitude to possessions from our own. They are generous far beyond British standards; they dislike the fetters into which ownership thrusts you; their instinct is to share everything that may come their way with their neighbours. In the village echelon of society, a stroke of luck—whether it emanates from a good crop or a lucky coup at gambling, and all Burmese are gamblers—is not an occasion for hugging one's winnings to one's bosom; it is the excuse for the best party that the money will stretch for. If your house burns down, it is not a major calamity:

your neighbours will rally round, just as you would do for them. If you are really in luck, build a pagoda. On no account hoard.

Bill Maung Maung was away on tour, as he had warned us he would be, but his wife Mary made us welcome—a beautiful girl with a flower in her hair, and looking so young that it was hard to believe she had three children away at boarding school: a boy at Maymyo and two girls in Rangoon. Two younger children, a boy and a girl, were at home. Bill and Mary had met and married in an internment camp during the Japanese occupation; Bill was already in the Government service, and suspected for various good reasons of being anti-Jap. They had been in Katha for less than a year, having come there from Rangoon; but Bill had had several postings overseas, and knew London, Washington, New York, Paris and Geneva. The house was littered with British and American magazines, and with many back numbers of the *Weekly Mirror*; and before the evening was over we were to hear on the gramophone the long-playing record of Michael Flanders and Donald Swann in *At The Drop of a Hat*, which we had somehow not associated with Katha.

Meanwhile we settled down to discuss plans. Maung Maung had suggested that we should have one day's rest in Katha, and join him on the next day in Banmauk, which he expected to reach at about the same time as we would. I was all for going to Banmauk, but the idea of a rest didn't appeal to me a bit; I was determined to be out and doing, or rather seeing. We had just had a day's rest in the launch, and didn't want another.

" What about going to Mawlu? " I asked. I wanted to see the " White City," where Mike Calvert had successfully blocked the main Japanese line of communication on the railway, for more than two months.

Of the three officials who had met us, and who were still
sitting in Mary Maung Maung's drawing-room taking part
in the discussion, the dominant one was U Hla Pe, the Sub-
District Officer, who was to be our frequent companion
during the next few days. It is always difficult to guess the
age of a Burmese. They continue to look very young until
they are middle-aged; and when at last they begin to look
old they are apt to do so suddenly, and to remain venerable
in appearance for years and years. I imagine U Hla Pe was
about twenty-six, good-looking, with a rather determined
face; we were to find him highly intelligent, and well-
informed both about Burma and the outside world. He had
never so far been abroad, but was anxious to travel. Before
joining the administrative service, he had been a schoolmaster. It was U Hla Pe who now replied.

" It will be quite easy to go to Mawlu," he said, " if you
don't mind an early start. There is a train from Katha at
seven-twenty and we shall have to wait an hour at Naba;
but we can be back in time for dinner in the evening."

Mary swore that it would be no inconvenience to her to
give us an early breakfast, and U Hla Pe was equally
emphatic that he didn't mind coming with us: Mawlu was
in his Sub-District, and he would like an excuse to visit it.
He would call for us shortly after 7 a.m., and Mary would
give us a picnic basket. There was no further talk about a day
of rest, and the three officials took their leave.

A handful of guests arrived for dinner. They included the
station doctor and his wife, who were leaving by steamer the
following day on posting to a new job somewhere down in
the delta, and a retired District Treasurer of charm and
culture, who had been caught in Katha when the Japs
arrived and had perforce worked for them throughout the
war. He had seen some of our Chindits being brought to
Katha Jail in 1943, where they were kept for several weeks

before being moved on; and had been able to get some little luxuries like tobacco and extra food sent in to them. He told us also a sad little tale of six French nuns, who were worked so hard as beasts of burden humping sacks of rice for the Japanese in Katha that four of them died. His account of war-time Katha provided a sobering note on which to go to bed.

VIII

WE HAD FINISHED OUR BREAKFAST and were all ready for the road when U Hla Pe arrived in a police car to collect us and take us to the station. He was wearing brown shoes, a European jacket, a green *loongyi* and a green pork-pie hat.

Also with us was Bill Maung Maung's factotum, Nyan Maung, who had waited on us at dinner the night before and brought us our breakfast this morning. He belonged to Lower Burma, but had married and lived for many years in Banmauk. His temporary position as our henchman he took very seriously. He had with him two sets of tin dishes, fitting into each other, and packed with cooked food: we saw a lot of these in Burma, and very neat they are, with a strap and a carrying handle at the top. Though already encumbered with these, he insisted also on carrying Laura's two Shan bags. These equally useful articles are to be seen everywhere, and I can't think why they haven't been introduced into Europe. They are made of stout black cotton with gaily coloured embroideries; they are square in shape, open at the top with a broad band to slip over your shoulder; and as there are no pockets in a *loongyi*, everybody of both sexes carries one of these bags.

The town was astir and the bazaar full of people. A procession of boys from the *poongyikyaung*, moving slowly along in single file with their bell, was accepting the matutinal gifts of food: this is one of the familiar sights of Burma. A Buddhist religious eats not for pleasure but to keep his body alive; he is supported entirely by the contributions of cooked food willingly given by the faithful, and he eats whatever is put before him. It is just as well that he is supposed to derive no fleshly satisfaction from it, since it must always be cold by the time he gets it.

The station-master was a jolly old boy in a Balaclava like Ba Ohn's and a brown woollen cardigan, who had actually seen me in Tigyaing; he had left his post on the railway, wherever it was, and gone down to Tigyaing as a nice quiet little place where there wouldn't be any bombing or other disturbance. He recalled our arrival there and our prolonged crossing of the river—it took us two or three hours to get everybody over—and the advent of the Japs just as the last two boat-loads were pushing off.

" They fired on you with cannon," he said, and I agreed; but I'm afraid it wasn't true: one solitary mortar had lobbed a few bombs out of the town and across the sandbank to our embarkation point, but they were all wides. The station-master, like the Chief Clerk the night before, said nice things about my men's behaviour, and the punctilious way in which they had paid for all they bought.

After ten minutes' gossip he showed us ceremoniously to our carriage, the little engine gave an important scream, and we clanked away slowly up the incline, on the twelve-mile journey to Naba. The gorge is deep and narrow, so narrow, indeed, that from inside a railway carriage you can only see a few yards up the hill on either side of the line; the extremities of the two halves of the range are looking at each other from a mile apart, 2,500 feet above your head. Railway, road and *chaung* have to share what little space there is, and cross each other repeatedly. In 1944 one of my columns contrived to get itself beaten up while moving into bivouac fifteen miles south-west of here, and most of their mules had stampeded with their heavier weapons; it was hereabouts that they sneaked back on tiptoe across the line, on their way to Aberdeen to reorganise and re-equip. I remember them reporting by radio what a beastly march they were having, and apologising for their slowness. Their colonel, who is still serving to-day as a major-general, had been shot through the butt of his revolver as he held it in his hand; his palm was full of bits of butt and bits of finger. He must have had a miserable time slithering down the one set of hills and scrambling up the other, with a heavy pack on his back and only a single hand to help him.

Our train trundled into Naba Junction, and we clambered down on to the tracks. There were no platforms, only a labyrinth of sidings, where the most conspicuous rolling-stock were long flats laden with teak logs, marked with hieroglyphs in red or blue keel. A dozen vendors of food had their stalls strung along beside the line; all were doing good business, and not only among the passengers, for many of the crowd were obviously there for no better reason than a gregarious instinct. There were a dozen individual soldiers in jungle green, with their military paraphernalia slung about them; we watched one of them demolish, in a succession of platefuls, enough rice to keep the average English preparatory school in rice-pudding for at least two terms. He cast a longing look at his source of supply as the south-bound train came in, and on my last sight of him as he climbed into it had added to his considerable burden two neatly-packed leaf-fuls to sustain him on his journey.

We ourselves were sipping tea with U Hla Pe and the Township Officer. Township Officer is the lowest " established " rung on the ladder of the administrative service: below him come the senior and junior headmen and elders, who administer their own native villages where they live and die; whereas the Township Officer is a career man, who may find himself serving anywhere, and follows his job from post

The Light Plane strip at the White City

Tales of the White City. Calvert's Headquarters were up the
gully behind me

Above left, Bonchaung Bridge, with wreckage of the old girders
in the bed of the stream

Above right, Maung Lu Kyaw the watchman (facing camera)
describing his flight on the day we blew the bridge. Anne
Samson is on the right

Below, U Hla Pe and the RAF bomb now serving as pagoda
gong

to post. A Sub-District may comprise three or four Townships, and there may be a similar number of Sub-Districts in a District. Above the District comes the Division, run by a Commissioner; and there are seven Divisions altogether in Burma proper. Bill Maung Maung, as Deputy Commissioner for Katha District, touched his hat to the Commissioner at Sagaing, 200 miles to the south; and his writ ran east almost to Bhamo, and as far north as Mawhun: at both these points his diocese marched with the Kachin State.

U Hla Pe and his subordinate were deep in official talk in Burmese, but Laura and I were happy watching the crowd and its habits, and in an occasional stroll up and down. After an hour our train arrived, a slow goods, and U Hla Pe ushered us into the brake van. There is no embargo in rural Burma on travelling by goods-train, and we could see people swinging themselves up on to the flats or into the wagons between us and the engine.

Away we went, along the eastern foot of the Kyagaung Range. I had once had a thirsty and anxious spell of three days on the western slope of it, two miles west of the railway, when I was forced to have water dropped on me by parachute in metal containers. It was odd to be drinking Indian water in Burma.

Soon we came to Pinwe, a little station with half a dozen houses which I had once visited. The only *raison d'être* for Pinwe is the loading of timber on to railway flats; it has no other significance. A constant source of contempt during the war was the unseemly grandiloquence of the British communiqués in this theatre; the only thing to be said in their favour was that the American ones were worse. When the 36th British Division was advancing southward, several months after we had left the area, it was announced that: " Our troops have occupied the important railway centre of

Pinwe." Similarly, I was once down on the Arakan front as a visitor. Everything was as quiet as the tomb, but one gun suddenly went off. I was standing near it at the time, and it made me jump and my eyeglass fell out. That night's communiqué reported " a quiet day, except for artillery duels."

At and around Pinwe, much derelict rolling stock and locomotives were lying in the ditches beside the line. At first I thought these must be relics of our own activities and those of the Royal Air Force, who were assiduous in their attentions on the railway; once they even shot up one of my own patrols, part of the price we had to pay for the secrecy of our operations. I was soon disillusioned: these wrecks were the inglorious pre-Ne Win trophies of the insurgents, who had done so much to impede the progress of Burma during these last few years. Railways and rolling stock are always the easiest and most vulnerable targets for rebels and guerrillas: they are impossible to defend, and successful attacks on them not only disrupt the economic life of the country, but bring a bogus prestige to the attackers and bolster their morale.

Our train had some shunting business to do among the sidings of Pinwe, and we were promised half an hour's wait; so Laura and I wandered over to watch a team of elephants loading teak, an entertainment of which I never tire. There were three of them, dragging logs from the fringe of the forest with chains, and then pushing them up a sloping wooden ramp on to railway flats standing on the sidings. An average teak log is 25 feet long by 5 ft. 8 ins., or 50 cubic feet, and weighs exactly a ton; which gives one some idea of the power reposing in these glorious and lovable beasts. It is a matter for rejoicing that they found a worthy chronicler in Elephant Bill Williams; and a matter of grief that he died when he had still so much to tell us.

North of Pinwe we came to a stretch of paddy, our field of vision widened, and I suddenly caught sight of an old landmark—well-remembered, although I had completely forgotten it until that moment. It was Mawhun Taung (*taung*= hill) twenty-five miles to the north, a bastion sticking out southwards from the main system of battlements of the Kachin Hills, four miles west of the railway: 3,592 feet of it, jaunty and defiant, cocking a snook at Burmese, British, Shans, Shan-Kadus, Japanese and all. And away to the westward I could see Kalat Taung, 133 feet higher, which used to guide our aircraft into Aberdeen while at the same time getting in their way with its tall, awkward shoulders. Hills always assume characters. In my mind, Kalat Taung, with its promise of sanctuary in our stronghold just below, was always bumbling, protective and amiable; and Mawhun Taung a likeable, combative bounder, whose sympathies were wholly with us. I could imagine Mawhun spotting me, and flashing across to Kalat the news that I was back.

I cried out with delight at Mawhun Taung, and explained to Laura and U Hla Pe why I was so pleased to see it. U Hla Pe looked at me curiously.

" I can see now that you really do love this country," he said; and from that moment onwards the relationship between us underwent a subtle change. It wasn't that he had been chilly before, but I think he now realised that it was something more than mere curiosity that had brought me back again.

We were now approaching Mawlu. Without question, the most dramatic and effective feat of arms performed by the Chindits in either year was the establishment and defence of the White City. It derived its name from the number of parachutes hanging in the trees all about it, for it had to be supplied entirely from the air at great risk to the gallant crews manning the Dakotas. The object was to cut, and to keep cut, the main Japanese supply line to their troops opposing Stilwell's Chinese in Myitkyina and Mogaung. We failed to realise at the time how far they would be able to step up their road supply through Bhamo to compensate them for the loss of the railway; but even so the Japs in the north came near to starving because of the White City.

The story should be read in full in Calvert's book *Prisoners of Hope*, where it is superbly told. He picked the place off the map, and it proved to be a winner. Having landed his brigade at Broadway—where he lost twenty-eight men killed in the process—he made a forced march at speed through the Kachin Hills, and pounced on the railway just north of the hamlet of Henu, a mile north of Mawlu, before the Japs even knew of his landings. West of the line was a wide stretch of paddy, where a Dakota strip was improvised in an hour or two; east of the railway, which here runs on an embankment, there was a little half-moon of tree-covered hills. The embankment and the hills together made a perfect natural fortress; a *chaung* provided water; and a stretch of three hundred yards of pasture between the embankment and the hills, and defiladed by both from fire, was just long enough and smooth enough to fly off light aircraft.

By the time the Japs had tumbled to what was happening, four 25-pounders and four Bofors anti-aircraft guns had been flown on to the paddy, dragged over the embankment and sited in the fortress. Immense quantities of barbed wire, digging tools and mines had been either flown in or dropped. The hills were quickly honeycombed with defences, tunnels, dug-outs. And there, athwart the main Japanese lines of communication, sat Mike Calvert and his men, tightening their grip every day. His normal garrison within the fortress was two battalions, plus gunners and sappers. Outside it were four to six " floater " columns, each of four hundred men, who lurked in the jungle, beating up or ambushing the Japanese forces as they sought to deploy for an attack. At one time the place was invested by four times the strength of the defenders, but it never looked like falling. More than once the Japanese drew away from it altogether in despair. The block was first set up on the 15th March, and finally evacuated in accordance with a change of strategy during the night of the 7th May, 1944. One gun got immovably stuck in the mud, and had to be abandoned; the rest were flown out from the Dakota strip, under cover of a skilful diversion.

At Mawlu Station (where Mike Calvert once amused himself by taking a single ticket to Rangoon) we alighted. I gave the engine-driver a note of greeting for Ba Ohn at Kadu, twenty-five miles up the line, and we walked along the broad street, the centre of an ever-growing crowd, to the house of the headman, U Tin Maung. All the buildings were new, for Mawlu had been razed to the ground in the fighting. For all that we had brought luncheon with us, Tin Maung insisted on our being his guests; and while his wife was preparing food, we sat around and talked, with U Hla Pe translating.

Tin Maung was quite young, perhaps thirty-five, and the son of the headman of Mike's day. We were now to hear the first authentic stories of reprisal. Tin Maung's father had died at the hands of the Japanese in revenge for the help which he had no option but to give to Mike; and his father-in-law, U Hte, the headman of a small village nearby, had been hung up by his arms while the Japs poured boiling water into him to make him talk. Thereafter he was interned for six months, and then came home and died.

All this was interpreted by U Hla Pe, with a grim face. I felt miserable talking to these two young people, who had suffered such appalling bereavements because of us; and much of my exhilaration at being back burned out to a cinder. There are 740 miles of railway between Rangoon and Myitkyina; and as far as these people were concerned, it was pure chance that the British had chosen to cut it at Mawlu, thus fatally embroiling their parents in what wasn't their quarrel. Yet they seemed to bear us no scintilla of ill-will, and uttered no word of reproach.

After luncheon we set out to walk to the White City; but within a few yards I saw a post office, and was overcome by an irresistible desire to send a postcard to Bobby Thompson in Kuala Lumpur; he had been a major figure alongside Mike Calvert on both expeditions, and I thought it would tickle him to get a communication post-marked " Mawlu." While Laura was recording this scene for posterity with one of her cameras, and practically strangling herself with the other, which hung round her neck, Nyan Maung electrified her by saying suddenly: " Can I hold that for you? " in English, which we didn't know he spoke. He revealed that he had been for some years servant to a British Forest Officer and his wife, but had had no occasion to speak English since Independence.

A few yards, and I saw to my astonishment a cinema— the first I had seen outside Rangoon. U Hla Pe said it had just been erected, as part of the Government's project to introduce modern amenities and a degree of sophistication in the wilds. I expressed dismay, but was assured that there hadn't been any films yet, which pleased me strangely.

Our walk to Henu was along a dusty mile of track, about twenty yards broad, running parallel with the railway. Laura, U Hla Pe, U Tin Maung and I were leading, but beside us and behind us were at least twenty people. As we walked through Henu our numbers were swollen still further, and Laura totted up a total of forty-five. To cross the *chaung* that skirts the southern edge of the old perimeter we clambered up the railway embankment and walked across on the bridge; the sleepers were laid between two long spans of concrete, and we looked down between them into the water below.

And there before us lay the White City. The little hills were green again, but there were no tops to the taller trees, only stumps where the Japanese shells and mortar bombs had broken them off short. A few water-buffaloes were grazing peacefully on what had been the Light Plane Strip. I had flown into the White City four or five times during the siege, usually from Aberdeen, two days' march away or twenty minutes' flying. One or two of the trips had been fairly frightening. Once the Japs were mortaring the strip as we took off; another time I brought back Peter Fleming and three wounded Gurkhas, and we only just got airborne by the skin of our under-carriage. Peter was sitting under the floor-boards, and couldn't see a damn' thing.

There was one man in our party who appeared to be the local buffoon, the sort of chap for whom everything always goes wrong. He had been pressed into work by Mike's chaps, and had spent fifty days of the siege inside the White City, digging, digging, digging, while according to his own account the Japanese bombs and shells went woomp-woomp-woomp. He was still aggrieved about it, but at everything he said the other forty-four members of our escort went into fits of laughter at him. I asked whether he had been properly fed, and whether he had been paid. More gusts of laughter when he said that all he had to eat was three packets of biscuits a day, and he'd only been paid ten *kyats* for fifty days' work. I would guess that initially he had done something, probably quite an innocent something, that aroused suspicion, and that he was regarded in consequence as what my small boy would call " a baddy "; otherwise he would have been on the proper pay-roll. But he was rather fun, and when we parted at the end of the day I slipped him another ten " chips," which everybody thought was splendid.

There was another man with us who had also been in the White City throughout the siege, apparently as a volunteer. He had obviously been a trusted member of the garrison, and he asked warmly after Taffy Griffiths, Mike's Burma Rifles officer. He offered now to act as my guide to the old Headquarters dug-out; but I wanted to see if I could remember the way on my own. I led the party across the airstrip into the dark little gully, whose shelter I had so often been glad to reach. As we entered it, the former trusty pointed out, beside the track, a weapon-pit where a Brengun had been found long after the evacuation. During the insurgent troubles, the Government had given generous rewards for all weapons handed in, to prevent them reaching the rebels, and the people of Mawlu and Henu had done pretty well out of their fossicking.

One of the men put a question to me through U Hla Pe. " Why did the British leave that Bren-gun there? "

It certainly sounded rather careless. My guess was, and remains, that it had been fitted up with a device so that it should go on firing at intervals after the garrison had slipped out, to give the impression that the place was still being held.

We went on up the gully and turned left; I knew I was getting warm, but at last I was baffled, and the trusty, delighted at putting me right, took over and led us to what I recognised as the authentic spot. The stout head-cover which had so long resisted Japanese mortar bombs had fallen in at last; and where the neat, log-lined walls had been there was now only a large hole in the ground. But there was the place where I had enjoyed many a mug of rum and tin of bully with that gallant band of soldiers, who with indomitable cheerfulness spent seven weeks in that minute perimeter, cocking a snook at the whole might of the Japanese Empire.

There was a lot of junk still lying about, which must have dated from that last night when the place was evacuated: the rules about the disposal of debris and rubbish had always been strict. Like any vulgar tourist, I picked up some souvenirs: a couple of spent bullets; the broken top of an old wireless battery, with the legend " MADE IN AUSTRALIA 442C " still clearly inscribed in red; and brought them home to Scotland. The forty-five stood around reminiscing, digging with their bare toes, picking up the odd piece of scrap and asking me what it was.

One question aroused more interest than any other. U Hla Pe laughed as he heard it, and turned to me to translate, while the crowd hung on his words.

" They want to know," he said, " if it's true that there's a lot of treasure buried here somewhere? Apparently they've been looking for it for years."

" If there had been," I said, " I wouldn't have waited sixteen years before coming back."

They laughed politely, but they were obviously disappointed, like a child whose last lingering hope that Father Christmas really does exist has been finally killed. After I got back to Britain somebody reminded me that we had all made a series of caches of rations and money, of which the sites had been carefully recorded and reported, intended for crashed air-crews: perhaps this had given rise to the legend. I never heard of such caches being exploited. By the same token I used to carry in my head the precise location of the cache where was hidden the liquor ration of the Officers' Mess of the 2nd Burma Rifles for March and April, 1942: it was so many yards on such-and-such a compass bearing from such-and-such a milestone on such-and-such a road. I have long since forgotten the directions, and a stamped and addressed envelope from any interested reader will be a waste of time and money.

The trusty took us down to the little glade where the dead were buried. It was he who had disclosed it to the representatives of the Imperial War Graves Commission, when they came in search after the war, to exhume the bodies for reburial near Rangoon. It was a pretty little place—soft, green, benevolent and far from sinister. But what a problem for the defenders: to find a burial ground within such a tiny perimeter! Any good dry-bob could have thrown a cricket-ball from that spot well into the former Japanese lines.

I would like to pay tribute to the work of the Commonwealth War Graves Commission, as it is now called. I have seen many of their cemeteries in remote corners of the world and never have I found one which wasn't impeccably cared for. But I was in trouble with the Army authorities several times in the years just after the war for refusing to reveal where I had buried some of my comrades, whose next of kin wanted them left where they were. I have no quarrel whatever with the Commission's sensible policy of concentrating the graves in a few chosen cemeteries where they can all be properly looked after. At the same time I have every sympathy with parents or wives who prefer that their sons or husbands should be left in peace, and their graves forgotten by all but God.

I visited another corner of the perimeter, near the *chaung*, where I remembered seeing Pat Hughes during the height of the siege. He and I were at Sandhurst together, where he was captain of the cricket team. In the White City he commanded a battalion of Nigerians, which had previously spent a week or two in Aberdeen. He asked me to write to his wife in Kenya, since he was too busy, to say I had seen him well and in good heart. I am by nature a poor correspondent, but that was one of the letters which I did write, and remembered to post. Pat told me how the evening before the Japs had got into his sector.

" But they didn't get out again," he added grimly. He survived this and other adventures to become a District Commissioner in Kenya after the war.

We visited also the old water-point, and the dressing-station, and the gully where the mule-lines used to be. Every now and then somebody would pull back the under-growth, to disclose another collapsed weapon-pit; and some-times the trusty would be able to tell us exactly what it had housed.

I confess to having been deeply moved, for to me the whole place had something of the quality of a shrine. Some of the gallant men I had known there were dead, and one of the best of them had suffered disgrace, a much greater mis-fortune; but they had made magnificent history here, and I had seen them doing it. There had been British troops in plenty, and Gurkhas and Nigerians; smaller numbers of Indians, Burmese, Kachins and Karens; Anglo-Burmans and Anglo-Indians; some Chinese from Hong Kong who had fought with Mike before, and even two Japs, American citizens, who were risking immeasurably more than any-body else. They used to crawl out and plug into the enemy's field telephone lines, so as to learn their intentions. Their usefulness was diminished after one of them with an irre-pressible sense of humour, whom I remember well, suc-cumbed to an overwhelming temptation the day the White City was abandoned: he told the Japs in their own language and on their own telephone just exactly what bloody awful soldiers he thought they were.

We all walked back to Mawlu in high spirits, less the Henu lot, who dropped off with much hand shaking as we passed through their hamlet. The trusty and the buffoon and everybody else were vieing with each other in their tales of the war. U Hla Pe must have been exhausted with several hours of non-stop interpreting. It was odd to hear among torrents of Burmese two recurring English phrases which seemed to have passed into the language of Mawlu: *W'itecity* and *Wingitexpedition*. The tea-party while we awaited our train at the station assumed the proportions of one of the major Highland Gatherings, and our send-off was prodigious; but I couldn't get out of my mind how the fathers both of the headman and his wife, who had shown us so much kindness, had died miserably because of the help they had given us. It was a fair wallop of an answer to those back-stage ignoramuses who used to say that the Burmese were all hostile.

Back we trundled in another goods train, and this time we had a two hours' wait at Naba. It was 8.15 p.m. before we reached Katha for another dinner-party with Mary Maung Maung as our hostess. Among the guests this time was the friend of a man on whom I had pulled a pistol to induce him to ferry us over a river in 1943. He seemed to harbour no grudge, since he had actually given my co-guest a copy of the book in which I described the incident in thoroughly uncharitable terms. He was now a Government official in Myitkyina, and I was sorry not to have seen him there, when I might have offered my belated apologies.

Next morning we were off to Banmauk, and our rendez-vous with Bill Maung Maung. U Hla Pe had his own job to do, and Banmauk was outside his jurisdiction, so he didn't come with us; but Nyan Maung did, and contrived to look extremely important. We expected to be away for at least two nights, so we took blankets and bedding; and we travelled in a blue police truck, with Laura and me sitting in front beside the driver. An escort of six armed policemen sat with Nyan Maung in the back.

Our route lay at first through the Naba gap, with the railway running beside us; the road was good, and the bridges metal. Instead of turning north at Naba, the way we had gone to Mawlu, we carried on to Indaw, which I had tried but failed to capture in 1944. It was a neat little town, which I knew well from the air, having reconnoitred it several times in a light plane. There, for instance, was the jail which I had sent a column to capture from the rear, in hopes of releasing some of Mike Calvert's men and a few of my own who (I had reason to believe) were being held there; but it was this column which got mauled and limped back to Aberdeen with its colonel wounded.

The big war-time airfield just north of the town, which was my main objective, had reverted to paddy. The lakeside hamlet of Inwa, which the two columns of the Royal Leicestershire Regiment captured and held for a couple of days in a brilliant little action, had disappeared altogether; its fields were choked with *bizat* and other rubbishy plants. Beyond it were the blue waters of Indaw, the Royal Lake, which only the Leicesters had managed to reach. At Thetkegyin, on the northern end of the lake, we paused outside the main gate of the stockade, and I sent one of the escort to fetch the headman; two other of my columns had had a rough time here, and I wanted to ask him about the battle. Unfortunately Nyan Maung's English wasn't as good as Kan Gyi Maung's had been, and whenever I tried to talk Burmese I found myself skidding into Arabic, which is not very useful in Burma. No, on reflection I take that back: I found it extremely useful during the war, when more than once I spoke to Orde Wingate over the wireless in uncoded Arabic, confident that even if we were heard it wouldn't matter, since no eavesdropper could understand. But Wingate's Arabic was far more elegant than mine, and sometimes I didn't understand it myself.

Still, we did establish from the headman of Thetkegyin one or two things I had long wanted to know.

" What was the first you knew about British troops being in your neighbourhood? "

" When some men of the Burma National Army came back from Auktaw to tell the Japanese in Thetkegyin that they were being attacked. The Japanese officers told us to stay in the village and not to go outside."

This was fairly interesting. If true it would mean that we had been able to march all the way from Ledo in Assam, the other side of the Patkai Hills—four hundred miles or thereby —without any forewarning to the enemy; and this despite the fact that we had had three brushes on the way before Auktaw, which is six or seven miles north of Thetkegyin. But then I realised that it wasn't true of the Japs, since we had learned from other sources that they had put troops into Thetkegyin and a screen of Burma National Army into Auktaw because they knew we were coming. The headman's story did at least reveal that the Japs had kept their knowledge to themselves until the last possible moment. I recalled that when we bumped the B.N.A. screen at Auktaw we took a prisoner, a former postal clerk from Sagaing, who swore that we were wholly unexpected; and in his then mood—he was terrified, poor little chap—he would certainly not have lied. Apart from that, the White City block had already been in existence for a couple of weeks.

" Did you see any British soldiers? "

" We saw some dead ones after the battle, and buried them. And there were three prisoners in our village. They were crying out for water, and we gave them some."

This certainly made sense. That countryside was as dry as a bone, except for two *chaungs* which meandered through it several miles apart, and for the lake itself. The Japs had dug in along the water, and whenever anybody tried to get

near it they found the approaches raked by machine-gun
fire. Some of the men went for two and a half days without
water, and when that happens you go mad. Some drank
their own urine, and when you do that you either go mad,
or are mad already. It wasn't their fault, but it was my
responsibility.

Two days is the longest I have ever been without water,
and that has happened to me twice. We in Britain are far
too accustomed to seeing the stuff pouring out of a tap, and
taking it for granted. From time to time I try to remind
myself that I must never do this again; but alas, the occasions become fewer and fewer. The recollection was horribly
vivid that morning when I was talking to the headman of
Thetkegyin.

" And what happened afterwards? "

" We were told by the Japanese that the British would
never come back any more. And they didn't, except for a
year or two. There were one or two British about for a bit,
but they never really came back. Do you know Mr.
Castens? "

I was fed up with Bertie Castens, and decided that the
time had come to push on towards Banmauk. I knew all
this country like the back of my hand. What I hadn't
walked over I had flown over in light planes on countless
reconnaissances. Heaven knows how many miles I flew in
these contraptions with their carefree American pilots,
visiting outlying columns or neighbouring brigades, in 1944.
One thought no more about nipping into one of them for a
quick hop than one does nowadays about hopping into a
jeep. We lapsed sadly in this respect after the war, and even
now the British Army lags far behind those days in its ideas
about individual aerial mobility. The brigadiers of 1914 had
chargers, and those of 1944 had light planes; on present
form, those of 1964 will still be in Land Rovers, a half-way

hovel between the two. In my brigade in 1944, every column commander who wanted one—and he was suspect if he didn't—could call on a light aircraft at an hour's notice to overfly the area he was about to traverse, or the objective he was about to attack. I developed such a taste for this casual flying that after the war I converted the financial " arisings " (as the Royal Navy calls them) from *The Wild Green Earth* into the purchase of a light aircraft, and learned to fly myself: whereby hangs many another tale, some of them true.

Our route now lay along the Meza River, a broad and lazy stream which I know and love for most of its length. It rises in the Kachin Hills not far from Indawgyi, and surrenders its identity to the Irrawaddy eight miles south of Tigyaing. At this time of the year it was low enough to be fordable at most places, and the ferries lay moored to the bank, idle and unwanted. Where there were bridges they were in good order, though wooden. We passed through several villages, all of them as placid as the valley in which they lie. They looked cosy and comfortable, each house within its fence, each village within its stockade, each river-bank with its complement of bathers and its rafts of bamboos ready to drop down-river for sale to communities less richly endowed with that tree-of-all-uses.

I stopped at Milestone 20, which I had long wanted to see, but had hitherto viewed only from the air. According to the map, it was the most succulent place for an ambush: the river and the road ran side by side in a sharp curve close under the hill. I had found a place in Manipur which seemed to be its exact counterpart, and had practised the operation several times over with my column on the eve of the first expedition. Wireless sets a mile along the road in each direction were to tell us when a convoy was approaching, and how many vehicles were in it; the ambush was to

Aung Ni, Thugyi of Manhton

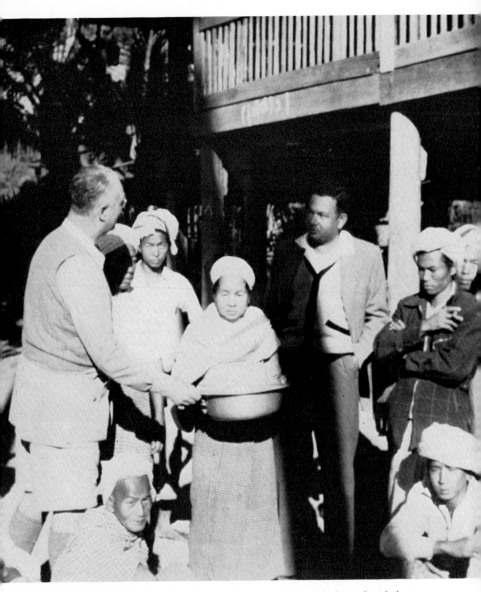

Meza House : Ba Tun and his mother with her aluminium
basin. Bill Maung Maung stands between them

pinch off the last six or eight, so as to be sure that our own strength outnumbered the enemy's; carefully-sited light machine-guns were to stampede the troops in the trucks on to the far side of the road, where they would find themselves floundering in a minefield laid there especially for their benefit.

We never got a chance to pull this off in 1943, but in 1944, No. 22 Column of The Queen's Regiment did it beautifully. This column was commanded by a cheerful and cynical war-time officer, Terence Close, who was one of the Bolshiest men I have ever had under command; he could pack into a single glance enough insubordination to sink a battleship. He won the D.S.O. for his performance at Milestone 20 and other comparable feats; and after the war forsook his profitable career on the Stock Exchange to follow his fortunes in that Army which he affected so much to despise. His death from cancer two or three years later was a calamity for a circle much wider than his many friends.

With characteristic frankness he told me afterwards that Milestone 20 on the Banmauk road wasn't half as good a place for an ambush as I had assured him that it would be. Now that I was seeing it with my own eyes, I was obliged to concede to his shade—and I could see his mocking look, more insubordinate than ever, from the safety of his present haven—that he was plumb right; but it was the map's fault, not mine. The road and river weren't hollowed out from under the hill as the map indicated; between river and hill was a flat two hundred yards of country through which the road ran in an undramatic fashion. But Terence and his men had contrived to make a good killing there all the same. Chet Khin had been one of his officers, and his close friend.

From Thetkegyin onwards the track had been abominably rough, but it hadn't deterred our driver, who kept the accelerator firmly down and flush with the floor despite the bumps. At 11.30 a.m. we drove into the police barracks at Banmauk. The guard turned out, a delicate compliment indeed. I stopped the vehicle, descended, inspected the guard, ascertained that the inspector in charge spoke English, made a little speech saying what a privilege it was for me to find a guard mounted, and asked the inspector to translate it, which he did. I then asked him to dismiss the guard, which he also did.

An embarrassing conversation then developed.

" May I ask who you are? " said the inspector.

I remembered Samson's pronunciation of my name.

" I am Brigadier Fuggusson," I said proudly.

" Oh," said the inspector. " We thought you were the Deputy Commissioner."

Laura laughed. I blushed.

Banmauk lies four miles west of the Meza, and in the eastern jaws of an eighteen-mile defile through the Mangin Range into the Mu Valley. We had passed by its western exit on our inward march in 1943, but our free passage through an area where the Japs were in strength was only achieved by the sacrifice of one of the Gurkha columns. Detached to attack the garrison of Pinbon, at the opposite end of the defile from Banmauk, this wretched column quickly found that it had bitten off far more than it could chew. They were ambushed two miles short of their objective and badly beaten up; they had great difficulty in disengaging, and were attacked again. By the time they got clear, they had exhausted all their ammunition, and having lost their wireless sets and ciphers were unable to get any more dropped to them. In the end they returned to India, and the column commander's decision to do so was endorsed by Wingate after the campaign.

But their aim was accomplished in that the rest of us got a clear run. It was a forced march all right. On three consecutive days my own column, which was detached from the others for the special task of blocking the railway in the Bonchaung Gorge, covered thirty-four, twenty-two, and eighteen miles, which is good going with heavy packs, though admittedly almost all of it was on road or track. It included crossing a 2,000-foot pass, through the range six miles south of Banmauk.

I knew Banmauk from the air just as I knew Indaw. The Japs had always had a garrison there, of anything up to five hundred men; whereas Indaw the day I attacked it had three thousand, though some of these were reinforcements on their way to join in the assault on the White City. Banmauk is delightful. The hills press closely on the town, and the air is beautifully fresh. After my little misunderstanding with the police guard, we were driven to a large and airy house of two rooms on the far side of the compound, where a table was set for luncheon by Nyan Maung. We did it full justice.

Afterwards we made friends with a woman with a baby in her arms; she was standing just outside our house pointing out to the baby the antics of some ducks in a puddle. It was a happy little picture: the ducks waddling and splashing, the mother imitating the noises and laughing, and the baby crowing with delight. While we were thus innocently engaged, there was a stir and a bustle of cars, and truck-loads of soldiers coming in at the gate.

The D.C., the real one this time, had arrived.

IX

BILL MAUNG MAUNG, Deputy Commissioner of Katha, was an imposing figure. He was six foot in height, and broad and powerful in build: clean-shaven, with a good jaw, and resolute in appearance. During the last fortnight his name had become familiar to us; everybody had spoken of it with respect; and I regarded him at first with a certain amount of awe. He too was a little shy of us at the start. He spoke in abrupt staccato, like Mr. Jingle, and his movements were quick and decisive. Long before nightfall our mutual shyness had evaporated; we found that our views on all sorts of things were identical, and that our sense of humour was pitched in the same key.

With his knowledge of European and American capitals, and his experience of U.N.O. and Geneva, and his long service at the centre in Rangoon, he belonged naturally to a much more sophisticated environment than Katha; but he was thoroughly enjoying his time in the appointment, just as a good and rising soldier welcomes every escape from the staff for a tour of regimental duty. His last such spell had been several years before as a Sub-District Officer in Arakan, during one of the many periods of unrest and rebellion which have been the plague of that unhappy country throughout history. He was obviously right on top of the job, and his handling of it was reminiscent of the best type of British official of pre-war days. His manner with his subordinates and the villagers was a happy mixture of firmness and chaff, and he was vigorous and incisive in all he said and did. When the Ne Win administration took over, and the District and Divisional officials were everywhere made subordinate to the military, there were some cases of friction, and others of the military taking a rather contemptuous view of their civil counterparts: exactly as one has seen happening in countries still under British rule in periods of disturbance. But not with Maung Maung: he and Saw Myint had worked hand in glove. Neither had shrunk from taking decisions which were strictly in the province of the other, and acting on them, in full confidence that their opposite number would agree and approve. *O si sic omnes.*

His absence from Katha these last few days had been due to military rather than to civil reasons. He had been out with a party of military police and soldiers in search of some Communist dacoits who were terrorising the villages between Kyaungle (where our Gurkha column was ambushed) and Pinlebu: the very area through which our thirty-four-mile march had taken us in 1943. So far he had been unsuccessful, but he had high hopes of a trap which he had set that very morning, and which might be sprung at any time in the next two or three days. Meanwhile he planned to spend that night at Banmauk; and to-morrow we would all go up the Meza to Aberdeen, my stronghold of 1944.

This was magnificent news. I had been warned in Rangoon not to be too sanguine about getting to Aberdeen, since the Communists—not locals, but incomers—had been active between the Mu and the Upper Meza; but I hadn't been entirely without hope, and had given Saw Myint a list of headmen who had co-operated with us. This had been furnished me by Bill Smythies; his two flimsy sheets of air-mail paper had travelled all the way from Sarawak, where he was now serving in the Forests, to Scotland, and thence in

my pocket-book to Myitkyina. Smythies had been a Forest
Officer in Burma, like his father and uncle before him, and
my Political Officer throughout 1944, including my occupation of Aberdeen. Indeed when, under orders from Wingate's successor and under protest from me, we were made to
evacuate Aberdeen, Bill went on strike, accusing me of
having led the people up the garden path and then abandon-
ing them to their fate and the Japs. He proposed to remain
behind with them; and I gave him my permission to do so,
because I knew he'd do it anyway, no matter what I said.

Saw Myint had sent the precious list to Bill Maung
Maung. There were nine names on it, of *Thugyis*, *Lugyis* and
Ywagaungs—headmen of big villages, or a group of villages;
village elders; and headmen of hamlets. Maung Maung
told me that two of them were dead, but he had alerted all
the others, and summoned the chief one to Banmauk.

So the plan was firm, or seemed to be; and Bill Maung
Maung excused himself on the score of having some work to
do with the Banmauk Township Officer. Laura and I
decided that a siesta wouldn't come amiss; but before we
had time to put this bold decision into practice, Nyan
Maung appeared at the door, with another man behind
him peering round his shoulder. Nyan Maung began saying
something, but before he got well launched the man behind
him brushed him aside, came into the room at a trot, and
went down on his knees in front of me, swaying back and
forth and mumbling.

He was old and wizened, and his clothes were covered
with dust; his bare feet were caked with it.

" He is very, very sorry," said Nyan Maung.

" What on earth is he sorry about? "

Nyan Maung made a hasty correction.

" I mean, he is *glad*, very *glad*. He is happy to see the
Thakin again."

The man looked up from his obeisance, and I suddenly recognised him. It was Aung Ni, the *Thugyi* of Manhton, the biggest of the villages in the little kingdom we had created up the Meza and called Aberdeen; he was the doyen of them all. I hauled him to his feet and pumped his hand; all his four teeth showed in a broad smile, and he made little moaning noises of happiness. He had naturally aged a bit, but he still looked tough; and indeed he and his wife had walked in from Manhton that morning, a good fifteen miles. He kept pointing at my eyeglass and grinning; and then he pulled at his own beard and pointed at where mine used to be; so I hauled out and gave him a copy of the famous photograph, which set him chattering afresh.

This dumb-show conversation was just about drying up for want of gestures we hadn't already exhausted, when Bill Maung Maung came back, and Aung Ni withdrew bashfully into a corner. With Bill was Major Mya Maung, the Burmese Commanding Officer of the 1st Kachin Rifles at Katha. Bill had dreamed up a better plan. He had finished his business here, so we would all go off to Aberdeen at once instead of staying in Banmauk, and save a day.

All was now bustle, with Bill telling everybody to get a move on. Nyan Maung put up our bedding-rolls, which he had undone only an hour before; Aung Ni was sent off at the double to collect his wife, with instructions to join us on the outskirts of the town; the military police and the soldiers were running out of their huts and throwing their kit-bags into trucks; and within a quarter of an hour we were on our way. I noticed as we picked up Aung Ni and his wife, who were both grinning from ear to ear at the prospect of a ride, that he was carrying a cross-bow.

There were several trucks in the convoy; Bill was driving the second one, with Laura and me beside him. We followed a track west of the Meza which I had never been on before;

but the country it traversed was exactly the same as the track I knew so well on the other side of the river. There was some teak, some *indaing*, and occasional stretches of paddy. Bill's initial shyness had dropped from him completely, and he made wry comments on his own driving as we hurtled across dry *chaungs* and straddled deep ruts:

" Oh My God."

" Here We Go."

" Nothing Can Stop Us Now But I Think It's Going To."

We paused at the foot of Kalat Taung, in the village of Pandaw, the southernmost of those we had taken under our protection, where the *Thugyi*, Po Than, emerged to greet us. He was very friendly, though apparently I had only met him once at the very beginning of our occupation: when Bill Smythies summoned all the headmen to a sort of durbar which I held, to promulgate the rules of the occupied area.

Greater Aberdeen, as one might call it, was shaped like a capital Y, with Pandaw at the foot; the two arms, each about eight miles long, ran up as culs-de-sac into the hills. At the top of the western arm was a narrow pass, by which we first came in, leading to the important Jap garrison at Mansi; but this was easily watched by a permanent outpost with radio, and the Japs never tried to force it. The eastern arm, running up the Meza River, ended in almost impenetrable and uninhabited hills; there was access from the east by various tracks, but there wasn't much water in that area, and little choice of route: so that this direction too was easily watched. Only to the south, in the direction of the Banmauk-Indaw road, was the valley open; by the time you reached Pandaw it had closed to a width of about three miles; but the enemy had a long way to come, and couldn't hope to cover the ground without our getting wind of him. So the defence of the place was easy and the joy of it was that

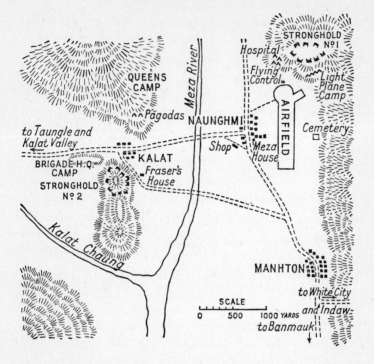

we ourselves could slip in and out at will; we were only two days' march from the railway at the White City, and two and a half from Indaw.

Aberdeen proper lay near the confluence of the two rivers whose valleys form the Y: the Meza and the Kalat. It had no well-defined perimeter, like the White City; it didn't need one. The air-strip, 1,200 yards long, ran north and south, with a prepared position suitable for two columns on a spur above it; and another similar position, and an intermittent home for Brigade Headquarters, lay less than a mile away on the other side of the paddy. Both commanded the air-strip by fire. Within this general area were two small villages, Naunghmi and Kalat; and Manhton, whose population I would guess to be about 700, was a mile south of Naunghmi.

We reached Manhton at 5.15 p.m. Aung Ni leapt down from his truck, and left us in no doubt that he was headman of Manhton in fact as well as in name. People went scurrying in all directions to do his bidding. We were to be billeted in his own house, and Laura and I stood and looked about us while our bedding-rolls were rushed up the outside stairs. It was a typical village of its kind, well-to-do and prosperous; the stockade was in good condition; the gardens were neat and cared-for; and the stilts on which the houses stood were sturdy and carefully selected. Aung Ni's house was commodious as well as smart, but there was something odd about the railing of the balcony. He saw me eyeing it, laughed, went upstairs and tapped it. The sound was unexpected: not wooden, but metallic. It was in fact twenty-five feet of air-frame from a crashed Dakota, and it suited its purpose admirably.

All the population who hadn't been fagged by Aung Ni stood in front of his house goggling at us. Such soldiers and police as were not being used to fetch and carry had disappeared to their billets. In a corner of Aung Ni's compound was springing up a neat bath-house of matting; and as soon as it was ready we took it in turns to go in and have a sluice-down with pitchers of water, brought in relays by soldiers and dumped at the door.

Since our return to Britain, some of our more curious acquaintances—I use " curious " in the sense of " inquisitive "—have asked delicately: " How did you get on for, um, sanitary arrangements? "

The answer is that they were splendid everywhere. Conditions in Manhton were probably the most primitive we encountered, but the " arrangements " were up to the high standard of common sense and cleanliness that we met everywhere else. Every house in every village stands within its own fence of palings; somewhere in the garden is a matting hut with an arrangement of planks over a deep hole; and in the hole is a large basket, three feet across and three deep. The end product of everybody's exertions arrives in the basket, which is recovered in due course, being replaced by another, and its contents applied to agricultural purposes. In the poorer quarters of the larger towns, no doubt, the arrangements are less effective; but in the whole course of our journey we encountered only one dirty latrine, and not more than half a dozen swarms of noisome flies. Of all the Eastern countries I have travelled in, Burma is far and away the cleanest, the most devoid of flies, with never a stink or stench. In even the remotest village, every house had an inscription in white paint, on door or stilt, recording the last time it had been subjected to treatment with D.D.T.; and in no case was the legend more than two years old. Once I saw a house on which the white-wash legend read " D.D.T.'d 1.1.60.—Peace on earth and goodwill towards men."

We ate an enormous supper of rice, chicken, cold fried eggs, sweet potatoes, dried fish, green vegetables of every kind, sitting around fires burning on the floor in the usual fashion: kindled on beaten-out kerosene tins. One would imagine that the fire risk in such a village, where all the buildings are of wood, must be considerable; but although no doubt it happens, I have no first-hand knowledge of a Burmese house going up in flames. Presumably the risk is so great that everybody is ultra-cautious by instinct.

The Ne Win Government had invested a lot of effort in national propaganda within Burma, as part of its drive to introduce unity and contentment to the country. It included special films and radio programmes. Personally I thought radio the curse of sophisticated Burma. In places like Rangoon, Mandalay, Maymyo, and Moulmein, loudspeakers

affixed to trees in public parks blare out at full blast, and
Laura and I were soon to learn that express trains were fitted
up with it as well, with no means of turning it off: it is as
intolerable as that continuous cacophony at Waterloo
Station in London. Bill Maung Maung had brought with
him to Manhton a mobile cinema for a one-night stand, and
a presentation Government-issue wireless set to enable the
lieges to listen to Radio Rangoon. I couldn't help feeling
that the visit of Laura and me had coincided with the sad,
first debauching of that peaceful place.

Somebody now, out of misplaced consideration for us,
tuned in the new set to the B.B.C. South-East Asia programme; and what do you think we heard? First, a detailed description of a new type of clinical thermometer, just
invented by us clever British; and then a talk by " a dis-
tinguished author," whose name I didn't catch, on the
subject of the poet Crabbe. If I had set out to lampoon the
image of the B.B.C. as projected by its most vicious critics,
I couldn't have done better than it did for itself that night.

In sheer embarrassment, Laura and I got up, went out on
to the veranda, down the stairs and into the village for a
walk. The street was empty. No sooner were we out in the
open air than we heard the raucous sound-track of Bill's
blasted mobile cinema; it was echoing all round the Upper
Meza Valley, and off the wooded slopes of Kalat Taung. It
spelt for me the Twilight of the Nats, the spirits of woods and
waters. We strolled along the broad dusty street in the
moonlight, and through the heavy wooden gates at the
northern entrance to the village. There on the paddy was
an enormous screen, and between us and it the head of every
man, woman and child in Manhton other than those few we
had left sitting around the fires in Aung Ni's house. They
had brought with them sitting-mats from out of their houses,
to interpose between themselves and the dew, and were pre-

pared to stay there till dawn if need be, just as they would for one of their own *pwes*. The Demon Cinema had them in its grip.

The film was an interminable record of the Independence Day celebrations, held in Rangoon a few days before our arrival. It went on and on and on, showing troops, tanks and armoured cars rolling past the saluting base, as well as hundreds of Home Guards of both sexes. Different cameras had been at work, and all their " takes " had been stitched together without editing, so that one saw the whole thing over and over again, only from a different angle. The people of Manhton were lapping it up, and when we left the audience was still growing; they must have been coming in from neighbouring villages, in order to see what on earth was going on in Manhton. All the dogs were howling at the bright lights and unaccustomed din; and Laura and I were in full sympathy with the dogs. But it was effective propaganda, and the message that Manhton and Rangoon were all part of the same country seemed to be getting across.

When Laura and I drifted off, back to Aung Ni's house, we found the fires dying down, and most of our travelling companions already in bed. Only one of the fires was being kept up, and round it a small group was still sitting, talking in low voices; one was a woman suckling a baby. We found our bedding-rolls laid out at the southern end of the large room, in parallel with several others: those of three Army officers, one police officer's, and Bill's. As Laura composed herself to sleep, she rolled over on an elbow and murmured to me: " If only my mother could see me now. . . ."

Our morning began with visits to the bath-house down in the garden which had sprung into existence so swiftly the evening before. It continued with an ample breakfast of chicken and rice and thin tea. There may not be much variety in a Burma diet; but for a few weeks, at any rate, it comes as a new delight and a fresh joy at any time of the day. It was always a misery when, in order not to offend, one had to eat and offer thanks for a European meal proudly submitted by the former cook of some vanished British family. It always ended with caramel pudding.

Bill drove us out of the village, past the scene of last night's film show, on the way to Naunghmi. It was his first visit to the Upper Meza, and I enjoyed the sensation of showing him the way in his own diocese. Half-way between Manhton and Naunghmi we came to a shallow *chaung*, with a steep bank on the far side.

" Can we do it? " asked Bill.

" Well, we used to do it in our jeep," I said. (I was proud of that jeep: it was flown in to us in the later stages of the 1944 campaign, and except for two or three more, owned by the American ground staff who operated the airstrips at Broadway and Aberdeen, it was the only one behind the Jap lines.)

" O My God, Here We Go," said Bill, and slammed into bottom gear, four wheel drive. The truck stood almost on its tail, its wheels spun, its engine roared; but suddenly we were horizontal again—and Aberdeen appeared before us, within its familiar rim of hills. Four hundred yards away, in all its trim neatness and beauty, lay Naunghmi, our old sanctuary; and a little blob of white at the southern entrance to the stockade showed that its people were expecting us. During the war, knowing that the air-strip was sure to be bombed, we encouraged the villagers to clear out, though they used to return by day, either to till their fields or to work for us, which they cheerfully did. We paid them handsomely for their services in Indian money, which they could spend in the shop we opened especially for them, and stocked with all the goods they'd been unable to buy in war-time.

The first man I spotted was Ba Tun. His grandfather had been the nominal headman in our day, but his father Maung Tin had been our principal doer and mouthpiece, playing a leading part in setting up and running our chain of agents in the Valleys and their fringes. I asked for him at once, to learn with sorrow that he had died five months before. But the old grandfather was incredibly still alive, though no longer able to leave the house.

Ba Tun, intelligent and quick off the mark, was all smiles and welcome. He was only seventeen when I knew him, and still looked little more than a good-looking twenty; but in fact he was thirty-four. He had been one of our most eager and trusted assistants, and I remembered him as soon as I set eyes on him. I asked him to take us to his house, where we used to hold our conferences over huge feasts organised by his father—Meza House, we called it; other brigade commanders and representatives from Force Headquarters would arrive to participate: the former by light aircraft from wherever they found themselves, the latter by Dakota from India. If anybody from India were attending, it had to be a night session, beginning after dark and ending before dawn: it was too dangerous to fly unarmed Dakotas in or out by daylight.

I needed no prompting to find Meza House. It stood on the southern fringe of the village, looking across the paddy towards Manhton. Ba Tun led Laura and Bill and me up the familiar stairs. The old man was totally blind, but he knew it was I, and held out a trembling hand; the old lady, Ba Tun's grandmother, was as spry as ever. I was inspired to ask her if she still possessed the blue china off which we used to eat; she was delighted that I remembered it, but it had all been broken long since. She produced instead, with a chuckle, a large aluminium basin, and plates, knives and spoons of the same material. Bill looked amused as he listened to her jabber, and then interpreted.

After the war was over, and the Japs and the British had both disappeared whence they came, half a dozen Chinese tinsmiths arrived. They set up a furnace, and proceeded to melt down the remains of the various aircraft which had crashed or been shot down in and around Aberdeen: seven Dakotas and seven assorted Jap fighters. These they had transformed into domestic utensils and crockery, making a fortune in the process; the Township Officer told me that articles from their workshop were to be found all over the Upper Meza. Later in the morning we were shown their graves: they had spent all the money they had made on opium, and smoked themselves to death *seriatim*.

Ba Tun pointed to a corner of the room, and said, through Bill as interpreter:—

" That's where you used to sit during meals and conferences, on the wheel of a crashed aircraft: do you remember? "

Now that I was reminded, I vaguely did. The room was full of ghosts, anyway: not only of people, but of plans. In this room it was broken to me, after Wingate's death, that the plan on which we had been working was jettisoned, and his whole strategy abandoned. The new conception was to cease operating behind the enemy's lines, and to move northwards, giving up everything that we had won, in order to help Stilwell's advance on Myitkyina and Mogaung. It was dictated by political considerations rather than strategic, but they would never have prevailed if Wingate had still been alive. The monsoon was due to break in a month's time, and we brigade commanders were unanimous that our proper strategy was to strengthen our grip rather than loosen it by drawing off to the north. Air supply would have to be intermittent, and dependent in breaks in the monsoon weather, lasting perhaps for only two or three hours; it would mean tying up aircraft to meteorological forecasts, but the results would justify it.

Wingate's successor, Lentaigne, wasn't present; the decision, which came from high up, was conveyed to us by Henry Alexander, Colonel Operations on his staff. Alexander was a close friend of mine since Sandhurst days, and still remains so; he was a fine polo-player, full of dash and combative by nature. We all knew that his heart was with us, but he couldn't give anything away.

" It's no good," he kept saying. " Even if you're right, the decision's been taken. It's no good kicking against the pricks."

We bullied, we wheedled, we pleaded. The most he would consent to do was to take out an appreciation, written by me in pencil, which I saw again a dozen years later in the files of the Historical Section of the Cabinet Offices: it never provoked an answer, and I don't suppose it got very far.

Lentaigne, who died suddenly some years after the war, was a first-class fighting soldier of an orthodox stamp. He was highly thought of, and he made a richly deserved reputation, first as a battalion and then as a brigade commander, on the original withdrawal from Burma in 1942. While our first expedition was slogging through Burma the following year, Wavell, convinced that whatever its fate might turn out to be the general idea was sound, caused a second Chindit brigade to be formed; and demanded as its commander the best brigadier the Indian Army could produce. With some reluctance they offered Lentaigne, a tall, spare, Irishman who was highly esteemed even outside the world of Gurkha regiments; within that world he was adored.

When Wingate emerged from the jungle he was incensed with Wavell, rather than grateful to him, for having raised this second Chindit formation. If there were to be a second Chindit brigade—and in fact there were shortly to be six— he reckoned he had the right of nominating its commander. I pleaded with him, quoting my rather bogus authority as a former member of the Joint Planning Staff in Delhi, saying that although I didn't know Lentaigne, I knew his reputation; that Wavell had given us one of the best officers in all the Indian Army; that to refuse Lentaigne would be not merely to lose a sterling commander, but would needlessly irritate Wavell, and alienate the Indian Army to a man. We had few enough friends anyway, not that Wingate minded that. This was one of the rare occasions when I managed to dissuade him from a course of action on which he had made up his mind.

Lentaigne remained in command of 111 Brigade, and I was sent down to him as second-in-command for two weeks, before getting a brigade of my own. My doubts about him began from that moment. I had none about his courage, his skill or his integrity; you couldn't spend half an hour in his company without being sure of those. But he was too forthright to conceal his conviction that Wingate was a mountebank, and his ideas on strategy and tactics lunatic. Wingate had done nothing to make him welcome or to win him over, and they disliked each other from the start.

Nobody knows, or will ever know, who Wingate intended to succeed him in the event of his death. It certainly wasn't me, because he told me so; and it certainly wasn't Joe Lentaigne. He told me one name, which would have been my own choice; apparently he told two other people two other names. Lentaigne was selected from on high as a man who could be trusted to obey orders, who would conform without question, and who would not claim to have inherited the right to force signals through to Winston Churchill over the heads of his commanders: a privilege which Wingate enjoyed, and occasionally exploited. The appointment of Lentaigne meant the end of the Wingate tradition and the death of the Wingate plan: which was exactly what the higher command intended, as it had every right to do. I bear no resentment now, but at the time it was a bitter pill to give up this considerable tract of country, over which we had established our domination at the cost of hard fighting, heavy casualties and much privation—and, I repeat, for political, not military, reasons.

There was another evening in Meza House which came back to me vividly. My second-in-command was " Katie " Cave of the Rifle Brigade, who was fourteen years older than I; he had been an R.F.C. pilot in the First World War, and subsequently many years commanding the Equatorial Province of the Southern Sudan, where I had last met him. His place was with Rear Brigade Headquarters in India, but he flew in to confer with me from time to time. On this particular evening I was waiting for him on the air-strip, and heard his Dakota losing height as it came in over the shoulder of Kalat Taung. The landing lights along the runway were switched on; but just as the aircraft was arriving we heard another noise, an angry buzz, and a Jap fighter shot across its course with guns blazing. The Dakota got down all right, with some damage, and only one man, coming in as a reinforcement, was wounded. I took Katie to Meza House, and poured out two handsome tots of rum; he seemed to need his much less than I know I needed mine.

At this moment of writing, Henry Alexander has just ceased to be Commander-in-Chief of the Ghana Army, having made a considerable name for himself in the early days of the United Nations intervention in the Congo; " Katie " Cave is a Catholic priest.

I asked Ba Tun whether the Japs had carried out any reprisals against Naunghmi for having harboured and helped us; and was greatly relieved to hear there were none. After we cleared out, the Japs came in some strength and dug trenches across the air-strip; but they were very jumpy, they always posted strong piquets, and they never stayed overnight. (They never came back after that; but, Ba Tun added grimly, the Communists came instead.) The community had suffered six deaths directly attributable to our stay. Two men had been killed in an air raid—I remembered that occasion; after our departure, three blew themselves to smithereens while dissecting with a *dah* a bomb from a crashed Jap aircraft: a fourth had survived to describe the gory details. In addition, a man from Inbauk, up the eastern arm of the Y, had been blown up mysteriously, they supposed on a mine.

The only Europeans they had seen since we moved out in May, 1944, were a party, presumably from the War Graves Commission, who had come a few years later to exhume our dead. There weren't many, because usually our killed were buried where they fell; but I had established a cemetery close under the hill on the east side of the air-strip. According to Ba Tun, there had been another, with ten graves, in the little gully north of the air-strip where the hospital had been; but a land-slide had covered them, at too great a depth for the exhumation party to tackle. The land of Burma had swallowed them up.

After a dish of tea we left the house, and walked through the village at the head of its population, to emerge by the side of the old air-strip, on which no fewer than 700 Dakota landings had been made. It had long since reverted to paddy, and it was hard to believe that it had ever been anything else: the *kezins* or bunds—the little turf walls that divide the fields into squares and keep in the water—had all been restored and were in good order. Ba Tun and I stood gazing across it at the hospital gully, and that other little gully next door to it where the light aircraft used to be pegged down at night. On a busy day, when there was a fight going on somewhere, these little planes would be flying in and out of the place like bees, returning with a load of two or three wounded men from some distant stretch of paddy near the battlefield, hastily converted into an emergency strip. We found by experience that it was always best to fly them on to India that night when the Dakotas came in, however badly they were wounded; their chances of recovery were much greater in a proper hospital with all facilities. But sometimes the Dakotas couldn't come, either because of bad weather conditions in India or Burma or over the hills between, or else because of intensified air activity by the Japs. By this time, in 1944, the Allies had air superiority, and were blasting away at enemy airfields everywhere in Burma; but the Japs were ingenious at switching their squadrons almost daily from base to base, sometimes locating them well forward at Shwebo or Mong Mit for an orgy of strikes, and sometimes tucking them out of reach away in Siam.

It was because of these frequent interruptions—often we had to turn back the Dakotas in mid-flight—that we were obliged to establish our own hospital, complete with an advanced surgical team capable of performing operations. There were no beds, but cover was provided by tarpaulins and the carcasses of two or three wrecked gliders, which had brought in the baby bull-dozers and graders which we used to make the strip Dakota-worthy. Almost all the patients were battle casualties. Malaria was so common, despite strict discipline and our daily dose of suppressive tablets, that we were forced to decree that malaria didn't constitute grounds for evacuation—unless it was cerebral, a form of the disease which was fatal more often than not. Ordinary cases had to sweat it out on their feet. The country around Indaw had a particularly evil reputation for being

spittle and fight for it: a flattering though not a pretty habit.

Downstream again was the hut where John Fraser and Bill Smythies used to live, with a tobacco-grower. Here their scouts and spies used to come and see them by night like Nicodemus. I asked for the old boy who was their host, but he was dead these three years. Apparently in addition to growing tobacco he was the local herbalist and medicine-man. I wonder whether he nursed a private grievance about the clinic we ran with our medical officers.

Bill Maung Maung wanted to get back to Katha that night, revisiting Banmauk on the way to hear how the operation against the Communist dacoits had gone; so we had to make our farewells. I took a long look round before leaving, and what the villager said to Bill was true: nothing at all had changed. Our sojourn in this peaceful valley might never have been. The only evidence that it had happened was a crop of aluminium utensils and a sur-prisingly affectionate regard for us. I don't suppose I shall ever see Aberdeen again, or Ba Tun either; but somehow our affinity is now lasting.

We stopped for half an hour at Manhton to load the trucks. We were evidently not the copyright-owners of the idea of giving children sweets. Major Mya Maung had an enor-mous tin of them, the size and shape of a kettledrum, from which he was scattering handfuls all over the street. Bill and Aung Ni and the Township Officer from Banmauk (whose parish includes the Upper Meza) were deep in discussion about something, when Bill suddenly called me over.

" Look," he said, " I believe you're the man to help us on this. We're discussing the alignment of a new road Aung Ni wants us to build. They're asking for a direct outlet from here to the railway, somewhere about Mawlu, instead of having to go south to the Banmauk-Indaw road and then east. You know the country between here and the railway as well as anybody: what do *you* think? "

This was highly gratifying. It so happened that the first time I did that particular journey Aung Ni had been my guide as far as Konhka on the Nami Chaung, which I remembered chiefly for its pagoda. The distance from Manhton to Mawlu was only twenty miles or so, but there were one or two really hellish hills, particularly the first one out of Manhton. My heart had sunk in retrospect the night before as we passed it driving in, and my pack seemed to be on my back once again.

I spread my quarter-inch map on the ground, and we all pored over it, though it didn't mean much to Aung Ni. Nor do I suppose that Bill really needed my views, but it was kind of him to make me feel so important. And when we got back to the Police mess at Banmauk, where we lunched, my advice was prayed in aid once again, this time on a matter of tactics.

Waiting at Banmauk was U That Tin, the Deputy Inspector-General of Police, whom we had already met at Myitkyina with U Bo. The Communists had failed to set off the trap laid for them in the Mu Valley, and Bill and That Tin were putting their heads together to concoct another plan. On the strength of my year as Assistant Inspector-General in the Palestine Police, shortly before the end of the Mandate, I enjoyed swapping with That Tin theories about terrorists and how to deal with them. But our problems had been urban, whereas his were rural, more akin to those of Malaya and Kenya, of which I had no experience apart from a short visit to Malaya during the Emergency; yet his was the more interesting for me. He was concerned with locating terrorists who were skulking in the very country where I myself had skulked; and it oughtn't to be difficult for me, said U That Tin, to put

myself into their skin and tell him how their collective mind
might be working.

I found this a fascinating exercise. But there was one big
difference between the dacoits and the Chindits. In our day
the occupying power was alien, and so were the skulkers;
the Japs were ruling by terror and intimidation, while the
British did all they could to ingratiate themselves with the
inhabitants by impeccable behaviour and by payment for
services rendered. Now the occupying power and the skulkers were both of the same race as the inhabitants. The
skulkers were even more unwelcome to the inhabitants than
we had been; it was they who used terror as their weapon,
and the Government which wooed the inhabitants with good
administration, generous subsidies and all-round benevolence.

The circumstances might have changed, but the country
hadn't; and the dacoits must have inherited many of the
headaches which had once been ours. These came flooding
back to me as I looked at the map on the mess table. There
were the defiles which had worried us in case they were
watched, and the secret tracks which the Japs hadn't known
about. I tried to find a pattern in what I was told about the
recent activities of the dacoits, and to equate it with their
probable aims and hopes and fears. Whether the few
suggestions I produced were ever tried, or were any good,
I still don't know. Certainly the Mu and Chaunggyi
Valleys, and the Mangin and Zibyu Ranges, were a wonderful setting for a game of Peep-Bo with lethal weapons; we
had learned that much in the war, if nothing else.

X

THE WEEK or so that we spent in Katha District was of more than ordinary interest, and that for several reasons. In the first place, it was the part of Burma I knew best. I had been through it and in it twice. What I hadn't walked over I had flown over in light aircraft at low level: we had discovered early on in 1944 that treetop height was the safest to fly at, since by the time the enemy on the ground was alive to your passage you were out of shot.

Secondly, the people of Katha were taking far more interest in the elections, due in two weeks' time, than the people in the north: although at Mohnyin we had been amused to see a small baby on all fours at the foot of a huge election poster, staring up with a puzzled expression at the more than life-size photograph of U Nu's face which adorned it. At Katha, Naba, Banmauk and Manhton, posters and handbills were much in evidence. The elections would decide which faction of the Anti-Fascist People's Freedom League would resume the reins of government from General Ne Win: the " Clean," led by U Nu, or the " Stable," led by U Ba Swe. These two odd appellations, which had stuck to the rival factions almost by chance, would have been better rendered as " Purged " and " Consistent." U Nu was leader of the Clean, and his election colours were Orange, the sacred hue of Buddhism: his opponents accused him of cashing in on his reputation for personal sanctity.

The fact that the elections were pending meant that people were inclined to talk. I don't mean that officials were letting their tongues wag, for they were all the soul of discretion; but the people themselves were in a communicative mood, and we got an idea of how their minds were working, just as a foreigner might during a general election in Britain. In Katha District, it looked as though U Nu was going to win in a hand canter.

Lastly, we were now something better than mere tourists: we were looking over the shoulder of a Deputy Commissioner as he made a progress through his District with his subordinate officials and his policeman, doing his job. His duties are many and varied, and his word is law.

The constitution of Burma is an odd mixture of parliamentary government and direct rule. Although at the time of our journey parliamentary government had been suspended in favour of military, Ne Win had only consented to take over on the strict understanding that it should be resumed as soon as he had restored law and order. Thus the edicts of Parliament, democratically elected, are carried out by exactly the same echelons of officials as in the British days; the more senior ones, indeed, were officials under the British, and still speak with affection of the individual chiefs under whom they learned their job. The only essential difference on paper is that the place of the Governor has been taken by Parliament.

There is no reason why the system shouldn't have worked, except that the quality of deputy was lamentably low, and that corruption spread like a fungus in the atmosphere of the time. Enlightened ideas and generous subsidies are of no avail unless they reach the people they are intended to benefit. By way of illustration, here is a tale, not from Katha District, of a pretty little case of graft.

A young Sub-District Officer in his first appointment was

directed by the local M.P. to award the contract for a proposed new bridge to one of the M.P.'s cronies. If he failed to do so, he was told, he would find himself posted to an uncongenial District where his wife and family would be unable to join him. The S.D.O. complied, and in due course the contractor, accompanied by the M.P., came to ask for his money. The S.D.O. demurred, on the grounds that he hadn't yet inspected the finished work; but the M.P. insisted that his friend should be reimbursed at once, and the S.D.O. paid up. When he went to look at the bridge, there wasn't one. The young man had the guts, although threatened with various woes, including assassination, to prosecute both M.P. and contractor, and they duly went to jail; but the S.D.O. had to be removed from the District for his own protection.

Under Ne Win, subsidies had continued, and even been increased; the difference was that they were now reaching those for whom they were intended. The only discontent that we encountered with his rule was among some up-country merchants, who had been interrupted in their traditional milking of the community cow. All imported goods, for instance, on which hitherto the merchant could make whatever profit he liked, now had to carry a card showing the official price.

The subsidies weren't always fully appreciated. I heard of a Kachin headman who was asked how many pigs he had.

"Twelve," he said.

"The Government will make that up to two hundred, for free," he was told. His face fell.

"For goodness' sake," he said, "don't let the Government do that to me. I should only have to look after them."

Again, there was an American agricultural adviser who was sent to demonstrate to a Burmese village how they could grow twice the normal amount of rice on their stretch of paddy. They thanked him effusively. The following year when he went back to see how they were getting on, they gave him a tremendous reception. Thanks to his advice, they had been able to grow exactly their usual crop of rice on exactly half the paddy with exactly half the effort.

It is no easy job to induce an agricultural community so naturally rich as that of Burma to grow more for export. Why should the people of Upper Burma be interested in export, terms of trade, balance of payments, foreign currency and so on? A tiny surplus in each village gives them enough to buy the few extras, mostly clothing and salt, which is all they want.

" I sometimes wonder," said one official, " whether we are justified in making people want more, when they are perfectly happy as they are. I have a nasty feeling that we are creating an artificial appetite for things they don't really need: just to make them grow and export more, so that we can earn more foreign currency and buy ourselves radiograms."

Bill Maung Maung told us of a visit he had lately paid to the Mu Valley. He had asked what price the villagers were getting for their paddy, and was told such-and-such a sum. He explained that this fell short of the price guaranteed by the Government, and that it would be made up to the full amount by subsidy. The difference was duly paid; but he heard later that the credit for it was being given, not to the generosity of the Government, but to the shade of a *poongyi* or monk who had been held in general reverence and esteem, and had died three years before. The powers of a live D.C. are as nothing compared with those of a really good dead *poongyi*.

In fact, the powers of a D.C. are considerable. Even a Township Officer has immense authority: when I think how pitiful in comparison are the powers of a brigadier in the

British Army I could weep. A Township Officer can try all cases in his Township, which may embrace more than twenty towns and villages, other than murder and rape. He can award a prison sentence of up to seven years. He is responsible for the collection of all taxes, for which he has a Treasurer to help him. He can advance Government money in loans without any security beyond the good name of the borrower: the only check is in the form of a carbon copy of the agreement, which is sent to the D.C.'s office, plus an occasional audit by travelling Treasury officials. The borrower must start paying off the loan at the end of three years.

One can see that such a system is open to abuse, to corruption, to favouritism, even to blackmail; but there is much to be said for a system that presupposes people are honest. I still harbour a grudge from the days of the Army of Occupation in Germany just after the war, when a commanding officer had to submit the work-tickets of his vehicles to examination by German clerks as a safeguard against his " cooking " them.

Among other little matters occupying Bill Maung Maung's attention in Banmauk was a threatened bus strike. In his estimation the owners of the daily bus service between Banmauk and Indaw, maintained by a couple of ancient vehicles whose chassis were obviously veterans of the Fourteenth Army, were profiteering grossly. He cut their fares there and then to a reasonable scale, and the owners duly struck. Bill let it be known that our convoy was returning to Indaw and Katha, and that free lifts were available for anybody who wanted one, which brought us the company of—among other people—some extremely pretty young women. They perched on top of the loaded trucks with every appearance of finding this a luxurious means of travel. Bill told us how the day before, on his way to Banmauk from

Pinbon, he had passed three Shan girls walking along the road, and asked them where they were going: to the *myo gyi*, or big city, they said. The thought of Mandalay crossed his mind, and he wondered if they realised what a long trudge lay ahead of them; but on pressing them he found they meant Banmauk, the biggest city in their ken.

I made Bill stop at Milestone 20, determined to show him the site of our ambush whether he would or no. A caravan of covered carts was resting under the trees from the heat of the day; the oxen were grazing and their drivers lying down, though they showed enough interest in us to rise up on their elbows and stare. The daily time-table of Burma is regulated by hot-weather conditions. There isn't much " heat of the day " in February, though it was quite hot enough for Laura and me; but the habit of resting at mid-day persists in the cold weather too. And because in the hot weather, markets are held from just before dawn until a couple of hours later, in order to dodge the heat, they are still held at the same hour in cold weather, with everybody shivering under blankets wrapped around them like plaids. It is an odd quirk, but no odder than our own British habit of building our houses with outside pipes, and feeling aggrieved when they burst every winter. I know of a local authority in Scotland which imported a number of pre-fabricated wooden houses from Sweden, but insisted in their specification that the pipes should be put outside instead of in, even though this meant additional expense, as well as exposure to frost.

The various vehicles of our convoy peeled off as we got to Katha, dispersing to their destinations. Most of our passengers, the would-be travellers by bus, had already left us at Indaw. This was the third time that Laura and I had arrived at the Château Maung Maung, and we felt very much at home. Mary was waiting for us, and Nyan Maung disappeared like a lizard into the back areas of the house, to emerge once again the butler, and offer us drinks. U Hla Pe was there, ready and eager to accompany us on whatever sortie we might be planning for the following day.

I was determined to see the bridge at Bonchaung. Colonel Saw Myint had expressed no objection; he had only stipulated that I shouldn't blow it up again. Bill reckoned he must spend a day in his office after several out in the field but that he could spare U Hla Pe to take us down to Bonchaung. U That Tin came in to dinner. He and Bill and everybody else were a bit tired after their week in the open air; so we made an early evening of it, and were all abed by ten o'clock.

Eight hours later, at 6 a.m., we set off by road through the Naba Gap to catch a train at Indaw: U Hla Pe, Laura, myself and the indispensable Nyan Maung, with his accustomed pillar of interlocking tins all stuffed with food for our midday meal. There is no road to Bonchaung: it can be reached either by rail or by a single track, that winds through the hills from west to east and is suitable only for Shanks's mare.

Between Indaw and Bonchaung is Meza Railway Station. This was another pin-point with sinister associations for me. During the war it was the headquarters of a Japanese battalion, expressly charged with the protection of the railway. We knew that its men were deployed along the line, in small standing patrols guarding " Vulnerable Points " or in mobile patrols travelling constantly between them; but we never knew quite how many were garrisoned at " Meza R.S.," as the map called it.

Laura now knew something about " Meza R.S." that I had for the moment forgotten. Bo Gyi Samson's daughter had just taken up her first appointment there as a Government midwife. In the chill of our early-morning drive to Indaw Station, Laura prevailed on U Hla Pe to send a message by railway telegraph bidding Anne Samson to meet us at Meza Station, and to be prepared for an absence from base of about five hours.

Once again we were travelling by goods train, in a truck modified to carry a few not very choosey passengers. Its sides were open, but there were wooden benches shaped like packing-cases on which to sit and stretch our legs. We clanked at a lolloping rhythm along a railway track whose alignment was dictated by the meanderings of the Meza River (which soon came to meet us like a loyal friend) on the west, and the curves of the range of hills on the east: from time to time the vagaries of the two allowed us a straight run through paddy.

At Meza Station, where a sizeable town had sprung up since the war, I swung myself out on to the step of our truck; there was no platform, and the step afforded a better view than if I had descended to the track. To start with, there was nothing to be seen but a swirling mob, but as it settled I saw a tiny figure making her way along the train, looking anxiously up at the wagons. She was neat, very attractive and minute: so small, indeed, that I wondered whether she could possibly be the offspring of the burly Samson; but I took a chance, jumped down and approached her.

" Are you Anne Samson? "

" Brigadier Fuggusson? "

We pulled her up into our carriage. She had already heard from the Bo Gyi that we might be coming her way, and had deduced from the peremptory summons which had reached her half an hour before that we must be in the offing. She was a little darling, terribly pretty, beautifully dressed, and desperately shy; yet not awkwardly so: she had natural good manners, her English was limited but good, and her pleasure at being sought out was obvious. Apart from her training as a midwife, she had never before been away from her parents; and here she was, all alone in Meza: the only Christian there and the only Karen.

The train blew its whistle, and we all rode on. Anne Samson sat demurely, answering questions but never volunteering a remark. She was obviously aware that U Hla Pe, as S.D.O., was ultimately her boss, and whenever he spoke to her, to put her at her ease, she was very much on parade. Whenever I sought to tell her something about the old relationship between her father and me, she said: " Yes, Daddy told me that," which was cosy, but didn't help our talk to burgeon. But Laura and I soon realised that she was enjoying our company, despite her shyness, as much as we were enjoying hers. The conversation languished, and we all looked out at the countryside: not through the window, for there wasn't a window, but straight into the good, green, fresh world of Burma.

Soon the hills closed in, and the train was running at twenty-five miles an hour through a long succession of cuttings. The paddy had disappeared, and the jungle encroached to within a few yards of the track. I bent myself double to peer under the roof, but even so could see only a little way up the tree-clad hill-side. After a few miles I felt the brakes go on, and the train begin to slow down; the gorge suddenly opened out, and the train came to a halt. A large board announced in Burmese and English that this was Bonchaung Station; and we descended.

Bonchaung Station was exactly as I remembered it. Our advance there in 1943 had been interrupted by a brush with the enemy, four miles to the westward, which cost me a good officer and ten good men. The task originally given me by Wingate was to block the railway two miles south of Bonchaung, where it ran through a narrow gorge, by blowing down thousands of tons of rock on to the line. My sapper officers told me that this would be a difficult operation to perform, and an easy one for the enemy to clear; and that we would get much better value both for our march and for the amount of explosives that we'd carried for 400 miles if instead we blew up the three-span steel bridge which carried the railway over the Bonchaung. I was far too much in awe of Wingate to ignore the gorge altogether; but I was persuaded, and rightly, to put the better part of our money on blowing up the bridge. So I sent one detachment to the gorge, and another to the bridge; and I intended to accompany the second. It looked like being the more spectacular affair, and I had high hopes of seeing a Jap train blown up while half-way over a bridge: an ambition which I wasn't to realise until fifteen years later, vicariously, when I saw the film *The Bridge on the River Kwai*.

In the event we blew both the gorge and the bridge, and I witnessed the blowing up of the latter: though my arrival was delayed through getting involved in the skirmish on the way. As a result I got lost, and arrived, not by the proper track which the main body and the demolition party had followed, but by some devious route which my soldier servant, Peter Dorans, and I were obliged to cut, over the hill. We found our sentry-posts facing in every direction, and the sappers hard at work on the bridge. The Japs failed to put in an appearance, and at 9 p.m., after four hours of preparation of which the last was in the dark, the bridge went up. We inspected the damage before moving off. The middle span and one of the side ones lay twisted in the river-bed fifty feet below, and both the stone piers were severely damaged.

The party I sent to the gorge also got lost and arrived there late but we heard their explosion about midnight. The officer in charge was careful not to make too ambitious a claim, but I couldn't dissuade Wingate from including in his report the phrase which he had always had in his mind: that " some thousands of tons of rock were brought down upon the line."

The station, where we alighted, was immediately north of the bridge; and Laura got her movie camera into action in time to film our train puffing over it as it went on southwards. Then Nyan Maung produced three rather seedy-looking men, the station watchmen: two were old and decrepit; the third, Maung Lu Kyaw, was just decrepit. They turned out to be the very same watchmen that were on duty the day we blew the bridge: one would have thought, somehow, that they might have lost their jobs, along with the princely wage of thirty-five *kyats* a month (about £2 15s.) plus food that went with it. We cross-examined them about the events of that exciting day.

Lu Kyaw was their spokesman, and he had plenty to say. Although my demolition party and their escort had seen no sign of anybody as they approached the station and bridge, there was apparently a detachment of twenty-five Japanese soldiers guarding it. The whole lot, including the watchmen, vamoosed as one man when they saw my leading troops coming up the track through the bamboo forest. They hadn't heard any news of British soldiers being in the country at all, nor had they heard the noise of our engagement four miles to the west: so they must have been pretty quick in making up their minds to run. The three watchmen and the Japs were all hiding in the jungle together when they heard our beautiful bang.

More Japs arrived in force the following morning, marching along the line from both directions, to find the bridge down and the twisted girders lying in the river-bed, which at that season was almost dry. The watchmen were not punished; but the Jap guards had been taken away under arrest, and were said to have been shot. They would certainly have been a considerable nuisance if they had shown fight. Although we would have outnumbered them by six or seven to one—I had sent out other detachments on reconnaissance or to make diversions—it would have been a fairly bloody business to turn them off the embankment on either side of the bridge if they had chosen to defend it; and they could have made our prolonged preparations for the demolition both costly and difficult by sniping from the jungle. There were no signs of any fox-holes or weapon-pits having been dug. I suppose they were so sure there were no British east of the Chindwin, that they had spent all their time twiddling their fingers in the station buildings.

We had always hoped that the Japs would be unable to repair the bridge before the monsoon, which was due in two months' time: this would mean that the railway would be out of action for eight or nine months. But alas, the R.A.F. reported trains running over it normally at the beginning of May. Poor David Whitehead, the sapper officer who actually did the nefarious deed on the 6th of March, had the mortification of travelling over the bridge as a prisoner before the end of April; he was lying on the floor of a steel goods wagon with seven bullet wounds in him; the only satisfaction he got was that the train was obliged to cross it dead slow. I myself had flown over it in a light air-craft during the 1944 campaign, grinding my teeth with annoyance to see it still standing.

Lu Kyaw confirmed that the Japs had brought in a hundred men from neighbouring villages as forced labour, and had worked them mercilessly to get a temporary bridge erected before the rains began; it had taken only twenty-five days to complete, despite many bombing raids by the R.A.F. A more solid one was built by the Japs after the monsoon, and the present bridge dated from 1952. I asked

Lu Kyaw about the damage done in the gorge, and as I expected he made light of it: "just a few rocks," he said, which took only a matter of hours to clear away.

We scrambled down the bank to the bed of the *chaung*. In the monsoon it would be a torrent, whereas now there was no more than a film of water over the sandy bottom. But the monsoon floods of all the intervening years had not been strong enough to carry away the wreckage of the old piers, which still lay there as a memento of our previous visit. We went for a short walk along the track to the west, and then back to the station. We asked the station-master, whose hut was embellished with a Rogues' Gallery of Wanted Men, when was the next train to Indaw? His answer dismayed us: there wouldn't be another for five hours.

What the blazes would we do at Bonchaung for five hours? Anne and U Hla Pe were far too polite to say what they thought of me for landing them with such a dull day. U Hla Pe made contact with some senior railway official on the telephone, to see whether Burma Railways couldn't find some light engine and truck to send along for us, but he drew a blank. We had to reconcile ourselves to a long, long wait, spinning out Nyan Maung's picnic luncheon for as long as it would last.

There wasn't much to amuse one at Bonchaung. There was a small police post, indescribably dirty: U That Tin would have gone up in smoke if he'd seen it, and even more so if he'd known I'd seen it; and a few houses grouped in a semicircle, for railway surfacemen and their families. An impromptu cabaret turn was provided for us by a pet monkey belonging to one of the railway staff: it shinned up a tree, chain and all, and made rude gestures at us from the top. A tempting display of goodies failed to entice it down; and in the end a boy went up and chased the poor beast to the end of a branch, from which it was shaken off

with a long pole, and caught as it dropped lightly on all
fours.

Then U Hla Pe spotted an old pagoda with a hermit's hut
beside it, on the edge of the clearing, and he and I walked
down to it. The pagoda was of red brick and shaped like a
beehive; it was crumbling away, and stood in a heap of its
own debris; the hut by contrast was clean and modern.
Both were enclosed in a single compound some thirty yards
across, surrounded by a fence of palings. We removed our
shoes at the gate, and went to ask the monk's permission to
visit the shrine.

I stood at the door while U Hla Pe made his three
obeisances. The hermit was sitting cross-legged on the floor,
reading an ancient book; his saffron robe left one shoulder
bare. He was a man of about sixty; his face, on which was a
pair of huge horn-rimmed spectacles, was intelligent and full
of authority. He looked well-bred and reasonably well-fed,
he was scrupulously clean, and there was an air of serene
certainty about him, as well as a total unawareness of the
proximity of the railway station. He removed his spectacles
when U Hla Pe spoke to him, glanced at me without showing
any sign of interest in the fact that I was a European, gave
his consent in a short sentence, resumed his spectacles and
went on reading. I noticed that there was nothing whatever
in the room but him and his book: no furniture, no rugs, no
plates or pots or pans.

Outside such a hermit's hut, as outside a *poongyikyaung*,
there is usually a gong, with a deep resonant note such as we
had heard sounding in the dark on our journey to Mohnyin.
As U Hla Pe and I, fortified by the monk's permission,
walked barefoot through his hut to the ruined pagoda
beyond, we passed his gong, which was slung between two
poles; and I saw to my astonishment that it was in fact the
rusty unexploded shell of a 250-lb. Royal Air Force bomb.

I have been familiar for as long as I can remember with the words of the 18th Paraphrase:—

> To ploughshares men shall beat their swords,
> To pruning-hooks their spears;

but the conversion of a Royal Air Force bomb into a temple gong in the service of the Lord Buddha was something I hadn't thought of.

In the pagoda was a deep, narrow cavity, as though in an old-fashioned oven or lime-kiln. U Hla Pe thrust his arm into it, right up to the shoulder; and withdrew a handful of exquisite little models, of iron or blackened bronze, about the size of toy soldiers. Twice more he groped, and by that time we had a dozen of them to look at. Each depicted some figure or incident in Buddhist legend: one was of the Lord Buddha under the fig-tree where he sat for forty-nine days. According to U Hla Pe they were of great antiquity, and I have no doubt he was right. He offered me one or two as a souvenir, and I was greatly tempted; I would certainly have treated them with reverence; but I felt they belonged to Bonchaung and the Buddha rather than to Ballantrae and me. We put them back into the cavity where they had lain for so long. There were two or three children playing round the place, who saw what we were up to; and perhaps they had fewer scruples, and perhaps these things would have been safer with me, here at home, after all; but I am happier on the whole to have had the handling of them, and then to have put them back.

The long day wore on, until at last our train, another goods, arrived up the incline from the direction of Wuntho and Nanhkan, where Mike Calvert cut the line on the same day as our operations at Bonchaung. (He hadn't had such juicy targets as a bridge and a gorge, but he had made a great nuisance of himself by destroying culverts and points and the like.) The five of us boarded a brake-van, which was occupied by only a single passenger.

We weren't alone for long. At the next station we were joined by a party of laughing Shan girls, very pretty, laden with vegetables and accompanied by an old crone who was grumbling. U Hla Pe cocked his ear to their talk, and began first to smile and then to giggle. They were all bound with presents for the big *poongyikyaung* at Indaw, where some boy relation of theirs was serving his novitiate (as all Buddhist boys must do at some time in their youth), and the old lady was complaining that they ought to have walked and saved their money. The girls kept teasing her.

" I grudge the fare! " she kept saying. " I'd rather have the money! Twenty *pyas*! (About threepence-ha'penny.) I'd rather have twenty *pyas* and walk than ride in this thing! I could do with twenty *pyas*."

Then she caught sight of Laura and me, and was struck dumb. The horrors of travel by rail were bad enough; the waste of twenty *pyas* was worse; Laura and I were the last straw.

At Meza we were told that the train would be stopping for twenty minutes, which gave us time to see the house that Anne was getting ready for her parents. It was small, but brand-new and spotlessly clean, and she was extremely proud of it, for all that it was sited in a noisy and rather squalid quarter near the market. It was void of any furniture except for a mattress and bedding and some cooking pots and tins; but this didn't necessarily denote poverty: country people in Burma just do not have material possessions beyond their needs. We all had tea together in a shop. Any fears we might have had about the train leaving without us were allayed by the guard having his tea there too, his official cap embellished with a pink rose from the station garden. We went on having tea until the engine whistled for us, when we climbed back on to our box-seats, and waved to the tiny figure of Anne until she was out of sight.

She was a little darling, and we hated leaving her alone, with so many problems to grapple with: of life and death, and of looking after her ageing parents. During the day, she had got less shy with Laura, and had made her many confidences. Her training as a midwife had been short and sketchy by British standards, and she was all by herself in Meza. She had to combat all sorts of old wives' tales about childbirth, and if she herself were ever to put a foot wrong her position would be untenable. For instance, it was the custom that, for many weeks after the baby was born, the mother must eat nothing but rice: no meat, no fruit, no vegetables; and the resulting malnutrition of mother and child often meant the death of the baby. If a mother were to yield to Anne's persuasion and eat fruit or marrow, and the baby were then to die, poor Anne would get the blame.

U Hla Pe promised to keep a kindly eye on her; but we were shaken to the boots to hear that her predecessor at Meza had actually been raped. We thanked our stars that the old Bo Gyi and his wife would be joining her soon. Later on, when we got to Mandalay, we put together a hamper of foodstuffs and various household utensils (not forgetting three bottles of good Mandalay rum) and sent them up by rail for the house-warming.

It was U Hla Pe who had made contact for us with Anne. We had also asked him to put us in touch with the two Englishwomen at Indaw, whom we had heard about from Dansey and the other B.C.M.S. missionaries at Mohnyin. He promised that we should be seeing them on our way back from Bonchaung to Katha, and he was as good as his word. When our train reached Indaw, we walked along to the Township Office. There was our vehicle, to take us back to Katha; there also, to my embarrassment, were these two women, looking uncommonly as though they were under arrest. They, like Anne Samson, had been summoned; and I fear they had been kept hanging about for hours awaiting our appearance.

They waved away the apologies I offered; and Laura, U Hla Pe and I accepted their invitation to tea. The Mission was only four hundred yards away, close to the railway line; and a pleasant little house, with a split-new church, as smart as paint but not yet consecrated, beside it. The old one had been destroyed during the war: almost certainly, whether directly or indirectly, by me. The three of us sat down to the sort of tea one might have in an English vicarage, with good china, little home-made cakes, and lettuce sandwiches. Miss Hand had been many years in Burma, Miss Soper was a recent arrival. They seemed entirely out of place in Indaw; yet they exuded the same air of serene confidence as the hermit at Bonchaung a few miles down the railway. We told them about Anne Samson at Meza, and they promised to look her up from time to time: a promise which has since been amply honoured.

Back in Katha that evening, Bill Maung Maung took his family and us to a *pwe*. A *pwe* is a theatrical show with a religious significance, peppered and salted with broad comedy and almost interminable in length, like a medieval mystery play in England. This one was presented by a well-known company on tour from Rangoon and Mandalay, glittering with star performers, in a large wooden hall completed only recently by public subscription.

There must have been five or six hundred people present, all accompanied by their children, and all sitting on mats spread on the ground: some people bring their own; others hire them as one hires " soft seats " at Lord's or Wimbledon. In either case you install your whole family thereupon: babies, picnic supper and all. We privileged persons of the

D.C.'s party sat on chairs at the back. The music was appallingly noisy, amplified without mercy throughout the hall by loudspeakers; and it took all the authority of the D.C., and several peremptory messages, to get the volume modified a little.

When we arrived, the show had already begun. The hall was dominated by an enormous golden Buddha at the back of the stage; the entire company was on its knees with its back to the audience, intoning the opening devotions; and the orchestra in front was blaring away. There was one huge instrument shaped and painted like a dragon; I was too far away to see what it was. There were cymbals and gongs, and xylophones, and heaven knows what else. The colour of the brilliant lighting kept changing every few seconds, until one's eyes were as weary, through continually having to adjust themselves, as one's ears. Jangle-jangle-jangle, flicker-flicker-flicker, jangle-flicker-jangle, boom-boom-*crash*. This praise of the Lord Buddha went on for fully twenty minutes, and then the curtains drew across to screen his image, and the play proper began.

If I understood Bill aright, it wasn't a complete play so much as a series of excerpts from a whole cycle of plays, of which we saw only two. The first comprised several scenes. It began with a truly magnificent figure springing on to the stage. This was the Peacock Prince, dressed from head to foot in peacock colours, and equipped with a tail which he could, and frequently did, display. He was soon joined by six slightly inferior but still splendid peacocks, to whom, in a high tenor voice of considerable quality, he sang a song declaring his intention to seek food in the forest. They then danced a graceful ballet and disappeared.

They were succeeded by the tragi-comic figure of a hunter who told us, partly in song and partly in humorous monologue, that he had been given ten days by the King to shoot a peacock for him; death was to be the penalty of failure, and this was the tenth day. He suddenly bethought him that he had once hatched a peacock's egg—on reflection, I suppose it must have been a peahen's egg—and set the peacock free. He summoned his daughter, and told her to go out into the forest and lure back the peacock with the beauty of her dancing. Exit hunter. Enter Peacock Prince. Dance between girl and Peacock Prince. Whether she lured him to his doom and saved her father; or whether she fell in love with the Peacock Prince and said To Hell with Father; I shall never know: because the piece ended at this point, and was succeeded by a knockabout turn, wildly funny even to me who couldn't understand the language, on the ancient theme of the country bumpkin outwitting the city slicker.

By this time it was nearly midnight; we had had a long day; and it was something of a relief when Bill suggested that honour was satisfied, and we might go home to bed. I wouldn't have missed the *pwe* for a month's pay, but the moment had come when bed was more alluring. Bill's two children protested, and were allowed to stay on as a treat with their twelve-year-old nanny; but Bill and Mary and Laura and I drove home, through a Katha dappled in the light of a moon which was now waning.

Urbanised, detribalised as we are to-day, moons no longer mean much to us. In Burma they are of moment. On this our journey the moon had been at its full on our second night at Mohnyin, just before Indawgyi, beaming its approval with much more serenity and efficiency than the stuttering electric-light machine. It was now in its last quarter; and so was our journey.

XI

WE NOW HAD THE HAPPY PROSPECT of another day on the Irrawaddy, tempered as it was with regret at leaving Katha. I had twice suggested that it would be fun to go to Hintha, a village between the Irrawaddy and the Shweli where we'd had a battle by moonlight in 1943, and I'd been ignominiously shot in the behind. (I wasn't running away: I was lying on my tummy.) The hint wasn't taken; in fact somebody told me that the village no longer existed; so I didn't press the point.

Tigyaing was another matter. I knew Christopher Sykes had been there in 1956, while gathering material for his life of Wingate; and when I asked Bill whether we too might visit Tigyaing he responded with enthusiasm.

" We'll all go," he said; " we'll make a family party of it."

It was decided that we should leave after an early luncheon. I still hadn't honoured my promise to Sein Win to visit the Kachin Rifles' mess; but an invitation came from Major Mya Maung, who had been at Aberdeen with us, for the Maung Maungs and Fergussons to lunch there before we sailed. From Tigyaing Laura and I would board one of the Irrawaddy steamers, and go on down-river to Mandalay.

Half the officers of the 1st Kachin Rifles were Burmese and the other half Kachin. Two Kachin wives were also present at the luncheon, no doubt to ensure that Laura and Mary Maung Maung should feel at ease. They were both dressed in Kachin full rig, bedecked with silver ornaments and pendants. Sein Win was there, all smiles; and I chaffed him for not having brought along Miss Katha, 1959. Another Burmese officer, the adjutant, was the younger brother of the leading actor, the Peacock Prince, at the *pwe* the night before: he was basking in the compliments of his brother officers.

And there was the R.S.M., who had been asked to luncheon for my special benefit. He was one of two Kachins whom John Fraser had allotted to me for my personal bodyguard in 1944, a Lance-Naik in those days: a powerful, smart, alert and cheery youth, with his carbine always at the ready, who accompanied me everywhere except when I was flying, and even then used to be waiting for me on the strip when I got back. He hadn't aged at all in the years between. He still spoke no word of English, and he couldn't take his eyes off me throughout the meal; I fear he was wondering how I had gone so grey and got so fat.

This was a festive rather than a formal occasion; but such ceremonial as there was followed exactly the pattern which was so familiar to me after nearly thirty years in the British Army. The mess waiters were impeccable in turn-out, and faultless in their serving of the meal. The regimental silver was out in full force, beautifully cared for and obviously cherished. I read some of the inscriptions: " Presented by Captain John Smith on Promotion "; " Presented by Major George Brown to The Officers, 1st Kachin Rifles, on leaving the Battalion "; " The Jones Trophy, for the Best Shooting Company." I couldn't help feeling how touched and proud these long-vanished officers whose real names escape me would have been to know that their gifts were still treasured as *lares et penates*.

Several of the party came down to the foreshore to see us off; Nyan Maung was already embarked with our luggage.

We were travelling in two launches: Bill, Laura and I in the army one which had brought us down from Bhamo; Mary, the two children, Nyan Maung and a couple of women, members of some welfare organisation of which Mary was president, were relegated to Bill's official launch, which was slower, smaller and less comfortable than ours. Not very chivalrous, I fear.

We said good-bye with real regret to U Hla Pe, who had been such a congenial host and travelling companion during the last few days. One of the boatmen cast off the stout grass rope that linked us to a stake in the sand, and the swift stream whipped us away. The gap between boat and beach widened, with Mya Maung and Sein Win at the salute, and U Hla Pe waving his green pork-pie hat, and the jagged, jungled line of the Gangaw Range behind them as a back-drop. Soon they were out of sight.

We were back on the Irrawaddy, with its sandbanks and its winking bits of tin. The first place of interest to me was seventeen miles below Katha: Inywa, where the Shweli flows into the Irrawaddy. Here Wingate crossed eastward-bound in 1943, and here also he made his first attempt to cross westwards on the homeward route a couple of weeks later. He hoped the Japs would think we were still pressing on, or alternatively that, even if they guessed we had turned back, they would not expect us to use the same crossing-place twice. He had with him his own H.Q., those of the Burma Rifles, and the three British columns—Scott's, Gilkes's and my own, though mine, acting as rear-guard, was now at less than half strength. Two of the leading platoons got across safely, and reached India; but at that moment the Japs intervened, and it was no longer possible to continue the operation. David Hastings, who had been a small boy at Eton when I was a big one, the son of Sir Patrick Hastings, the best-known K.C. of the day, was killed as he clambered

Aberdeen : Ba Tun standing on the old Dakota strip

Aberdeen : the bridge across the Meza, with Kalat Taung in
the background

Tigyaing : Tun Sein (*left*) and myself, on the boat in which we
crossed the Irrawaddy in 1943

up the west bank; Scott got a bullet through his map-case as he stood on the eastern side.

Now, as we sailed past in the comfortable security of the launch, I could see through my binoculars the spot, identifiable from a group of huts, where I had emerged on to the paddy in search of a crossing-place accompanied by Duncan Menzies: it was only five days before his death. We had met a patrol of the Burma Rifles Headquarters on the same mission. It was my first meeting with the Jemadar commanding it, a Karen called San Shwe Tou. He impressed me favourably with his equanimity in the face of crisis, and with his calm and collected appraisal of the situation; and his men had confidence in him. San Shwe Tou was among the survivors of the campaign, and I prised him out of Peter Buchanan to serve in my own brigade on the second show. He was a great singer, and while in India between campaigns organised the Karen choir which broadcast to Burma during the Japanese occupation, and made a gramophone record of which I still possess a copy. I had already learned since my return to Burma that San Shwe Tou had been killed in that unhappy action at Nyaunglebin, where Karens fought against Karens. San Shwe Tou was on the rebel side; among those killed on the Government side were the admirable Saw Moody, as a lieutenant-colonel, and the Madrassi mess caterer Sivalingam, who had served me with many a pink gin.

The launch swept us inexorably past this spot of leaden memories. I had spent the last few days among scenes where our fortunes had been at their highest; the incidents of Inywa had seemed at the time to be our nadir, though in fact we were to sink lower yet. I looked at it glumly, resenting its beauty and prosperity, and remembering how much we had suffered in the woodlands beyond it. I was fully content to go on down the river without stopping.

But I was looking forward to Tigyaing. Tigyaing was one of our highlights: a really exhilarating day, when we whisked our whole column animals and all, (bar one horse, which bolted), across the Irrawaddy right under the pug noses of the Japanese. There we had been helped far beyond our hopes by the Burmese inhabitants. Even before blowing up the Bonchaung bridge, I had chosen Tigyaing as a likely crossing-place, and sent John Fraser on ahead to have a look at it. It appealed to me because it was marked on the map as a Steamer Station, and we reckoned there ought to be plenty of boats there. I calculated furthermore that the Japs would never expect us to be so bold as to seize and use such a prominent place; and this bluff paid us immensely well. John reported back to me by wireless that there were no Japs nearer than Tawma, eight miles south on the Meza and close to its junction with the Irrawaddy. Their numbers were reported to be between fifty and five hundred. Whichever figure was correct, they would have a march of not less than two hours to reach us after the earliest moment they could possibly hear that we were at Tigyaing. So we took a chance, and swaggered openly in column of threes into the town by daylight. We got the column across scatheless in a mere three hours; and the Japs arrived in time to open fire on the last two boat-loads only, by twilight. It was what the Duke of Wellington would have called a close-run thing; but it came off handsomely.

Bill Maung Maung had proposed to leave Katha at one o'clock, in order to reach Tigyaing by daylight. But Burmese ideas about time bear a close resemblance to those held in the Highlands of Scotland. (I quote the Bishop of Moray, himself a Gaelic-speaker from Glencoe: " We have a saying in the North: ' the Lord made time, and plenty of it.' ") These ideas about time, and the hospitality of the Kachin Rifles, combined to delay us; we sailed late; and I

felt I was going to be defrauded of the daylight view of
Tigyaing which I had promised myself and Laura.

But things turned out admirably. Our launch approached
the town, round the last bluff of the river, just as the sun set,
and at the identical moment of the day when I had last seen
it. The shadow of the hill on which the pagoda stands, where
I sited Tommy Roberts with his machine-guns to cover the
approaches over the paddy from Tawma, was reaching out
across the river as we swung round to come in to the beach.
The shadow of the houses was long on the sandbank, close to
where we had embarked; and only the *hti* of the pagoda, its
topmost pinnacle, three hundred feet above us, was lit up by
the setting sun. The usual soft blue smoke of evening was
rising, and such wind as there had been was no more.

We swung round and beached gently on the sand, the
launch's nose upstream like a salmon's, just south of Pagoda
Hill. Here again the bed of the river had changed; and
whereas in 1943 there was half a mile of sand to cross, and a
lagoon to wade through between the village and our embarkation point, there was now only fifty yards or so between
the beach and the houses. The crew ran out a plank to the
shore, where a group of ten or twelve men awaited us.

Bill was the first to walk the plank and to be greeted
officially by the Township Officer and an unmistakable
Bengali, who turned out to be the doctor, one Banerji.
Laura and I followed. As I stepped on to the beach, I saw
one of the men start as though stung by a wasp, and stare
at me with his jaw dropping. Then he dug his elbow into
his neighbour's side, and pointed at me, still looking incredulous. It was none other than the boatman who had
ferried me over under fire.

I grinned and nodded, and then he was sure of me. He
darted forward, the sand spurting under his bare toes, and
grabbed at my hand. The last time I'd seen him was on the

far bank, parting from him in the darkness and asking him
anxiously through one of my Karen N.C.O.s whether he
would be all right. He was slightly fussed, the more so
because his partner, frightened at the bullets which skimmed
all around us across the water, had jumped overboard soon
after we pushed off, and swum back to the bank.

It was several minutes before Tun Sein—which I now
discovered was his name—subsided from his first pitch of
excitement at this happy reunion; and there and then, on
the bank, with a fair-sized crowd around us, he continued
the story from that moment. He had paddled his boat back
across the river to Tigyaing itself, and not, as I thought he
would, to some other point downstream where he would miss
the Japs. He was worried in case he might be fired on; so as
soon as he was within a few hundred yards of the shore he
began calling out:—

"Don't shoot! Don't shoot! I'm only a poor Burmese!"

They had grilled him a bit, but he protested that we had
pulled pistols on him (as indeed we had) and that he had no
choice but to do our bidding, which they accepted: I would
have expected them to make an example of him, duress
or no.

Twice or thrice during our stay in Tigyaing I asked Tun
Sein to bring his less courageous colleague to see me, so that
I could assure him there was no ill-feeling; but he never
appeared. Others showed less delicacy. One such was the
doyen of the water-front, who told me without embarrassment that it was he who initiated the message to the Japanese
at Tawma that we were in Tigyaing. He insisted that he had
delayed doing so until he was sure we would have completed our crossing by the time the Japs arrived. If so, I can
only say that he has missed his vocation: he should have
been a handicapper on a race-course: their arrival coincided precisely with my own departure, when with the

water up to my chest I helped to shove Tun Sein's boat off
the sand and hauled myself into it.

By the time Tun Sein and I had finished our first orgy of
reminiscence, our bedding-rolls and other baggage had all
been loaded on to bullock-carts, and the slower launch
bringing Mary Maung Maung and her contingent had also
arrived. We were all ready to set off to our lodging. This
was a newly-built maternity centre on the landward side of
the town, where two tracks converge: I remembered the
place exactly, since we had marched past it in 1943, and it
was close to where I had set up my headquarters for the short
duration of our stay. Its two bare, unfurnished rooms were
empty, and we slept there in comfort for a couple of nights,
undisturbed by confinements; Bill and Laura and I in one
room, the other women and children next door. I rejoiced
that the electric light machine of Tigyaing had broken down,
and that the neon tubes on shops and pagodas were tempor-
arily useless: glowing charcoal fires and hurricane lamps in
the dark recesses of the shops were more to my taste.

Our first and most constant visitor was the Chinaman,
Ah Hyi. Christopher Sykes met him when he was up in
Tigyaing four years earlier; he wrote to tell me that Ah
Hyi had been asking after me, and enclosed a letter from him
written in Chinese. I got it translated by some pundit in St.
Andrews University, and in due course answered it in
English. Back came a reply, also in English, to say that he
was a very poor man, with rows and rows of children, and
please would I send him some money? I decided that the
moment had come when, as editors say, "this corres-
pondence must now cease," and it did.

Ah Hyi had come into my life the day we crossed the
Irrawaddy. In those days he kept a " chow shop " for the
benefit of fishermen and boatmen: a matting affair which
he erected every dry weather on the edge of the sandbank,

and withdrew a few hundred yards inland to the shore proper when the river rose in the monsoon. Confronted without warning on a day in March, 1943, with 300 British, Gurkha and Karen soldiers, he had made a brief and ephemeral packet of money, selling us hot meals on the spot and stores for future consumption. When the Japanese arrived on our heels he wisely disappeared into the jungle, returning to Tigyaing only when the dust died down. After a period of penury, he switched from keeping a chow shop into keeping a piece-goods store; and he was now the most prosperous merchant in Tigyaing, though he hotly denied it.

He arrived at the maternity centre at the double and in a tremendous state of excitement, just as we were settling in and undoing our bedding-rolls. Tun Sein had been to his shop and said: " The *Thakin Gyi* you hired me for is here." From that moment on, until we left Tigyaing, he was always turning up: sometimes embarking on long stories, sometimes just sitting and devouring us with his eyes and rubbing his hands with pleasure. He was a gay little man with an endearing giggle, who could write English of a sort although he couldn't speak a word of it: I have in my note-book several communications which he wrote to me under my nose, and to which I had to reply in verbal English, translated into Burmese by Banerji the doctor. It was from him and from others that we pieced together the story of the Japanese reaction to our passage through Tigyaing.

The Japanese party which fired on us had been very small, not more than a dozen. The garrison of Tawma reacted to the news of our arrival by sending an advance party at once, following up in a strength of about 200 an hour later. The leading patrol opened fire on us as we were embarking, with their rifles, their light automatics and their single mortar. When the main body arrived they sent across a patrol in pursuit of us to Myadaung, the town on the far bank; but they omitted to provide it with an interpreter, it failed to press on, and came back empty-handed and without reliable information.

From then on they kept a garrison in Tigyaing, whose patrolling was constant and active. They had been suspicious about the attitude of the inhabitants to our brief passage, but mercifully there had been no serious reprisals. Even the head policeman, about whom I was worried, got away with it. He was a Karen, who did all he could to help us with advice; stipulating only that we should throw all his rifles into the river and lock him up in his office so as to keep him right with the Japs.

Ah Hyi claimed the credit for having engaged Tun Sein and the other boatmen on our behalf, and Tun Sein confirmed it, although the double-crossing doyen of the waterfront maintained his rival claim. Ah Hyi was beyond doubt a stout-hearted little chap, and it stands to his credit that he was popular in Tigyaing, despite the twin disadvantages that he was both Chinese, and the richest man in the place. He had certainly prospered of late years, and Bill, prompted by Banerji and the Township Officer, proceeded to tease him about his reputed affluence, with not declaring his income and not paying his taxes. Ah Hyi wriggled and giggled, and gave back as good as he got.

Ah Hyi maintained further that he had filled one of my spare socks with sugar. This may well be true, and if so I detect the hand of my soldier servant Peter Dorans. Socks in those days fulfilled a variety of purposes for which they were not designed: Wingate himself was reputed to strain his tea through his.

There were several inquiries for a Karen soldier, Saw Ohn Maung, who had been wounded and left behind during the evacuation of 1942; he had settled in a village just outside

Tigyaing and become a popular figure, but he joined up with us as we passed through, to share our fortunes. We hadn't a uniform for him, but we armed him with one of the rifles we took from the police. I hadn't seen him since the moonlight scrap in Hintha, when almost all my Karen platoon got separated from me.

While we were in Tigyaing, I discovered from two different people, non-officials, that I had been misled about Hintha. I mentioned to somebody that I was sorry it no longer existed.

" Who told you that? " he said. " I was there myself a week ago."

And somebody else told me that her son was in prison, through having got mixed up with the Hintha people (if I understood her aright). I suspect that it was giving aid and comfort to Communist rebels, and was thought too unsettled for me to see; but I was being so royally treated in every other respect that it would be ungracious to cavil at this one omission.

Next morning Bill had business to do up the valley, and set off on foot with the Township Officer. Banerji the doctor took on the duties of being our guide and interpreter. He was a typical Bengali, slim and frail in physique, anxious to please; he had been two years in Tigyaing, having come straight from Calcutta as soon as he qualified. There is an acute shortage of doctors and dentists in Burma. Efforts are being made to induce more Burmese to go in for these professions, but meanwhile the gap is filled chiefly by Indians on contract, such as Banerji. He was a nice chap, rather homesick, and distressed as a devout Hindu to be compelled to witness the daily slaughter of cattle for meat. With two or three other Indians living in the neighbourhood, he had scraped together enough money to tender for the contract to run the local *abattoir*, which was a Government monopoly: they hoped to win it, and then to refuse to kill anything but goats. But they had failed to keep their innocuous plan secret, and had been out-bid by a beef-eating rival: so poor Dr. Banerji was more unhappy than ever.

With Bill away, we went out with Banerji for a walk in the town. Our presence was known to everybody, and they were all competing to make us welcome. I stopped at one shop to buy a *dah*, and they tried hard to make me accept it as a gift. I have often stamped out of an oriental shop in the course of bargaining, refusing to pay the price asked; never before have I been pursued into the street by the shopkeeper saying that they will accept my money after all.

There was one man I particularly wanted to see. His house was only a few doors from the maternity centre where we were lodging; and in 1943, as we marched in from the direction of Bonchaung, this man stood on his balcony calling out: " God save the King! Long live the King! " I begged him to stop; I explained that we were only passing through, and that he would certainly be reported to the Japs and would suffer for it; but he went on despite my warnings, proclaiming his loyalty at the top of his voice, and his pretty daughter promised us her prayers. He gave me his card, which described him as a retired senior official of the post office, and I promised to report him to the Burma Government in exile in Simla, when and if we got out. Unfortunately the note-book into which I put it got swept out of my breast pocket by the waters of the Shweli River; and although I broadcast the story far and wide, and told it to His Majesty the King when he did me the honour of receiving me after I got home in 1945, I could never remember the man's name.

As soon as I asked about him in Tigyaing, there was a chorus. " It was U Tha Hla! " He was now living in Mandalay, but one of his sons was schoolmaster at Tawma, going out there every day on a bicycle and returning to Tigyaing in the evening. We arranged for him to be intercepted and brought to see us at our billet that night.

Meanwhile we went off to lunch with Ah Hyi and his wife and children. Although he no longer kept a chow shop his hand had not lost its cook's cunning. We ate among the bales of clothing and the innumerable items of his motley stock in full view of the street, where a crowd watched our every mouthful. His eldest boy was at school in Mandalay, but five other children were at hand, and Ah Hyi himself was bubbling over with pleasure at being our host, and the prestige among his neighbours which such a position conferred on him. He deserved every shred of it, for he had risked a lot on our behalf; and as a Chinese he could expect no mercy from the Japs if he aroused their suspicion. They had in fact removed another Chinese from Myadaung, who had never been heard of again.

After luncheon we went down to the water-front and boarded the army launch—my wife and myself, Banerji, Ah Hyi and Tun Sein. I wanted to cross to the other side, and Tun Sein was to point out exactly where he had put us ashore. It was by a tree a few hundred yards below Myadaung, the small town right opposite Tigyaing; by the time we had got there in 1943 it was practically dark, and I could not have spotted the place now without Tun Sein's help. It was here that I had shaken hands with him and blessed him with more sincerity than I have ever blest anybody; the escape which we had just had was very narrow indeed and but for him we should have been dead men, or prisoners. I myself would have been dead, since after long thought I had made up my mind never to be taken alive. Like all other Chindit officers, I carried enough morphia for a lethal dose several times over.

Ba Ohn had said to us at Kadu, " Sir, in those times life is nothing." He hadn't meant quite that. Life to me has always been very dear, and never more so than when it hung on a thread. I used often in Burma to think of those posthumous lines of A. E. Housman:—

Here dead lie we because we did not choose
　To live and shame the land from which we sprung.
Life, to be sure, is nothing much to lose;
　But young men think it is, and we were young.

The most awful decision which came our way on these expeditions of ours was what to do with the men who were so badly wounded that they had no hope of living, or even of being seen by a doctor. It had been drummed into us all that nothing must jeopardise the success of the expedition: that must always be the first consideration. The old tradition of the North-West Frontier of India, that no dead body, let alone a wounded man, must be allowed to fall into enemy hands, had to be jettisoned. The most that could be permitted was a pause to make a wounded man comfortable. But how for instance do you make a man comfortable whose body has been split open from neck to groin two hundred miles behind the enemy lines five miles from a road, and who is still living? Problems like these are certain to confront you, and you will be well-advised to decide them in principle before they arise.

Perhaps as I am no longer a serving officer I can safely disclose that on the first expedition I had a soldier flogged. He left his post and went to sleep as a sentry, at a particularly dangerous moment, and I could think of no other way of dealing with him. In *Beyond the Chindwin* I told the story and set the reader the problem, without revealing my own solution; and I still get an occasional letter asking what I actually did.

Now It Can Be Told—at least, I hope so. I interviewed

him, and gave him the choice of two alternatives. Either he would be furnished with a map and left to find his own way back to India with his rifle and ammunition and his own rations, which he was carrying on him anyway; or he would be flogged. He said at once that he preferred to be flogged. I gave him ten minutes in which to think it over; and as I expected he still preferred to be flogged. He duly received ten strokes on the buttocks, through his trousers, from a knotted parachute rope while bending over a fallen tree. The punishment was administered, good and hearty, by a reluctant serjeant-major in the presence of myself, the adjutant, the doctor, his platoon commander, his platoon serjeant, his section commander, and one private soldier witness selected by himself. I then dictated a statement to every officer in the column, saying what the man had done; how he had risked all our lives; the choice I had offered him; the choice he had made; and the manner in which the punishment had been administered. I finished up by saying that the whole thing was utterly illegal, but that I took full responsibility. I ordered the officers to read out the statement to their men before we moved off, so that every man-jack in the column would know exactly what had happened: the truth, and no rumours.

The results within the column were all that could be desired. The man himself came up immediately after his punishment, said that he had asked for it and was sorry, and that I would have no cause for complaint in future. Nor did I: he pulled his weight splendidly, and was eventually killed while displaying gallantry to such a degree that I would probably have recommended him for a decoration. The other men thought the whole episode extremely funny, and " I'll get the major to flog you if you do that again " became common conversational currency. We had no more slack sentries. Outside the column the story spread; and

the following year another column commander, not in my
brigade, did the same thing for the same reason to two other
men.

He was less fortunate than I was. One of the men wrote
home to his parents, who wrote to their Member of Parliament, who wrote to the War Office, who created an uproar,
which resulted in a court-martial for the officer. By this
time the war was over, but the scandal was not. I was subpœnaed for the defence; the other man who had been
flogged was subpœnaed for the prosecution. To his lasting
credit, he flatly refused to give evidence: he maintained that
his commanding officer was a very fine chap, that he himself
was ashamed of his lapse, and that the other man, in his
opinion, ought to be ashamed of himself for sneaking to Mum
and Dad. From this position he declined to budge.

We all assembled at a court-martial centre in Curzon
Street in Mayfair: the accused, the witnesses, the five
officers who comprised the court, a Judge-Advocate and
various counsel and officials. There had been a good deal of
publicity in the press, and fifty or sixty curious members of
the public watched us all going in. I felt at the time that the
whole thing was thoroughly unreal. What relevance had
Curzon Street, and the Member of Parliament who raised
all the stink, to the problems of a jungle track 7,000
miles away and behind enemy lines? What would the
Member of Parliament have done in similar circumstances?

The witnesses were all marched into the court, and sworn.
I looked at the five Members behind their bastion of green
baize tables, and found that I knew them all, though I had
been so long abroad that I had seen none of them for five
years or more. I noted with pleasure that in front of each of
them, and of the Judge-Advocate, and of the counsel for the
prosecution and for the defence, lay a copy of *Beyond the*

Chindwin. It probably meant that I was going to be cross-examined on the passage which I had written with so much caution and discretion, and in which I had set the reader the problem; it certainly meant that I had netted a quid, at half-a-crown a copy, in royalties at the public expense, which was all to the good.

In the end, none of the witnesses ever came into court. Counsel for the accused put in a plea in bar of trial on the grounds of condonation. The meaning of this piece of legal jargon is simpler than it sounds. If an officer does something wrong, and his superior, knowing all about it, overlooks it and takes no action, that officer cannot afterwards be called to account for what he did, since it has been condoned. How far this goes I am not sure; I doubt if it covers murder. But apparently in this case counsel for the accused propounded the fact that what I did became common knowledge in Wingate's Force; that Wingate publicly expressed his approval afterwards of what I had done; and that this constituted condonation of what the accused officer had done. At all events, the accused got away with it—technically; but he had lost his job and his acting rank while awaiting trial, his career sustained a jolt, and he was out of pocket to the tune of four figures. Among other things, the War Office was able to bring prosecution witnesses home from India at the expense of the Treasury, while such witnesses as the accused wished to bring home had to have their expenses paid by him.

The Member of Parliament who made all the fuss was a former temporary soldier himself; I see from *Who's Who* that he was wounded twice in the First World War, and he is therefore beyond the reach of a sneer. But the episode was not a happy one.

All this is a far cry from Myadaung and the Irrawaddy; but perhaps it serves to illustrate the gulf between the

Irrawaddy and Curzon Street. Tun Sein stabbed his finger at the tree below which we had landed, and the launch chugged a little farther upstream to put us all ashore at Myadaung. We found the headman's house close to the shore, and settled down to have tea with him. We were soon joined by a sophisticated and jolly old gentleman in a panama hat, and an old lady too, who told us the events of the day of our crossing as seen in Myadaung, through Banerji as interpreter.

They knew no more than rumours of British troops being back in Burma until my leading elements arrived across the river, landing by the tree. These had moved up the bank into the town, and finding it empty had directed later flights to land in the town itself. The process had gone on for two or three hours, and the whole population was en-gaged in the business of preparing and selling cooked rice to the troops; the old lady complaining good-humouredly that she never got her spoon back. One of the Myadaung men was drowned while helping ours to get our mules ashore. Just at dusk they heard the shooting over at Tigyaing, and an hour later a Jap patrol arrived on our tail. They had asked questions about us in bad Burmese, which the Myadaung people were able to pretend convincingly that they couldn't understand; the Japs were jumpy, and stayed only a few minutes before going back across the Irrawaddy.

Some weeks later a small British officer in spectacles had come back all by himself, asking in dumb-show to be put across the river. The man in the panama hat had given him a meal and made him have a sleep in his house, and then sent him over in a boat; but he heard later that the officer was captured on the other side of Tigyaing. I thought I knew exactly who this was: David Whitehead, my sapper officer, the man who actually blew the Bonchaung; he was

one of those who survived captivity and told me his story
after the war. A guide he took on between Tigyaing and
the Meza suddenly ran away and left him, while a fusillade
broke out from behind the bushes and he was wounded in
seven places. The panama hat man was delighted to hear
that David was still alive, and sent him warm greetings
through me. Unfortunately since I got home I have compared notes with Whitehead, and he tells me that he crossed
several miles farther north; so I have no notion of who this
other officer can have been.

At the beginning of our talk, which was conducted in
front of the usual crowd, children with satchels had been
passing on their way to afternoon school. Now there was
a commotion, and at least three hundred children came
running down the dusty street to halt in front of the house.
Apparently some of them had told the headmaster that there
were a couple of Europeans at the headman's house; and as
none had ever seen a European before, the headmaster had
bidden them scamper off and get an eyeful. So I made them a
little speech through Banerji about how good their parents
had been to us in the old days, and so forth, until the
headmaster rounded them up and took them back to work.

Returning across the river in the launch, we found Bill
Maung Maung, travel-stained but not weary, having tea;
he had walked some fifteen miles since breakfast, had had a
wash, and changed into a *loongyi*. He was now determined
to walk us up the pagoda hill. We had to leave our shoes and
socks at the bottom, for the whole hill is sacred ground.
Legend says that one of the ancient Burmese kings was
rafting up-river, when a man and a woman came to him to
do homage, the one carrying an umbrella for him and the
other a sceptre. When he asked where they dwelt, they
pointed to the pagoda hill; and the king said: " Hence-
forward this place shall be called *Hti-Gyaing*," or Umbrella-

Two old friends : *right*, Chet Khin in Karen dress ; *below*, Saw Lader with his father, wife and sons

U Tha Hla

Sceptre. The *hti* or umbrella is the topmost symbol of every pagoda.

I have always reckoned myself a connoisseur of views, with a short list of the truly magnificent. This includes the view from the Pali in Honolulu; over St. George's Bay from the hills above Beirut; the Bay of Carthage; Strathmore from Tullybaccart; and a few others. To this class I add without hesitation that from the pagoda at Tigyaing. It stands three hundred feet above the town on a promontory jutting out into the river, so that the Irrawaddy sweeps round three sides of it. You can see the river for twenty miles upstream and twenty down. To the north-east are the many flat miles of the Indaung Reserve Forest; to the north the peaks and glens of the Gangaw Range; to the west the smiling Meza Valley, with its rich stretches of paddy; and wooded hills to the east and south. At each point of the compass there stands on guard a gigantic *Chinthe*, where

> "... we petty men
> Walk under his huge knees and peep about."

And below lies the snug little town of Tigyaing itself. It was exactly twenty-four hours since our arrival, and once again the evening smoke was curling up, and the boats on the water-front being secured for the night—boats with high bow and stern, and a matting canopy amidships. The crew of our own launch were leaning over the rail looking into the water, the size of midgets.

Half-way down the hill is another, smaller pagoda, balanced on a rocking stone, and a *poongyikyaung* said to date from the 13th century. I am never at my best in bare feet, and was happy to get down again and into my shoes and socks. At our billet we found Ah Hyi, inevitably, and U Tha Hla's schoolmaster son; the latter very shy, the former as rumbustious as usual. U Tha Hla's son had been only a small boy when we passed through, but the occasion was the highlight of his youth. He confirmed that his father was alive, though now very old and blind, and gave us his address in Mandalay; his sister was in Rangoon; one of his uncles was a civil servant, and a former colleague of Bill's.

We were due to sail next morning on the steamer. Nobody knew precisely when it was due, and there was a rumour that it had lost time through being stuck on a bank; but Tun Sein undertook to give us ample warning, since it was always sighted from the pagoda when still a fair distance upstream. At about 9.30, Tun Sein arrived, complete with bullock-cart, to pick up our luggage; and we proceeded sadly down to the water-front. There were hateful good-byes to be made. We had good hopes of one day seeing Bill and Mary and their children: they might come to Britain, or we to Rangoon: one day at least we shall hope to be able to pay back some fraction of all their kindness. But to Ah Hyi and Tun Sein, who had put their lives to hazard on our behalf, this was probably a final good-bye: they were both near tears, which I always find infectious.

The gangway was drawn in, the bow was paid off, the powerful current flowed between the steamer and the beach, and we were slipping away downstream past the boats, while the little crowd on the beach waved and waved. Then I went to our cabin, and found a bag of oranges, a hundred cigarettes, one of those razor-blade knives, a cigarette-lighter and a packet of family photographs—farewell presents from Ah Hyi.

XII

THE STEAMER was a twin of the one we had overtaken between Bhamo and Katha: a two-decker with a rounded bow. There were only a few inches of freeboard between the water and the lower deck, which was crowded with passengers and their baggage. At the forward end of the upper deck was the first-class saloon, spreading across the whole beam of the vessel, with big windows giving an all-round view. Just abaft it were four sleeping cabins. Two were occupied by officers of the Army; one was shared by Laura and me; and in the fourth, to our indignation, were two Englishwomen, one the wife of a business-man in Rangoon, the other of a professor at the university. I give them full marks for enterprise: they had got fed up with never seeing anything of the country, and had broken away from the city for a fortnight's jaunt. Laura and I resented them only because we had become accustomed to feeling that we were alone off the beaten track. They were in fact two pleasant people.

We were given luncheon by a sad and seedy old Indian waiter with a hacking cough. An allegedly European menu was on offer, but we preferred the Burmese. It seemed to us excellent, though the two officers rejected it in favour of food brought them by their own orderlies. After luncheon, which we finished long before eleven o'clock, we watched the passing pageant of the river scene. There was no open deck to sit on, but you could cross from window to window, or lean over the rail.

On the river itself there was plenty to see: fishing boats, ferry boats, and the long teak rafts drifting down the current. Sometimes we would pass a rafting station at a *chaung*-mouth, where the logs, having floated down from some inland forest, were being lashed together for their onward journey. On the rafts themselves were the matting houses, with the smoke from the fire finding its way wispily through the roof; the raftman straining at his huge steering-oar; and his children fishing, or chasing each other up and down, or waving at the steamer. They reckon to take forty-five days from Mandalay to journey's end, when the raft is broken up, and the value of each individual log attributed to the contractor whose mark is on it. Then the raftman and his family travel home *de luxe* slowly against the stream, on the lower deck of a steamer. It would be a wonderful life for a philosopher. The worst that can befall you is to run out of rice or cheroots; and all you need do then is to haul on your steering oar, and fetch up at the bank to get more.

We passed one raft whose raftman was evidently doing a bit of trade on the side. It (or does a raft aspire to " She "?) was adorned from end to end with large red earthenware pots. They looked precariously balanced, and our course was shaped so as to pass within fifty yards. I half expected our wash to topple them over. But our serang, and the raftman, and the raftman's children looked wholly unconcerned; the raft was so long, and therefore so stable, that it didn't react to our passage at all.

Every few miles there was a steamer station, though to begin with there seemed nothing to identify one until the steamer pulled in to the shore. The banks of the river down here, as opposed to the hundred miles between Bhamo and Katha, were usually high. From our privileged eminence on the upper, first-class deck, the eye could usually see groups of houses above bank level, but they didn't all rate the

importance of a steamer station. As we became more
expert, we learned to spot the bales of merchandise and
bags of rice lying on the beach close under the bank,
awaiting our arrival.

By the time the steamer was drawing in, and the crew was
throwing her heaving-lines ashore, a crowd would have
gathered from nowhere and be pouring down on to the beach
—passengers, lookers-on and sellers of food. From the lower
deck, two planks were run out from ship to shore, each only
a foot wide, and neither with any such refinement as a hand-
rope. It was strictly one-way traffic. For the next ten
minutes, with an urgency astonishing in such a timeless
country as Burma, people would be running up and down
these gang-planks like ants going in and out of an ant-heap.
Those coming on board carried enormous burdens on their
backs, staggering with their weight but always running;
the splash that seemed inevitable never happened. Those
going ashore ran still faster to seize and swing on to their
backs another monstrous burden. At the same time, paying
no attention to the activity about the steamer, upstream and
downstream the bank would be crowded with bathers,
washing their clothes and themselves, and performing that
dexterous change of *loongyi* which I have already described.

Two pictures in particular remain in my mind from the
many steamer stations which we saw during that unforget-
table descent of the Irrawaddy. The first is of a tiny but
tireless woman at one such stop, who was not only directing
and supervising all the work in a shrill voice, but doing the
lion's share of it herself. The other is of a very impoverished
Indian woman, with her small daughter, who had brought
heavy containers of food to sell to any Hindu passengers who
might be on board. There were none. Her Burmese
competitors beside her did a roaring trade, the customers
bustling and jostling each other to buy rice and chicken and

ngapi before the ship sailed. Nobody bought from her; and my last memory of that particular stop is of her and her daughter toiling painfully up the path from the beach with all their containers still full, as poor as when they came.

We sailed on all day and late into the night. When darkness fell, we switched on our searchlight, to find the wands that indicated the channel, and to induce the little bits of tin to flash back at us. At last the ship tied up, and Laura and I went to bed, to be kept awake for hours by the tearing cough of the poor old Indian waiter, which racked the ship throughout the night far more than her engines by day. We got to sleep at last; and when we awoke we had already been steaming some time, and had missed the passage of the Third Defile. The vast unfinished pagoda of Mingun was just coming into sight ten miles away: it was intended to be the biggest in the world, until the king who was building it died and his successors lost interest. From afar off it looks so huge that I, never having heard of it, thought at first that it was a natural feature, something like Dumbarton Rock; with awe I realised it was man-made. On the water's edge, in front of it, stands a scale model in white, resembling a wedding-cake, to show what the completed pagoda was to have looked like; and the model itself is big enough to be seen from a couple of miles away.

At 11.30 a.m., twenty-six hours after leaving Tigyaing, we nosed our way in among the numerous craft along the waterfront of Mandalay: our voyage was at an end. This famous city has been described so often that I decline to do it again. To anybody who may go there I would warmly recommend a visit to the Arakan Pagoda; but on the whole the city disappoints, despite the glamour which still attaches to its name. The glory is departed.

So, for the matter of that, have almost all the Europeans. John Slimming, with whom we stayed, was an excellent host, and our two or three days in Mandalay were a round of parties. Keith Gregory gave a luncheon for us, and John a cocktail-party, to which came the Commissioner (who bore a marked resemblance to Lord Monckton) and several officers from District Headquarters. Among them was Colonel Tan Yu Saing, whom I had last seen as a courageous subaltern in the White City.

I had two or three old friends in Mandalay whom I saw constantly during our stay: Major Carroll, an Irish-Burman who served with me as a corporal-interpreter in 1944; Wally Unger, a Germano-Burman, who had been a subaltern in the Burma Rifles during the war, and a lieutenant-colonel in the Burma Army after it; he had since qualified and was practising as a dentist. But closest friend of them all was Saw Lader, known throughout his time in the Burma Rifles as " Sunshine ": because his smile used to spread from ear to ear.

Sunshine was a Karen, a regular soldier, and a Jemadar when the war broke out. When it finished, he was a captain, with the Military Cross and the Burma Gallantry Medal. It was he who found my adjutant, Duncan Menzies, tied to a tree and dying, having been shot in the stomach by the Japs who had captured him; and he who brought Colonel L. G. Wheeler of the Burma Rifles to give Duncan a lethal dose of morphia and end his suffering. Wheeler did what Duncan asked him, and was himself shot a few seconds later by a Japanese sniper, falling and dying in Sunshine's arms. They had served together for many years.

My last contact with Sunshine had been an invitation to his wedding in Toungoo in 1946, when I was serving in Jerusalem and therefore not very handy; but apparently on the great day I sent him a cable, which is still preserved among his archives. Since then he had been closely involved with Chet, and like him had lain for a while under sentence of death; but he too had been reprieved, and was now employed full-time in the service of the American Baptist Mission. In fact he was on a tour in the Shan States on its behalf, in company with Bo Gyi Samson's son, when he got the message from John Slimming that I was coming to Mandalay, and had done me the honour of coming back to see me. He was remarkably un-bitter about his post-war experiences. On a recent visit to Rangoon he had been invited to luncheon with General Ne Win, and found himself received once more on a friendly footing by a gathering of former brother officers asked to meet him.

One day John Slimming drove us up the hill to Maymyo for a picnic luncheon: it is a two-hour drive, and the view out over the Irrawaddy Valley from the lip of the hill is another one to remember. This is the first stretch of the so-called " Burma Road " that runs on through Lashio into the mysteries of China. Maymyo is a hill-station remembered with nostalgia by many old Burma hands, including soldiers: there was always a British battalion there before the war, and all the usual sops for the British in exile, such as a club and frequent race-meetings. A permanent European population, official and civil, of several hundred was swollen in the hot weather by families coming up from the plains. Now there was only a single pure-blooded European left in the place, an old German of over ninety.

We ate our picnic in the park, sitting under a tree. Although we were nearly four thousand feet up, the sun was hot, and I wouldn't deny that when we were full of John's victuals and his *vin rosé* we spent a pleasant drowsy hour lying rather than sitting. The park was beautiful and exotic, yet quite unlike Burma. There were severe formal roads running through it; there was an ornamental lake; the grass was partly mown; and the place was gay with English oaks, bougainvillæa, jacaranda and cherry-blossom, and pretty

girls strolling about. It was easy to conjure up a vision of
Maymyo as it was in the old days. There should have been
rolling victorias, drawn by high-stepping horses, and occupied by women in flowered dresses with parasols. There was
still an iron bandstand with a pyramidal roof, but no longer
a band to play in it.

During that peaceful afternoon my mind was occupied
chiefly with the events in Maymyo of February and March,
1949, of which my knowledge was by now almost complete.
Little by little during this present journey there came together like pieces of a jigsaw puzzle the detailed story of the
events which led to the disarming of the Karen officers and
their men. By the time I left Rangoon I knew it all; but
since it reached its tragic climax here in Maymyo, this is the
best place to tell it.

After Independence came to Burma, there were many
bands of rebels in the field. They represented every colour
of the spectrum, from straight Communists—though even
these were split into various factions—to Saw Ba U Gyi's
Karen National Defence Organisation, usually known as
K.N.D.O.s. These last had erupted so suddenly that their
early successes were startling. They began by capturing the
important town of Bassein, on the western flank of the Delta.
Soon they were threatening Insein, which is closer to Rangoon than Slough is to London.

The fledgling Burma Government was faced with the fact
that almost all its senior officers were Karen. Smith Dun
was Chief of Staff and *de facto* Commander-in-Chief;
Henson Kya Doe, who had been one term junior to me in my
company at Sandhurst in 1931 when I was Senior Under
Officer, was Vice-Chief; Saw Donny was Quartermaster-
General; Chet Khin commanded the only mobile brigade,
which was quartered at Meiktila; Lader commanded the
Officers Training School at Maymyo; and Sammy Shi

Sho was Chief of the Air Staff. All these were old friends of mine—and all were Karen. The only Burmese in high military places were Aung Thin, Wingate's old confidant, who was commanding Southern District as a brigadier at Insein; and Ne Win, also a brigadier, who had just handed over the command of Northern District at Maymyo.

All these officers had been with the British throughout the war, except for Ne Win and Kya Doe. These two had been closely associated with Aung San, the national hero of Burma, when he turned on the Japs in March, 1945, and helped to expel them. Ne Win had been an ally of Aung San's for some years; Kya Doe had been engulfed as a major when the Japs first arrived, and had worked for two years in obscurity as a coolie before Aung San dug him out and signed him up. He was detained as a hostage by the Japs shortly before they eventually withdrew, and was lucky to escape with his life.

When Ba U Gyi's rebellion flared up so suddenly, Smith Dun, as Chief of Staff, called a conference at Rangoon, from which the only senior absentee was Ne Win, who failed to turn up. The clash of instincts among the Karens present must have been agonising, for many friends of theirs and mine had thrown in their lot with one or other set of rebels, mostly with Saw Ba U Gyi's. But they took the line that they had eaten the Government's salt, that their duty was clearly with the Government, and that they would suppress rebellion from whatever quarter it might come. The meeting broke up, and the officers returned to their various commands. A handful of other more junior officers was to choose otherwise when the moment came, but all the senior ones remained loyal.

A few days later, on the 19th February, Chet Khin at Meiktila was visited by a Burmese officer carrying a letter from Smith Dun. It instructed him to hand over his brigade forthwith to the bearer, and to go on indefinite leave to Maymyo. With his wife, his infant daughter and his sister-in-law, he drove to Maymyo in his own car, and put up in an hotel. Next morning he heard, at first with disbelief, that Meiktila, which he had left in good order the previous day, had fallen to the rebels. He went at once to Northern District Headquarters, and found them trying in vain to raise Meiktila on the wireless. Meiktila radio was as dumb as a log of teak, a fact which seemed to confirm the rumours.

Chet's departure from Meiktila had been so abrupt that he'd had no time to tell any of his friends that he was leaving. His wife and sister-in-law were distressed to think that their parents, living near Rangoon, would hear of the capture of Meiktila and deduce that the whole family was in rebel hands. Chet tried to send a telegram from Maymyo Post Office, but found that none were getting through. It occurred to him that the only way to communicate with Rangoon was to send a message by the pilot of the daily aircraft, which was almost due.

So Chet and his wife drove out to the airfield, three or four miles from Maymyo. They noticed as they went that there seemed to be an unusual amount of activity in the air; more aircraft than usual were coming in to land, and taking off for the south. And then by the roadside they spotted an Anglo-Burman Air Force officer whom they knew, and pulled up to exchange ideas about what on earth was going on. They had barely begun to speak when several trucks, full of armed men, came along the road from the direction of the airfield; and out jumped Naw Seng, an able, intelligent and popular Kachin captain in the Army whom they all knew. They were consequently staggered when he told them they were his prisoners. Naw Seng was the man whose name Laura and I had first heard a few weeks earlier; he had defected with the bulk of his command to the Karen rebels, and his men included the " Missing Lance-Naik," whom we had been seeking at Kadu.

Naw Seng ordered Chet and his wife back into their car, a station-wagon, and put three of his soldiers in behind them, giving them orders to shoot if Chet should make any effort to escape. So it came about that Chet was seen by a number of witnesses driving his own car, full of armed men, along the road to Maymyo in Naw Seng's convoy, to all appearance a willing party to the coup. It was this unlucky fact, coupled with subsequent events, that so nearly took him in front of a firing-squad.

It was already known in Maymyo that one body of rebels was marching up from the south, but the developments at Meiktila had taken everybody by surprise. Among the rebel booty at Meiktila were several Dakota aircraft, which Naw Seng had been quick to seize. The rapidity with which he organised an air-lift to capture Maymyo by an aerial *coup de main* shows him to have been an able as well as a bold commander. He brought with him as a prisoner Chet's successor in command of the Meiktila brigade, who had enjoyed that appointment for less than twenty-four hours.

Things at Maymyo were already chaotic. At the Officers Training School, Sunshine Lader, who had attended Smith Dun's conference in Rangoon, had received orders to send away all Burmese, Shans and Kachins under training, and to disarm all Karens; he asked urgently whether the Karens should not also be sent away, but got no reply. Meanwhile, Lader too had been suspended from duty; and Smith Dun had also arrived in Maymyo on indefinite leave, having been ordered by the Government to hand over his appointment as Chief of Staff to Ne Win. He took no part in the events of the next few weeks, preferring to lie low.

Exactly what those events were is still disputed, but the main outlines are clear. Chet, Lader and the more respons-

ible officers and men refused all blandishments to join Naw
Seng, who managed nevertheless to recruit extensively among
some of the more ebullient Karens and Kachins. There was
much tension and excitement. Naw Seng's men were in
triumphant mood and elated at their success so far; the
city fathers and civilian officials were apprehensive of
looting and riots, and begged Chet to take them under his
protection. It must have been a most perplexing problem:
he had no status, he didn't want to take service with the
rebels, and no doubt he felt it would be shirking responsibility to stand idly by and do nothing. In the end he took
the plunge, rearmed those Karens who had remained loyal,
and constituted himself a sort of neutral Military Governor.
He established control and administration, took over command of the police, organised a supply system, and at Naw
Seng's request took over also the 2,000 or so Government
troops who had been disarmed. Among the several hundred
loyal Karens who stood by him in these actions were Lader,
old Bo Gyi Samson, and John Hla Shein, who served
with me as Jemadar in 1944 and was now, like Lader, a
major.

There were in Maymyo just over 250 British men, women
and children. Half of them were civilians; the other half
belonged to a detachment of the British Services Mission
with their wives and families, enjoying as well they might
their life in that singularly beautiful town. It had now
suddenly become sinister and dangerous.

In command of the detachment was Brigadier The Earl
of Caithness (now Her Majesty's factor at Balmoral and
Colonel of the Gordon Highlanders); his official appointment was Adviser at Northern Burma Sub-District, although
for the last few turbulent weeks his advice had not been
noticeably in demand. The capture of Maymyo found these
families scattered in various parts of the town, but Caithness

quickly concentrated them in two areas; and it was just as well he did, for an attempt was soon made by Government forces to recapture the town. Sporadic fighting, with occasional quite sharp little actions, continued for several days; in the course of it one British woman was killed by a stray bullet, and a major severely wounded. After the 7th March there was a lull of three days, with the insurgents in possession of the town, and also of the airfield, which had changed hands several times.

Caithness had kept in constant touch with Chet, and now invoked his good offices to get the British flown out. Chet arranged this with Naw Seng, and during the 8th, 9th and 10th of March, British aircraft were allowed to land and take off. Everybody except a small rear party was evacuated; and the wounded major, a sapper called Whitney, was flown out five days later, as soon as he was fit to be moved.

In mid-March Naw Seng's rebels moved off, though there was no certainty that they mightn't come back. Other rebel parties were still milling around in the neighbourhood. As the threat had not entirely vanished, Chet retained his little *ad hoc* army complete with its weapons. He himself tried to communicate with the Government authorities, but found to his growing dismay that they were ignoring his messages. He sent emissaries, including John Hla Shein, down the hill to Mandalay to treat with the garrison there, but their advances were spurned. Then he got wind of a force moving down against him from the north under the command of Lezum Tan. He sent him a letter insisting that he was not in a state of rebellion, and appealing to him as an old friend and brother officer to meet him man to man to discuss arrangements for handing over Maymyo. He got back in return a message to say that friendship was friendship, but duty was duty; and realised with a sinking heart that he and his troops were regarded as rebels, and that whereas he was talking in terms of " handing over," the authorities were demanding his " surrender."

No resistance was offered, and Lezum occupied Maymyo without a shot being fired. Nearly thirty officers and seven hundred men handed over their arms and were interned. Two years later they were brought to trial before a court-martial. There was no lack of witnesses to testify that Chet had been seen in company with Naw Seng; that he had worn uniform, carried arms, and administered Maymyo during the rebel occupation. And unfortunately two murders had been committed by uniformed Karen soldiers—" we had our hot-heads," said Lader—during his administration. The proceedings dragged on for a year, in the course of which the leading counsel for the defence died. When at last they ended, the officers received various terms of imprisonment: except for Chet Khin, Lader and John Hla Shein, who were condemned to death. The sentence was soon commuted to imprisonment for life; but in fact they served only three or four more years, and were then released.

It is a dismally sad story, but in fairness to the Burma Government of the day it must be conceded that their apprehensions were not unnatural. The pre-war Burma Army had been almost entirely Karen, Kachin and Chin; its integration with the members of Aung San's Burma Defence Army, who were mostly Burmese, might be complete on paper, but it was very recent. It was inevitable, with Saw Ba U Gyi in the field and doing uncomfortably well, that all Karens should be suspect; and after Naw Seng's defection some of the Kachin Old Guard were suspect also. The Karen officers with few exceptions, and some Kachins, were retired on pension. So were a few of the Anglo-Burmans, though by no means all: one became Deputy Chief of Staff of the Army, and another—he who had been caught by Naw Seng with Chet Khin on the way to the airfield—served on to become Chief of Staff of the Air Force, in which Sammy Shi Sho, a Karen, also rose to high rank. But those Karens who were unfortunate enough to be involved with Chet lost their pensions, as well as the annuities which went with their decorations. Naw Seng is still at large with many of his men, and is probably in China.

The Karen rebels still carry on their hopeless struggle spasmodically in remote corners of Karenni, emerging from time to time to blow up a train or the like; their numbers are small, and they live a precarious life as outlaws on the run. Saw Ba U Gyi was killed some years ago in an ambush, by an officer whom I met in the course of this journey: I fear that the equivalent of thirty pieces of silver played some part in the affair. To suggest that he was misguided is not to impugn the memory of a brave man; but so long as the broken remnant of his followers remains in the field, it will be difficult for the Karen people as a whole to play their part in furthering the fortunes of the Union of Burma. The vast majority is anxious to do just that, and the Karen people have many qualities to contribute to the service of the state. There will have to be a measure of give and take.

It will certainly be my constant prayer that they may have a happy issue out of all their afflictions: I owe them too much to wish them any less. I derive encouragement from reflecting how impossible it must have seemed to our own ancestors that the English and Scotch should ever pull together.

Before leaving Mandalay we saw U Tha Hla, the man who had called out " God Save the King! " at Tigyaing. John Slimming sent a car to bring him and his wife to the house, and Laura and I awaited them in John's garden, bright with roses, cannas and phlox. The car drew up and the old couple alighted. He was almost entirely blind, wearing spectacles tinted green; but he had great dignity, and his wife, an elderly lady of extraordinary beauty, guided him gently with her hand under his elbow. She was a Mon, a member of the oldest race in Lower Burma. He too was a handsome man, and obviously under the stress of deep emotion.

I put him in a chair in John's cool drawing-room.

" May I give you a cigarette? " I asked.

The most charming smile broke over his face, and he made a slow sweeping gesture with his right hand.

" Let us not waste time in smoking! " he said. " Let us spend it in talking! "

He then produced his left hand. It held a copy of my *Beyond the Chindwin*, with his thumb in the page where I described our encounter. It had obviously been read and re-read many times, and the whole passage was underlined in red ink. I explained how I had told the story to the King, and he listened rapt, with his face transfigured with pride; then it clouded.

" What a pity that he never heard my name! " he said sadly.

My fears for his safety had happily not been realised: in fact he was one of the few people who had genuine cause to be grateful to the Japanese. During their occupation of Tigyaing, his wife (to use his own phrase) had been " sick unto death," and he had begged help from a Japanese medical officer serving with the garrison. This doctor turned up trumps, diagnosed the disease, and prescribed a course of seven injections, which he said she must complete in order to recover. She had only had three when " the British forces swept the Japanese away."

The daughter, that pretty girl who had promised to pray for us, sought out a British M.O. and implored him to come and see her mother. It might so easily have happened that this M.O. was too busy or too harassed to help; after all, he couldn't have known what U Tha Hla had done for us;

but he found time to visit the family. He couldn't identify the Japanese treatment, but he prescribed another one, and gave them an ample supply of the necessary drugs. The mother recovered completely.

She sat there now with her hands in her lap, watching our faces as we talked; she could speak no English.

" I remember your daughter well," I said, " but I don't remember seeing your wife."

U Tha Hla laughed.

" Do you know why? " he asked. " She was busy cooking for your men. She was cooking, cooking all the time you were in the town. She has never cooked so much in all her life. And your men insisted on paying us, though we didn't want their money."

He translated rapidly for her benefit, and she smiled for the first time. We had half an hour together, and he gave me his daughter's address in Rangoon. Then hand in hand the two went down the garden, climbed into Slimming's car and were driven away, a very good and gallant couple.

We left Mandalay by rail at three o'clock one afternoon, with twenty people to see us off. The train was fast and comfortable; the carriages were brand-new, representing war-reparations from Japan. We were back in a world of sophistication, but homesick already for the lumbering brake-vans of Naba junction and a sight of U Hla Pe's pork-pie hat. At Rangoon we found ourselves front-page news, in both English and vernacular press. Photographs taken at Myitkyina with Saw Myint, and at Mandalay by a group of journalists produced by Slimming, appeared over gratifying captions on the general theme " Fergusson rides again." We felt very important.

The time had come for Laura to return to Scotland. I was to stay on for a few days, to cover the impending elections for a London paper, and then to travel home circuitously by

Malaya, Manipur and the frontiers of Tibet. But we determined before Laura left to gather together as many former Chindits as we could find in Rangoon for one glorious final party. The Brookings lent us their house, the Allens their patronage; and we sent the summons throbbing out along the grape-vine.

What a gathering it was! There was Aung Thin, D.S.O., the stout jolly Burmese, a pillar of the Rangoon Turf Club before the war and Wingate's right-hand man on the first Expedition (on which, incidentally, he was the senior man in point of age). There was Mya Aung, one of the youngest men on the second show as a captain: still looking remarkably youthful. There was Mathew, a Karen Anglican parson in a white cassock, who had been a padre in the White City. There was Charles Cowie, and Dingle Bell, and Chet Khin, and John Hla Shein, and many another. There was a number of wives, all looking rather bewildered. There was Shan Lone and Kya Doe, not Chindits but old friends; and there was U Tha Hla's daughter, the one who had prayed for us.

She took a bit of persuasion before she would agree to come. U Tha Hla had told me that she was chief clerk in the Rangoon Telegraph Department, so it hadn't been difficult to make contact with her on the telephone; but she was terribly shy. In the end she agreed to attend on the understanding that she might bring a chaperone; and I sent a car for her. She arrived, as lovely as ever, to shed great distinction on the evening, which was not devoid of loud and libellous reminiscence.

So ended our joint pilgrimage. The following day Laura took flight, and left me waving good-bye forlornly on the airfield. Already our time up-country had begun to seem like a dream. Rangoon was steaming hot, and the latest newspapers from home reported Scotland snow-bound.

The newspaper publicity had brought me a letter from Saw Po Po Tou, a highly intelligent Karen Colour-Serjeant living in Moulmein. I had last seen him when we ventured together into the sleeping village of Hintha in 1943, and saw four men sitting round a fire.

" They're Japs! " said Po Po Tou.

" Nonsense! " I said, and addressed them in Burmese.

He was right, I was wrong, the battle began, they were killed, I was wounded, and I'd never seen him since.

I sent him a telegram and took an aircraft to Moulmein. It seemed as good a place as anywhere to witness the elections. A flight of an hour and a half took me across the Pegu River, the estuary of the Sittang and the broadening Salween; and there awaiting me on the strip was Po Po Tou and Saw Donny, another old Karen friend who had been Q.M.G. at the time of the purge. He had not been implicated in the tortuous events at Maymyo, and had been able to retire on pension, to a chicken farm. There he had been raided by dacoits, and lost most of his property. Now he and his wife were living in the Moulmein Hospital, of which he was the Secretary and Administrator.

Po Po Tou's career had been a trifle more *mouvementé*. Separated from my column in the midnight confusion of Hintha, he had made his way home by devious routes, a distance of some 600 miles, spending a short time on the way as a Jap prisoner. After Independence he had joined Saw Ba U Gyi, and remained with the rebels in the jungle until 1958, when he accepted the amnesty. He was now working as a timber contractor, and his wife was a school-teacher in Kawkareik. He had changed very little. The scanty beard that grew out of the mole on his chin had lengthened a few inches, but otherwise he was the same man, with the same pawky penetrating humour, that had endeared himself to us all in barracks, bivouac and battle.

I spent three happy days in his brand-new two-storey teak house, with its rooms all opening off each other, separated by neat red cotton curtains. At least fifteen relations and friends of all ages were sharing it with him, and I never lived in more cheerful and hospitable company. I made my number with the local authorities, both military and civil; I visited hospitals and schools, staffed entirely by Karens or Anglo-Indian Catholic Fathers; I called on Po Po Tou's father, a charming white-bearded patriarch who had long served T. D. Findlay & Co.; and on a retired Burmese Commissioner, who told me at length how he had once spoken to Queen Mary. I spent an hour among the shipbuilders, who did their work entirely by eye, building on the same lines and on the same spot as the Dutch and the French were doing in the 17th century. I lunched with a millionaire on the water-front. I witnessed the polling, which was dull as ditch-water.

There is no single European in Moulmein to-day,[1] though their former houses, exquisitely built of teak, still stand along the water-front and inland, in gardens still exquisitely tended. Here too, as at Maymyo, one can imagine the victorias trotting up and down: the British were in Moulmein sixty years before Colonel May founded Maymyo. On my last evening, Po Po Tou and Donny drove me up on to the Ridge to see the sun go down, a rite observed by Europeans for more than a century, but now no more.

Three miles to the west, with the sun setting behind it, was the massive island of Chaungzon. It splits into two the broad mouth of the Salween, the " Dark River " of which no European as yet has seen the source. On our right hand, beyond the northern channel, lay Martaban, for centuries the home of pirates. At our feet was the evening smoke of

[1] I was wrong when I wrote this: one retired English colonel still has a house there.

Moulmein, and beyond it a myriad masts. A few sailing vessels were out on the water. Immediately behind us was the great brooding pagoda, and beyond it and below rolling miles of forest, with hills in the distance towards Siam, seventy miles away. To our left was the long channel down to Amherst, by which I should soon be sailing. I could see what a wonderful capital city Moulmein would have made, if the Karen pipe-dream of an independent country could ever have come true. I had to remind myself that this had never been more than a hopeless illusion.

There is a small British vessel, the *Petaling*, which for many years has picked her way month by month among the islands, ports and anchorages between Penang and Rangoon, all along the Tenasserim Coast. I discovered that she was about to call at Moulmein, on her way to Rangoon, and took passage in her. Her master was Captain Harkness, of Glasgow, who might have stepped straight from the pages of Neil Munro; or of David Bone or Shalimar, both of whom knew these waters.

He treated me royally: I spent most of the journey on his bridge or in his cabin, accepting a dram from time to time, and listening to tales that were pure Conrad. He was much too pleasant a character to be drawn by Somerset Maugham: whom, incidentally, Laura and I had met in Rangoon a few days before. The world has no greater treat to offer me than a passage in a small ship in romantic waters; and we reached Rangoon all too quickly in a day and a night.

I had some farewells to make, and an interview with U Nu, who had won the elections with a four to one majority, and was once again Prime Minister of the Union of Burma. A day or two later I left Burma—by air, in 1960 as in 1944. Not asleep this time, but wide awake; not from the bumpy grass of a natural airfield far behind the enemy lines, but from the smooth smart runway of Mingaladon Airport; not with my pack under my head, but with a baggage check in my pocket-book. We soared above the golden summit of the Shwe Dagon, the busy wharves of Rangoon, the oil-tanks of Syriam, and the lower reaches of the river, dotted with ferry-boats and sampans.

But this to me could never be Burma. My Burma lay hundreds of miles up the Irrawaddy, where life in the villages had resumed its old rhythm as though we had never disturbed it, and where people and places and sounds and smells and colours were exactly as I had preserved them in my memory all these years. The dream was real after all.

EPILOGUE

Having waited so long to accomplish my pilgrimage, the last thing in the world that I expected was to find myself back in Burma within two years; but so it happened. At the end of November 1961, I was flying back to Britain from Netherlands New Guinea, and managed to break my journey in Rangoon, with a few days to spare.

After twenty months of civil government under U Nu, there was again widespread disturbance in the country, and I had some difficulty in getting permission to fly up to Myitkyina. Kumje Tawng was away on tour; but at six o'clock one December morning, after two chilly nights in Myitkyina, I boarded a slow goods train, and trundled off down the line with my feet dangling over the side of a flat. This time I knew what and whom to look for. The station-masters in turn alerted my friends by telegraph, and I made a sort of Progress all down the Railway Valley: holding court with, among others, the missionaries at Mohnyin, and Myi Tun Hka, grinning all over his face, at Kadu. Ba Ohn had retired to Katha; but by the magic of the telegraph he met me at Katha Station, and escorted me down to the steamer past the shops with their roaring pressure lamps, through the velvet darkness of a Burmese night.

At Tigyaing I spotted Ah Hyi on the beach as usual, and had time for a quick cup of filthy tea in his shop during the half-hour before the steamer whistled to summon us back aboard. He looked more prosperous than ever, and our conversation was punctuated by his directions to a clerk concerning a pile of invoices which our steamer had brought him. Dr. Banerji had been posted elsewhere; Tun Sein, alas, was away in hospital with some lung infection, but his young brother came to greet me. I stayed two nights in Sagaing with the Maung Maungs, Bill having been promoted to Commissioner; and saw Samson and Sunshine Lader in Mandalay.

In Rangoon we had another Chindit reunion. Being by nature good mixers, we invited some non-Chindits to join us, and gave them a demonstration of a column on the march. Aung Thin was detailed to impersonate a mule: he entered into his part with zest, kicking out manfully as he was led round the garden on all fours by Colonel Tan Yu Saing as muleteer, with a head-rope improvised from the girdle which Padre Mathew kindly provided from his cassock; while Chet Khin said " Gee-up ! "

I made no attempt this time to see U Nu, but I had half an hour with General Ne Win, who was his usual cheerful self. For all that the country was beginning to seethe, with the Karen troubles still going on, and fresh outbreaks in Arakan and among Kachins and Shans, Rangoon seemed tranquil. Two of the leading soldiers who were thought to be impatient of civil rule had been sent abroad to Ambassadorships, and out of the way of temptation. I left Rangoon in the second week of December, a little depressed about how things were going, but with no inkling that any change was imminent.

On the 2nd March 1962, just before the proofs of this book reached me, there was a *coup d'état* in the small hours of the morning. By the time the begging-bowls were going the round of the streets, Ne Win had resumed the government, and U Nu and his Ministers were in arrest. Among Ne Win's seven or eight leading supporters were Colonels Saw Myint and Tan Yu Saing; and Tommy Clift, the Air

Force officer, now Chief of the Air Staff, who had been arrested by Naw Seng along with Chet Khin on that unhappy morning near Maymyo thirteen years before.

A stone thrown into the pool at the capital must always send some ripples up-country, but I doubt if they have made much impact on the Upper Meza, for instance, or around the Indawgyi. The history of Burma continues to unfold, as unpredictable as ever.

INDEX

INDEX

Index

Index

Index